Reading Skills
for College Study

Reading Skills
for College Study

JAMES F. SHEPHERD

Queensborough Community College,
The City University of New York

HOUGHTON MIFFLIN COMPANY BOSTON
Dallas Geneva, Illinois Hopewell, New Jersey
Palo Alto London

This book is dedicated to Sam, Jane,
Steve, Mike, Eileen, Luis, Séan, David, Sunny,
Uncle Leon, and Hal.

Printed in the U.S.A.

Library of Congress Catalog Card Number: 79-89520

ISBN: 0-395-28503-8

[CONTENTS]

[TO THE INSTRUCTOR]

Reading Skills for College Study consists of a collection of passages much like those that students will find in their textbooks. These passages are accompanied by instructions, by worksheets, and by exercises chosen to teach students (1) how to read textbooks with greater understanding, (2) how to study efficiently by underlining and making useful notes on textbooks, and (3) how to answer both objective and essay questions on college examinations.

For each one of the thirty-eight passages, students are provided with multiple-choice questions, a written exercise, and a discussion question. On the worksheets called Reading for Understanding, multiple-choice questions serve several key purposes: they develop the student's ability to find the central thought of each passage and to use context to find or to infer the meanings of unfamiliar words; they improve literal and inferential comprehension; and they develop proficiency in answering similar types of multiple-choice questions that frequently appear on college tests. On the worksheets called Reading for Studying, written exercises provide guided instruction in underlining, in making various kinds of summarizing notes, and in answering essay questions. In the section called Reading with a Critical Eye, discussion questions on each passage help students learn how to judge a writer's methods and motives and how to evaluate the truthfulness, accuracy, authoritativeness, appropriateness, and general worth of what they read.

Part 1, How to Use This Book, gives an overview of the purposes of *Reading Skills for College Study*. In an orderly sequence, Parts 2 through 12 develop the student's ability to distinguish the various types of information found in textbooks.

The textbook selections, reprinted as they appeared in their original sources, cover a wide range of subjects and share the following characteristics:

They are expository.

They can be read and understood without specialized knowledge.

They present topics selected to interest college students.

They present information that stimulates class discussion.

In comparison with most textbooks that first-year college students are required to read, the reading difficulty of these passages ranges from easy to average levels. Since college textbooks are typically more challenging to read than high school textbooks, the passages were carefully chosen for characteristics that facilitate comprehension, such as:

high interest

informative introductions

good organization

helpful interior headings

clear definitions of important terminology

In addition, questions and exercises were chosen to ensure that most students will acquire skills without experiencing undue frustration. Nevertheless, *Reading Skills for College Study* teaches the skills necessary for typical college-level reading: the text is not intended for students who have severe reading deficiencies.

The passages are arranged in the sequence that best serves the instructional purposes of the text, and therefore most of the easier passages are found toward the front of the book—in an order determined by field testing. However, throughout *Reading Skills for College Study,* the more difficult passages are deliberately interspersed with the easier passages to replicate the *variation* in reading difficulty students will encounter when they read a typical group of textbooks during a term of college study.

Reading Skills for College Study provides the fundamental skills for helping today's average first-year college student develop a realistic understanding of the abilities required to do well in college. It is written in a format that allows for maximum instructional flexibility; it may be used both for classroom instruction and for independent study.

In *Reading Skills for College Study* students learn study skills by studying passages that have been selected for their widespread appeal; my intention is that they transfer these newly acquired skills to the reading and studying of all types of college textbooks.

I am grateful for the helpful suggestions that students provided when the materials in this book were field tested. I am also indebted to the useful comments of the following reviewers: Judith Clark, University of Wisconsin Center-Washington County; Katherine M. Fuller, Division of Special Studies, Gainesville Junior College; and Susan F. Rice, Department of English, Xavier University. Many of their suggestions are reflected in the final work.

Finally, I thank the faculty of Queensborough Community College for awarding me a fellowship leave that allowed me time to write this book.

J.F.S.

[TO THE STUDENT]

Reading and studying in college have always been more challenging than reading and studying in high school. But it has only been in the last few years that most colleges have made a systematic effort to help students adjust to the greater demands of college reading. *Reading Skills for College Study* will teach you the basic tools for reading and studying in college that many generations of students had to learn on their own.

The selections, questions, and exercises that appear in this textbook are the ones that students selected from many possibilities as the most interesting and instructive. In preparing *Reading Skills for College Study,* many students helped me in my efforts to provide you with opportunities to improve skills in the most productive and pleasant way possible. It would please me if this text provides you with an agreeable way to improve your reading and study skills.

J.F.S.

Reading Skills
for College Study

[O N E]

How to Use This Book

source of selections

Reading Skills for College Study contains selections from textbooks used in the study of college subjects. The passages represent most of the subjects that you will study in college, and they all were chosen to be interesting and informative, no matter what subjects you prefer.

Each selection is followed by ten multiple-choice questions called Reading for Understanding and a written exercise called Reading for Studying. Part 11, Reading with a Critical Eye—toward the end of the book—contains an additional "thought" question for each selection.

Part 1 provides an overview of ways to use these selections, questions, and exercises to improve your reading and studying of college textbooks. The explanations in this overview will become more meaningful if you first read one of the textbook passages and then answer several questions on it.

purpose of reading
Guide lines

For example, read the selection entitled "Studying" on pages 11–14. (For ease of reference you will want to tear out pages 15–16 and have them in front of you as you work through the remainder of Part 1.) As you read the passage, refer to the Reading for Understanding questions that immediately follow; at this early stage they will serve as guidelines to your reading. Then answer the Reading for Understanding questions, keeping the following in mind:

1. When you answer the questions, refer to the passage to make certain your answers are correct.
2. Asterisks (*) in the right-hand margin of "Studying" are there to help you locate the words tested in questions 3, 4, and 5.

READING FOR UNDERSTANDING

The multiple-choice questions are *not* a test of your memory; rather, they are a measure of your ability to read with understanding. If you are able to answer a high proportion of the questions correctly for each passage, you will also be able to understand college textbooks of average difficulty. Therefore, refer to the passages to find the answers to the questions unless you are absolutely certain you know the correct answer without referring to the passage.

The summary questions. When textbook writers discuss any subject, they usually place a summary of what they will say near the beginning of the discussion; often they write headings to help you find the major points they will make in the discussion. Before you read any passage in a textbook, you should survey the passage to find and read the summary. If you know the basic points of a passage before you read it, you will be able to read it with better understanding.

Now refer to your answers for questions 1 and 2 on page 15.

The correct answer for question 1 is "b." In summary, the passage "Studying" presents a method that can be used to remember and recall information for tests. It is true that the passage also gives information about reading quickly, underlining, and making written notes, but each of these points refers only to a *part* of the passage—none is a summary of the complete passage.

The correct answer for question 2 is "b." The summary is stated best in the second paragraph. Notice that the second paragraph lists the five headings used in the passage, giving a complete preview of the major points that are made in the passage.

The vocabulary questions. When you read your college textbooks, you will encounter many words you do not know. You will need to find the meanings of most of these words if you are to read with reasonable understanding. Three methods can be used to find the meanings of unknown words: (1) you can look up their meanings in a glossary or dictionary, (2) you can use word structure to find their meanings, or (3) you can use context to figure out their meanings.

Glossaries and dictionaries. A glossary is a brief list in which difficult and technical words used in a book are defined. The glossary is usually found in the back of a book, just before the index. Examine your college textbooks to see if they have glossaries; if they do, use the glossaries as a valuable source of definitions for technical or otherwise difficult words.

Every student should own at least two dictionaries—a paperback dictionary to carry to classes and a desk dictionary to use at home. I especially recommend *The American Heritage Dictionary of the English Language* and *Webster's New World Dictionary of the American Language.* Other widely recommended dictionaries for college students are *Funk and Wagnalls Standard College Dictionary, Random House Dictionary of the English Language,* and *Webster's Seventh New Collegiate Dictionary.* These five dictionaries are among those most often recommended to students by college English teachers. Purchase a good paperback dictionary and a desk dictionary, and use them when you read all of your college books.

Word structure. The second method for finding the meanings of ~~oo of lat e Gk.~~ words is analyzing the prefixes, bases, and suffixes that the words contain. See pages 25-28, "Word Structure," for further explanation.

Context. If you have to turn to a dictionary every time you encounter a word you do not know, your reading is likely to be slowed to the point where you become frustrated and lose interest. You should learn how to figure out the meaning of a word in its *context*—examining the surrounding words to discover what they tell you about the unknown word's meaning. Questions 3, 4, and 5 will help you become skillful at using context to find the meanings of words.

Now refer to your answers for questions 3, 4, and 5 on pages 15–16. Notice that the words *studying, converse,* and *perceive* are printed in **boldface** type and followed by asterisks (*); three asterisks in the right-hand margin of "Studying" will guide you to the contexts in which these particular words appear. This method is used throughout *Reading Skills for College Study* to help you locate the contexts for words in the vocabulary questions.

The correct answer for question 3 is "c." *Studying* is the process we use to remember and recall information. This meaning is stated directly in the context in which *studying* appears.

The correct answer for question 4 is "a." *Converse* means "opposite." You can determine this by substituting *opposite, identical, spoken word,* and *discussion* for *converse* in the passage. Only *opposite* makes sense:

> Students who have never used these steps for study often believe it would be very time consuming to study in this way. Actually, the **opposite** is true; these steps make it possible to learn more in less time.

The correct answer for question 5 is "d." *Perceive* means "understand." Its meaning may be figured out by using the same method used to discover the meaning of *converse*:

> Many students who can immediately **understand** the value of surveying and marking books have difficulty *understanding* why they should make written notes for study.

Whether you found question 3, 4, and 5 easy or difficult to answer, there are over one hundred similar questions in this book to help you become more expert at finding the meanings of words from context. There is no more useful vocabulary skill than the skill of using context to find word meanings; by avoiding constant reference to a dictionary, you will be able to increase your comprehension and improve your reading speed.

The comprehension questions. You will benefit most from answering the comprehension questions if you understand the two important purposes they serve:

1. *They provide a measure of the extent to which you read with understanding.* When you answer these questions correctly you practice and improve your ability to comprehend what you read in college textbooks.
2. *They provide examples of the types of multiple-choice questions that appear on college tests.* You are likely to find that multiple-choice questions on college tests are more difficult than the ones on high school tests. The questions in this book should help prepare you to understand and answer the kinds of questions on multiple-choice tests you will be taking in college.

When you answered questions 6, 7, 8, 9, and 10 on page 16 you may have noticed that the questions are listed in the order in which their answers are stated or suggested in the passage entitled "Studying." This procedure is used throughout the book to help you answer the comprehension questions. You will know, for example, that if the answers for questions 6, 7, and 8 are all directly stated in a passage, the answer for question 6 will be found someplace before the answer for question 7, and the answer for question 7 will be found before the answer for question 8.

Also the questions have been carefully written to make certain that there is only one correct answer for each question. The correct answers for the comprehension questions are not found by guessing; they are found by using the following procedures:

1. *If there seems to be more than one correct answer for a question, select the answer that is directly stated in what you have read.* For example, all the answers for this question are correct:

> The suffix -*er* is used on the ends of words that
> a. name people who have a certain occupation.
> b. name people who live in a certain place.
> c. name things that serve a certain purpose.
> d. are used to compare two things.

All the answers for this question are correct: *painter* names a person who has a certain occupation; *New Yorker* names a person who lives in a certain place; *roller* names a thing that serves a certain purpose; and *taller* is used to compare two things. In such situations, the correct answer is always the one that is stated directly in the passage that you read. If the passage stated that the suffix -*er* is used to name people who have a certain occupation, and it did not mention any other uses of the suffix -*er*, then the correct answer would be "a." This comprehension question measures your understanding of what you have read about the suffix -*er*—not what you might have known about the suffix -*er* before you read the passage.

The comprehension questions in this book are similar to ones that you will answer on college tests, on reading tests, and on tests that you may take when you seek employment with a large organization such as a government agency. Comprehension questions measure your understanding of what you read, not what you already know or believe to be true. If you do not answer comprehension questions on the basis of what you read, you may answer many of them incorrectly.

2. *Read questions carefully before you answer them to make certain that you understand exactly what they are asking.* Although comprehension questions are based on information you read, they often are written in such a way that you cannot answer them correctly by simply matching words in a passage to words in a question. For example, this statement might appear in a passage: "Approximately 40 percent of all

high school graduates go on to college." And this question might be written to test understanding of the statement:

> What percentage of high school graduates do *not* go on to college?
> a. 20 percent
> b. 40 percent
> c. 60 percent
> d. 80 percent

Notice that the correct answer is "c," *not* "b." The statement tells what percentage of high school graduates go on to college (40 percent), but the question asks what percentage does *not* go on to college (60 percent).

Some students complain that this type of question is "tricky." However, questions of this type appear frequently on college tests, reading tests, and tests you will take if you apply for a job in a large organization. There is nothing "tricky" about them if you read questions carefully before you answer them to make certain you understand what they are asking.

3. *If the answer for a question is not stated directly in a passage, find the answer by reasoning, using the information given.* Comprehension questions often require that you use reasoning to draw a conclusion that is not directly stated in a passage. For example, a passage might explain *sex-typing* simply by stating, "It is the act of parents encouraging boys to do things associated with men and encouraging girls to do things associated with women." The following question might be written to measure your understanding of that statement:

> An example of *sex-typing* would be parents encouraging
> a. a girl to ride a bike.
> b. a boy to care for a dog.
> c. a girl to clean the house.
> d. a boy to cook the meals.

Even though the answer to this question is not given in the statement, it can be arrived at by reasoning with the information that was presented. The correct answer is "c"—an example of sex-typing would be parents encouraging a girl to clean the house. Housecleaning is generally associated more with women than with men. The other answers are not correct: riding bikes and caring for dogs are associated as much with women as with men, and cooking meals is associated more often with women than with men.

The comprehension questions in this book are designed to increase your skill in understanding what you read.

Refer to your answers for questions 6, 7, 8, 9, and 10 on page 16.

The correct answer for question 6 is "d." The answer is found by reasoning. The paragraph under the heading "Survey the Chapter" states that all the items listed in the answers for question 6 should be surveyed, but the question asks you to form a judgment as to which item is likely to be *most* helpful. The purpose of surveying is to preview or to get an overview of what you will read, and a summary is, by definition, "a presentation in brief form." So the most helpful part to read for the purpose of surveying would be a one-paragraph summary.

The choices for the answers to the last four questions were written in such a way that there seems to be more than one correct answer; however, only one answer is correct for each question. The correct answers are the ones stated directly in the passage—the questions measure your understanding of what you have read. Remember, if there seems to be more than one correct answer for a question, select the answer that is directly stated in what you have read.

The correct answer for question 7 is "b." In the first paragraph following the heading "Read the Chapter," it is directly stated that marking textbook chapters is done best after the first reading.

The correct answer for question 8 is "a." In the second paragraph under the heading "Read the Chapter," it is directly stated that two factors make material difficult to read. The first factor is whether the reader is familiar with the subject matter.

The correct answer for question 9 is "c." It is directly stated in the last paragraph following the heading "Underline or Highlight the Chapter" that if an entire page is marked it is the same as if nothing on that page is marked.

The correct answer for question 10 is "c." In the last two sentences of the passage, it is directly stated that recitation is important because when individuals recite they do very much what they do when they take tests; in other words, they practice doing what they do on tests.

Conclusion. You will benefit most from answering the multiple-choice questions if you keep in mind their purposes:

1. Questions 1 and 2 (summary) will help you develop the habit of always looking for the writer's summary of a passage. Having the summary of the passage in your mind will help you organize your thoughts and read with better understanding.

2. Questions 3, 4, and 5 (vocabulary) will help you develop the ability to find the meanings of words in context so that your reading will not be slowed by the need to refer to a dictionary every time you come across a new word.

3. Questions 6, 7, 8, 9, and 10 (comprehension) will help you to develop better comprehension of what you read and to learn how to answer multiple-choice comprehension questions on any test. Remember the directions given earlier:

a. If there seems to be more than one correct answer for a comprehension question, select the answer that is directly stated in the material.

[handwritten marginal note: The best way to understand a chapter is reading the summary]

b. Read comprehension questions carefully before you answer them to make certain that you understand exactly what they are asking.

c. If the answer to a comprehension question is not directly stated in what you have read, find the answer by reasoning, using the information that is given in the passage.

Reread these explanations whenever you have difficulty answering the Reading for Understanding questions correctly. And use these suggestions to do your best on any multiple-choice test that measures your understanding of what you have read. This includes tests you take in college courses, reading tests, and tests you take when you seek employment in a governmental agency or other large organization.

READING FOR STUDYING

Passages 2 through 38 are each followed by an exercise called Reading for Studying. These exercises will help you learn how successful students underline in their books and make notes as they read so that they can use their notes when reciting in preparation for tests.

The passage entitled "Studying" on pages 11–14 states that many students believe that the best way to study textbooks is simply to read them over and over. Actually, however, study is most effective when a student underlines important passages, takes written notes, and uses those notes for recitation in preparation for tests.

The Reading for Studying exercises teach these abilities by first giving you very specific directions for underlining and taking notes. Beginning with selection 12, you are given less guidance so that you will become more self-sufficient in using these methods in textbooks you study for other college courses. As you progress through this book, you will find that the Reading for Studying exercises also help you learn how to organize definitions found in textbooks (Part 8); how to take notes when passages make comparisons (Part 9); and how to prepare for writing answers to essay questions (Part 10). These exercises will help you practice these important skills—skills familiar to well-organized students.

By the time you have done most of the Reading for Studying exercises, you will have a good understanding of what you can do to be well prepared for tests—an important goal of this book. But the most important purpose of *Reading Skills for College Study* is to teach you to apply what you learn from this book to the study of textbooks in all your college courses. You are the only one who can achieve the most important purpose of this book; you are the only one who can use what you learn here to assure yourself a more successful college career.

READING WITH A CRITICAL EYE

In Part 11 (page 323), called Reading with a Critical Eye, you will find questions that develop the skill of reading with critical judgment.

Sometimes students complain that they have difficulty concentrating on reading textbooks, particularly those they find boring. However, this complaint is seldom heard from students who engage in "conversations" with the writers of their texts—by carefully evaluating written material. These students judge writers' motives and methods; they evaluate the truthfulness, accuracy, authoritativeness, appropriateness, and general worth of what they read. For example, when reading "Studying," such readers might ask:

> Is it *true* that many students have difficulty accepting the idea that they should make written notes to learn information in their textbooks?
>
> Do my experiences convince me that this may be an *accurate* description of how to study?
>
> Do I have any reason to accept this information as *authoritative*? Is the writer an expert on the subject of studying?
>
> Is it *appropriate* (suitable, proper, or fitting) that the writer communicate this information to me?
>
> Is there anything in this passage that is of *worth* (value or use) to me?

When you ask such questions, you read with a critical eye, and with increased understanding because the questions require you to attend carefully to what is written. With this increased understanding will come greater enjoyment of what you read.

Use the Reading with a Critical Eye questions in Part 11 to increase your ability to evaluate and to judge what you read. All the questions in that section are appropriate for stimulating class discussion; some may also be used for additional practice in giving written answers.

RECOGNIZING TYPES OF INFORMATION
IN TEXTBOOKS

One of the primary purposes of this book is to help you learn to identify seven basic types of information that are commonly presented by textbooks. College textbooks are likely to explain:

1. *methods* of doing certain things. PROCESS
2. *sequences* in which events occur or appear. ORDER
3. *categories* of items. CLASSIFICATIONS
4. *reasons* that things are as they are. CAUSE & AFFECT

5. *points of view.* OPINION
6. *definitions* of important words.
7. *comparisons* among items. CONTRAST

You will be taught to examine textbook passages in order to decide which of these types of information are presented. When you are aware of the type of information being presented, you will be able to organize what you read—and therefore you will learn more efficiently.

KEEPING RECORDS OF PROGRESS

In Part 12, Records of Progress, you will find *record forms* on which you may record your scores for the Reading for Understanding questions. Read the comments on page 332 about these scores and then record your scores for the multiple-choice questions for the passage entitled "Studying."

Record forms have been provided so that you may also keep records for the Reading for Studying exercises and the Reading with a Critical Eye questions.

[1]

Studying

Many students believe that the best way to study for a test is to read and reread the material upon which they will be tested; they believe that reading is studying. Actually, reading and studying are two different things. *Reading* is the process we use to understand ideas that are presented in writing, but *studying* is the process we use to remember and recall information.

The typical college assignment is to study a chapter in a textbook. Research and the experiences of successful college students make it clear that the most efficient way to remember and recall information in textbook chapters is to follow these steps:

1. Survey the chapter.
2. Read the chapter.
3. Underline or highlight the chapter.
4. Make written notes from the chapter.
5. Recite from written notes.

Students who have never used these steps for study often believe it would be very time consuming to study in this way. Actually, the converse is true; these steps make it possible to learn more in less time.

SURVEY THE CHAPTER

Surveying involves previewing or getting an overview of what you are about to read. You can read a chapter in a textbook more efficiently if you spend a few minutes looking through the chapter, examining the headings, pictures, diagrams, the summary, and so on, to get a general idea about the chapter's contents. It usually takes less than five minutes to survey a chapter, but this is time well spent, because it gives you excellent preparation for reading.

READ THE CHAPTER

After you have surveyed the chapter, read it through. As you read, find the important statements that you will want to go back and under-

Adapted from James F. Shepherd, *College Study Skills*, pp. 34–38. Copyright © 1979 by Houghton Mifflin Company. Used by permission.

Transfer of Learning

To help

An important issue in optimizing learning is the extent to which the learning of one thing facilitates the learning of something else. If everything we learned was specific to the situation in which it was learned, the amount of learning that would have to be crammed into a lifetime would be phenomenal. Fortunately, most learning is readily transferable, with some modification, to a number of different situations.

Defn of transf. of positive Transfer

2 kinds of transf

The influence that learning one task may have on the subsequent learning of another is called transfer of learning. The term positive transfer is used when learning one task does facilitate learning another. If one is a good tennis player, it is easier to learn to play squash; this is positive transfer. But transfer is not always positive; when interference occurs, we have negative transfer.

Negative Transfer

There are numerous examples of negative transfer in everyday life. When driving a car with automatic transmission after having been accustomed to one with a stick shift, we may find ourselves depressing a nonexistent clutch pedal. When changing from a pedal-brake to a hand-brake bicycle, we may still try to press back on the pedal when we have to stop quickly. And the transition from driving on the right-hand side of the street to the British procedure of driving on the left is difficult for many American visitors to Great Britain. The original habit is so overlearned that even after driving successfully on the left for some time, an individual may revert to right-side driving when required to act quickly in an emergency.

influ of over learning

Figure 1. An Example of a Textbook Page Marked for Study.

(From James F. Shepherd, *College Study Skills*, p. 64. Copyright © 1979 by Houghton Mifflin Company. Used by permission. Originally published in Ernest R. Hilgard, Richard C. Atkinson, and Rita L. Atkinson, *Introduction to Psychology*, 6th ed., p. 253. Copyright © 1975 by Harcourt Brace Jovanovich, Inc. and reprinted by permission.)

line or highlight. It is usually not possible to mark a book accurately while doing a first reading; good marking is usually done when you read a chapter for the second time.

How quickly you read a chapter depends on (1) how familiar you are with the subject matter and (2) whether the information is presented in a clear and understandable way. Familiar subject matter written in a way that is easy for you to understand will be read most quickly; unfamiliar subject matter written in a way that is difficult for you to understand will not be read very quickly.

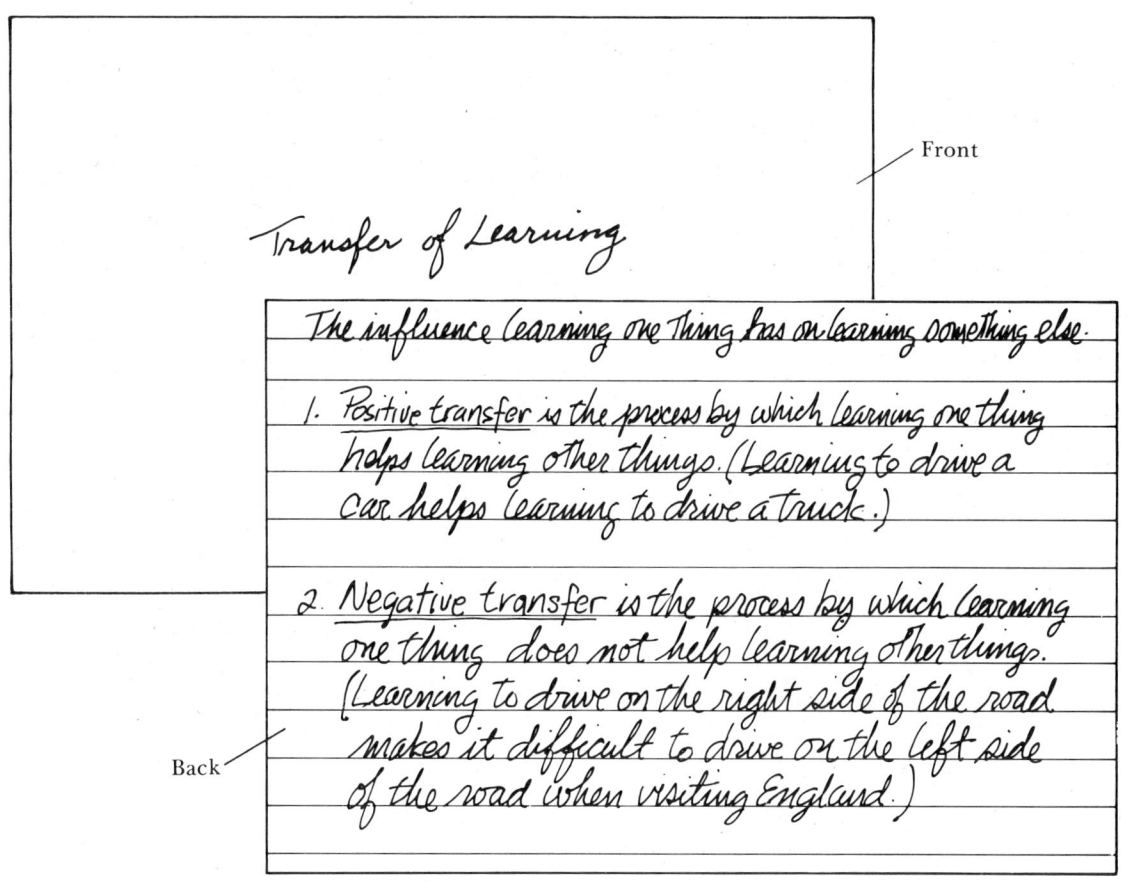

Front

Transfer of Learning

The influence learning one thing has on learning something else.

1. Positive transfer is the process by which learning one thing helps learning other things. (Learning to drive a car helps learning to drive a truck.)

2. Negative transfer is the process by which learning one thing does not help learning other things. (Learning to drive on the right side of the road makes it difficult to drive on the left side of the road when visiting England.)

Back

Figure 2. An Example of Notes for Studying.

These notes are based on the underlined passages in Figure 1. (Figure adapted from James F. Shepherd, *College Study Skills*, p. 65. Copyright © 1979 by Houghton Mifflin Company. Used by permission.)

UNDERLINE OR HIGHLIGHT THE CHAPTER

After you have read the entire chapter once, read it again to underline or highlight the most important information. Figure 1 shows an example of *underlining*. Notice that the important words to learn have been circled, and lines have been drawn under the most important statements. Also, notes in the margin summarize important points.

Underlining may be done using a pen or pencil, and neat underlining often requires the use of a ruler or other straightedged instrument. Most people cannot draw straight lines without using a straightedge as a guide. This is one reason many students prefer to mark their books using a highlighting pen.

Highlighting is done with special felt-tipped pens containing watercolor ink that does not damage books (pens with yellow ink are most popular). If the passage in Figure 1 were highlighted, highlighting would be placed over the words that are now underlined.

Whether you underline or highlight, do not mark too much information in your books. If an entire page is marked, then it is the same as if the page were not marked at all. To become good at marking books you must learn to find and mark *only* the most important statements.

MAKE WRITTEN NOTES

Many students who can immediately perceive the value of surveying   *
and marking books have difficulty understanding why they should make written notes for study. Nonetheless, most successful students make written notes from their markings in textbooks and study from their notes—not from their books. Once they have made written notes on a chapter, they do not have to reread the chapter unless they need to clarify or improve their notes.

Figure 2 shows written notes for the passage in Figure 1. The notes are written on the lined side of a three-inch by five-inch index card (a *study card*). The words *transfer of learning* are written on the blank side of the card. Of course, notes for study may also be written on notebook paper.

RECITE FROM YOUR NOTES

The fifth and most important step in studying is recitation—repeating information to yourself so you can remember it easily. To recite the information on the sample study card in Figure 2, you would read "transfer of learning" from the front of the card and then try to recall the information on the back of the card. Recitation is the most important step in preparing for tests: when you recite, you do very much what you do when you take a test. When you take a test, you give answers to a teacher's questions; when you recite, you give answers to your own questions.

[1]

Studying

READING FOR UNDERSTANDING

Summary

1. In summary, this passage presents a **method** that can be used to
  a. read textbooks more quickly.
  b. recall information for tests.
  c. underline things in textbooks.
  d. make written notes for study.

2. The summary is best stated in the headings and in the
  a. first paragraph.
  b. second paragraph.
  c. third paragraph.
  d. fourth paragraph.

Vocabulary

C

3. Studying* is the process we use to
  a. understand the things we read.
  b. examine things we do not know.
  c. remember and recall information.
  d. read and underline textbooks.

4. Converse* means
  a. the opposite.
  b. the same.
  c. a spoken word.
  d. a discussion.

Summary	Number right _____	X 10 =	_____
Vocabulary	Number right _____	X 10 =	_____
Comprehension	Number right _____	X 10 =	_____
		Total score	_____

_C_   5. To **perceive*** is to
       a. work hard.
       b. think about.
       c. describe.
       d. understand.

Comprehension

 6. Which of the following would be the *most* helpful to examine during your
       survey of a textbook chapter?
       a. all the headings in the chapter
       b. any pictures, diagrams, or photographs
       c. the tables, charts, or graphs
       d. a one-paragraph summary of the chapter

 7. The marking of a textbook chapter is *best* done
       a. during the first reading.
       b. after the first reading.
       c. with a pen or pencil.
       d. with a highlight pen.

_A_   8. The speed with which one reads a chapter depends on whether the chapter is
       written so that it is easy or difficult to understand and whether the reader
       a. is familiar with the subject matter.
       b. has low, average, or high intelligence.
       c. has been in college for several years.
       d. has learned to use good study methods.

 9. It is best if only the most important points in textbooks are marked, because
       if an entire page is marked
       a. the page will be very confusing to read.
       b. the minor points will be underemphasized.
       c. it is the same as if nothing is marked.
       d. a bookstore will not purchase the book back.

_C_   10. The primary reason that recitation is the most important step in studying is
       that when students recite they
       a. pay attention to the most important facts.
       b. learn more than they do in other ways.
       c. practice doing what they do on tests.
       d. can avoid the necessity for reading.

[T W O]

Methods in Textbooks

How to?

One of the seven ways information is commonly presented by text-books is by an explanation of methods. *Methods* are the procedures, processes, or ways of doing something. Some textbooks are devoted almost entirely to explaining the ways things are done. For example, textbooks for mathematics courses primarily explain how to solve various kinds of mathematical problems; textbooks for foreign language courses primarily teach students how to speak and write a foreign language; and textbooks for speech courses explain how to prepare and give speeches.

The passage entitled "Studying" presents a five-step method that actually can be used for studying chapters in college textbooks:

1. Survey the chapter.
2. Read the chapter.
3. Underline or highlight the chapter.
4. Make written notes from the chapter.
5. Recite from written notes.

Sometimes, though, textbooks provide information about methods and do not sufficiently explain how you can actually use those methods. For example, an introductory psychology textbook may tell you that the method psychologists use to identify normal behavior includes determining whether individuals (1) understand their motives and feelings, (2) have control over their own behavior, and (3) use their abilities in productive ways. Introductory psychology textbooks give information about the methods psychologists use, but they do not prepare students to use those methods as practicing psychologists do. In some of your college courses you will learn how to actually use certain methods; in other courses you will learn about methods that are used.

The two selections in Part 2, "Job Success" and "Word Structure," explain methods you may be able to use. As you study these passages, pay special attention to understanding the methods they explain.

The rest of the textbook selections in *Reading Skills for College Study* are followed by ten Reading for Understanding multiple-choice questions and a written exercise called Reading for Studying. Reading with a Critical Eye questions for the remaining passages are in Part 11.

[2]

Job Success

To succeed in a job you must get along with your employer and your fellow workers. Studies of success and failure in work have shown that lack of ability to do the job is the cause of only about 15 percent of all firings and dismissals. Among the common reasons given for firing a worker are too frequent absence from work, habitual lateness, making trouble among fellow workers, dishonesty, unreliability, and loafing. Undoubtedly these bad habits were acquired earlier in life.

To get along with others on the job you need to show interest, consideration, and courtesy toward them. Keeping a job and advancing to better positions and better pay depend on your displaying three factors: good judgment, a willingness to do more than the actual requirements of your job, and continued improvement in your work and self-development.

In general, employers expect that you will do the following:

1. *Do your work well.* Employers may like you personally, but if your work is continually unsatisfactory, sooner or later you will be demoted or discharged.
2. *Show interest in your work.* Employers can tell whether you have an interest in your work or whether you regard it only as a way to make money. If you show that you like your work, are interested in it, and put good effort into it, it is easy for employers to help you.
3. *Be prompt and on the job.* Employers or your direct supervisor notice if you are late or absent from the job. When either of these occurs, it means that they have to make other arrangements that cost time and money.
4. *Look the part.* Employers notice the appearance of their workers. They are embarrassed by employees who dress peculiarly or appear lazy and indifferent about themselves and their dress.
5. *Be open to suggestions for improvement.* Every person occasionally needs criticisms and suggestions for improving his or her work. If you can accept and work on these suggestions, even if they are not given very tactfully, the employer has an easier job and more friendly feelings toward you.

19

6. *Avoid practical jokes on the job.* Some people have lost their jobs because they "horse around" and play practical jokes. Playing practical jokes, particularly around power equipment, increases the possibility of accidents. This does not mean that employers want a cheerless, humorless worker; rather they want workers who know the time and place for humor.

Getting along with fellow workers is also an important asset in holding a job. Following are some of the expectations people have of those who work with them.

(handwritten margin note: 4 fellow worker expectation)

1. *They expect you to like them.* Everyone wants to be liked. The best way to get along with fellow workers is to show an interest in them.
2. *They expect you to take part in the talk.* You should not be too sensitive to the teasing and sharp remarks sometimes thrown at you by your fellow workers. They expect you to "take it" as well as "dish it out." They expect you to be one of them.
3. *They expect you to mind your own business.* Some workers develop a feeling that there is something special about their job. They know certain things about what they do that no one else knows, and they feel uneasy if other workers look into their activities too closely. If you find a co-worker who is friendly and wants to show you something about his or her job, then by all means take advantage of the opportunity. Just remember that not everyone likes to share his or her special knowledge.
4. *They expect that you will not criticize them.* It is a bad mistake to make a damaging remark about a fellow worker to the boss or anyone else. A good rule to follow is to pass on the praise, but not the blame.

(handwritten margin note: on the job expectation)

When you get a job, you are expected to show good judgment in your relationships with your fellow workers and the public with whom you come in contact on the job. You are expected to handle emergencies and to make decisions. By taking initiative and by showing that you can be trusted to do a job that needs to be done, even if it is not necessarily your job, you show that you are ready for greater responsibility and authority.

[2]

Job Success

READING FOR UNDERSTANDING

Summary

 1. In summary, this passage presents a **method** for getting along
   a. with an employer and fellow workers.
   b. at the place where one is employed.
   c. and being interested in one's work.
   d. with the person one is employed by.

 2. The summary is best stated in the
   a. first sentence.
   b. second sentence.
   c. third sentence.
   d. fourth sentence.

Vocabulary

 3. **Habitual*** means
   a. practiced.
   b. continual.
   c. inhibiting.
   d. informal.

 4. When people are **demoted,*** they are
   a. told to do better.
   b. put in a lower job.
   c. taken off the payroll.
   d. watched very closely.

Summary	Number right _____	× 10 =	_____
Vocabulary	Number right _____	× 10 =	_____
Comprehension	Number right _____	× 10 =	_____
		Total score	_____

21

5. If people are **indifferent,*** they are
    a. unconcerned.
    b. disagreeable.
    c. reluctant.
    d. comparable.

Comprehension

 6. What percentage of people who lose their jobs lose them for some reason other than the lack of ability to do their jobs properly?
    a. 15 percent
    b. 35 percent
    c. 65 percent
    d. 85 percent

 7. Most people who lose their jobs lose them because of
    a. the lack of necessary vocational training.
    b. the lack of required educational background.
    c. practical jokes they played while working.
    d. bad habits they learned when they were young.

 8. The things employers expect of workers are very similar to the things
    a. landlords should expect of tenants.
    b. teachers should expect of students.
    c. husbands should expect of wives.
    d. shoppers should expect of salespeople.

 9. In summary, the way to get along with an employer is to be
    a. willing to do whatever you are asked.
    b. agreeable and not ask for higher pay.
    c. cooperative and interested in your work.
    d. a good worker and not to joke around.

10. In summary, the way to get along with fellow workers is to
    a. be interested in them, but not criticize them or pry into their business.
    b. like them and learn to "take it" as well as to "dish it out."
    c. mind your own business and not criticize the things they do.
    d. constantly think of kind comments to make them feel good.

[2]

Job Success

READING FOR STUDYING

Underline the following in the passage: (1) the first sentence, (2) the sentence just before the list numbered 1 through 6, (3) the sentence just before the list numbered 1 through 4, and (4) the numbered sentences that are printed in *italic* type.

Summarize this information on the lines below. The words *how to* are used in the headings to emphasize that the passage presents a method.

HOW TO SUCCEED ON A JOB

How to Get Along with an Employer:

1. Do your work as well as you can.

2. How to show interest in your work.

3.

4.

5.

6.

How to Get Along with Your Fellow Workers:

1. _____

   _____

2. _____

   _____

3. _____

   _____

4. _____

   _____

Word Structure

ADV. TO WORD STRUCTURE (handwritten)

If you understand English word structure, you will often be able to discover the meanings of unfamiliar words without consulting a dictionary—especially when the unknown words are derivatives or are constructed from combining forms.

DEFF. OF DER. EXS. (handwritten)

Derivatives are words that contain an English base word and a prefix, suffix, or combination of prefixes and suffixes. *Unkind, kindness,* and *unkindness* are examples of derivatives. *Unkind* contains a prefix and a base word; *kindness* contains a base word and a suffix; and *unkindness* contains a prefix, a base word, and a suffix.

Combining forms are Latin and Greek word parts such as the *biblio-* and *-phile* in our word *bibliophile. Bibliophile* is defined to mean "one who has a love for books." Its meaning is closely related to the meaning of *biblio-,* which is "book," and the meaning of *-phile,* which is "having a love for."

The following discussion explains methods you can use to find the meanings of derivatives and the meanings of words that are constructed from combining forms.

DERIVATIVES

To find the meanings of derivatives, you must be able to find the base words they contain, and you must understand about the affixes (prefixes and suffixes) that appear in them.

How to recognise derr. (handwritten)

Base words. Derivatives do not always contain a prefix, and they do not always contain a suffix, but they always contain a base word. The following derivatives all contain a base word, but only one has a prefix *and* a suffix: re*appear, appear*ance, re*appear*ance.

Content of derr. what is diffic. EXS. (handwritten)

A major difficulty in finding base words is that sometimes the spellings of base words are changed before adding suffixes; sometimes final *e*'s are dropped or final *y*'s are changed to *i*'s. For example, the *e* was dropped from *mature* to form the derivative *immaturity*: im/matur/ity. When *e*'s have been dropped, they must be replaced to find the

Adapted and abridged from James F. Shepherd, *College Vocabulary Skills,* pp. 15–99. Copyright © 1979 by Houghton Mifflin Company. Used by permission.

correct base word. The base word in *immaturity* is *mature,* not *matur.* In the derivative *recertification,* the *y* was changed to *i*: re/certifi/ cation. When *y*'s are changed to *i*'s, they must be changed back to *y*'s to find the correct base word. The base word in *recertification* is *certify,* not *certifi.*

Prefixes. Prefixes are word parts that are added at the beginnings of base words to form new words. If you know the meanings of prefixes you can use them to figure out the meanings of derivatives in which they appear. For example, knowing that the prefix *pseudo-* means "false" helps you to figure out the meaning of *pseudoscience.* Knowing   * that the meaning of *non-* is "not" will aid you in discovering the meanings of the more than ten thousand derivatives in which this prefix appears. Figure 1 gives the meaning of prefixes that are most useful to know. It would be very worthwhile for you to learn this list.

Suffixes. Unlike prefixes, suffixes do not usually add any specific meanings to base words; even the most familiar suffixes have many different meanings.

Fortunately, the wide range of meanings associated with each suffix does not present much difficulty, because one can usually find the meanings of derivatives without knowing the meanings of suffixes. For example, it is not necessary to know the meaning of *-ity* to find the meaning of *particularity* in this sentence:

John's *particularity* is evident in the way he dresses.

The base word in *particularity* can be used to understand that John is *particular.* Keep in mind this important principle: when derivatives contain suffixes, *use the meanings of base words to find the meanings of derivatives in the contexts in which they appear.* You can see how important it is to become skillful at finding base words in derivatives.

COMBINING FORMS

Combining forms are *word parts* that are joined (combined) to create words. *Octagon* is an example of a word made by joining the two combining forms *octo-* and *-gon. Octo-* means "eight," and *-gon* means "a figure having a designated number of angles." An *octagon* is a figure having eight angles (the shape of the familiar red stop signs we see on street corners).

In Figure 2 you will find examples of a few of the many hundreds of combining forms. Students often ask, "Which of the combining forms are most important for me to learn?" This is a question difficult to answer: some combining forms are important to the study of chemistry;

Prefix	Meaning(s)	Example
1. un-	not	*un*happy; not happy
	do the opposite	*un*lock; do the opposite of lock
	remove	*un*chain; remove the chain
2. non-	not	*non*living; not living
3. in-	not	*in*direct; not direct
im-	not	*im*perfect; not perfect
		*im*measurable; not measurable
il-	not	*il*legal; not legal
ir-	not	*ir*regular; not regular
4. dis-	opposite of	*dis*appear; vanish
5. mis-	wrongly, badly, incorrectly	*mis*spell; spell wrongly, badly, or incorrectly
6. mal-	wrongly, badly	*mal*functioning; functioning wrongly or badly
7. pre-	before	*pre*war; before a war
8. post-	after	*post*war; after a war
9. inter-	between	*inter*state; between states
10. trans-	across	*trans*atlantic; across the Atlantic
11. pro-	favoring, for	*pro*war; favoring war
12. anti-	opposing, against	*anti*war; against war
13. hyper-	exceedingly	*hyper*active; exceedingly active
14. re-	again	*re*write; write again
15. pseudo-	false	*pseudo*science; false science
16. ex-	former	*ex*-president; former president
17. semi-	partly	*semi*public; partly public

Figure 1. Most Useful Meanings of Prefixes

some are important to the study of botany; some are important to the study of physics, and so on. The best answer to this question is to learn the meanings of the combining forms that will help you the most in the college subjects that you study.

You can learn the meanings of specific combining forms by using a good desk dictionary. If at least two or three words in a subject that you are studying begin or end with the same spelling, consult a dictionary to see if the spelling is defined as a combining form. If it is, you should learn its meaning. For example, in a chemistry course, you probably will encounter the words *glycol, glycine, glycogen*—and others beginning with the spelling *glyc-*. If you consult a good desk dictionary, you will find that *glyc-* means "sugar." Knowing the meaning of this combining form will help you understand the meaning of other words that begin with the spelling *glyc-* in a chemistry textbook.

Combining Form	Meaning	Example
anthropo-	man	*anthropology* is the study of the origin and development of man.
bi-	two	A *bicycle* has two wheels.
-cide	kill	*Infanticide* is the killing of an infant.
-cracy	rule	A *gynecocracy* is government by women.
deci-	ten	The *decimal* system is based on units of ten.
gyneco-	woman	*Gynecology* is the medical study of women's physiology and diseases.
hema-	blood	*Hematic* means blood colored.
hydro-	water	*Hydromania* is the abnormal craving for water.
-logy	study	*Theology* is the study of God.
mono-	one	A *monocle* is a glass for one eye.
patho-	disease	*Pathology* is the study of disease.
-phobia	fear	*Hemaphobia* is the fear of blood.
pyro-	fire	*Pyrotechnics* are fireworks.
quadr-	four	Four couples dance in a *quadrille*.
quint-	five	Five people sing in a *quintet*.
seismo-	earthquake	A *seismoscope* is an instrument used for measuring earthquakes.
theo-	God, gods	*Theomorphic* is to have the form of God or a god.
tri-	three	A *tricycle* has three wheels.
uni-	one	*Unique* things are one of a kind.

Figure 2. Examples of Some Combining Forms

[3]

Word Structure

READING FOR UNDERSTANDING

Summary

_____ 1. In summary, this passage presents a **method** for
   a. using combining forms to increase vocabulary.
   b. creating words from various kinds of word parts.
   c. using word structure to find word meanings.
   d. learning and remembering meanings of prefixes.

_____ 2. The summary is best stated in the headings and in the
   a. second paragraph.
   b. third paragraph.
   c. fourth paragraph.
   d. fifth paragraph.

Vocabulary

_____ 3. **Affixes*** are
   a. prefixes and suffixes.
   b. people who study words.
   c. certain types of suffixes.
   d. some types of base words.

_____ 4. **Derivatives*** are words that always contain a
   a. prefix.
   b. suffix.
   c. base word.
   d. prefix and suffix.

Summary	Number right_____	X 10 = _____	
Vocabulary	Number right_____	X 10 = _____	
Comprehension	Number right_____	X 10 = _____	
		Total score_____	

_____ 5. A **pseudoscience*** is
    a. an important science.
    b. an obsolete science.
    c. a genuine science.
    d. a false science.

Comprehension

_____ 6. The base word in *redistribution* is
    a. redistribute.
    b. distribution.
    c. distribute.
    d. distribut.

_____ 7. The base word in *disqualification* is
    a. qualifi.
    b. qualify.
    c. disqualify.
    d. qualification.

_____ 8. A *semiautomatic* machine is
    a. not really automatic.
    b. certainly automatic.
    c. half automatic.
    d. partly automatic.

_____ 9. *Hydrophobia* is the abnormal
    a. craving for water.
    b. craving for power.
    c. fear of water.
    d. fear of power.

_____ 10. A *theocracy* is a
    a. religious country.
    b. rule by God.
    c. thematic principle.
    d. God-like king.

[3]

Word Structure

READING FOR STUDYING

Underline (1) the first sentence of the passage, (2) the first sentence following the heading "Derivatives," (3) the first *two* sentences following the headings "Base Words," "Prefixes," "Suffixes," and "Combining Forms," and (4) the first *three* sentences of the last paragraph. Then **summarize** this information on the lines below. The words *how to* are used in the headings to emphasize that the passage presents a method.

HOW TO USE WORD STRUCTURE
TO FIND THE MEANINGS OF WORDS

Derivatives

How to tell if a word is a derivative

Derivatives always contain a base word and a prefix or suffix, or some combination of prefixes and suffixes.

_____

_____

How to find the base words in derivatives when *e*'s are dropped or *y*'s are changed to *i*'s

_____

_____

_____

_____

_____

_____

How to use the meanings of prefixes to find the meanings of derivatives

_____

_____

_____   _____

_____

How to find the meanings of derivatives that end with suffixes

_____

_____

_____

_____

Combining Forms

How to find the meanings of words that contain combining forms

_____

_____

_____

_____

How to find the meanings of combining forms

_____

_____

How to find combining forms that are important to learn

_____

_____

_____

[T H R E E]

Sequences in Textbooks

In addition to explaining methods, college textbooks frequently give information about sequences. A *sequence* is the order in which things follow each other in time, space, rank, complexity, or some other dimension.

The classic examples of sequences in time are found in history books: a discussion of history necessarily refers to the order in which events have occurred. For example, in order to think intelligently about the history of the United States, we must have some understanding of the order in which our presidents were in office and the sequence in which the country fought its major wars. This type of sequence is called *time order, sequential order, chronological order,* or *temporal order*; all four terms have the same meaning.

Knowing the sequences of places and objects in space is also important for organizing information and experiences. Geography and astronomy are two fields of study in which *spatial sequences* are especially important. When we know the order of planets in space, for example, we know that a rocket flying away from the earth must pass the orbits of Mars and Jupiter before reaching the planet Saturn.

A third type of sequence is *hierarchical order,* in which items are often arranged by rank or complexity. For example, a sociology textbook might contain information about various occupations that people rank high or low according to prestige: the occupations of physician and college professor are thought of as having a *high* level of prestige; those of electrician and police officer as having a *medium* level of prestige; and those of street sweeper and bartender as having a *low* level of prestige. In biology, forms of life are organized in a hierarchical sequence, beginning with the least complex and advancing to the most complex forms. In this arrangement of animal life, the one-celled protozoa are at the bottom, and apes are very near the top of the hierarchy.

Textbooks also make use of *logical sequences*—sequences that progress according to a rational ordering of events or tasks. The method in the selection entitled "Studying" is arranged in a logical sequence:

1. Survey the chapter.
2. Read the chapter.
3. Underline or highlight the chapter.
4. Make written notes from the chapter.
5. Recite from written notes.

The passage explains why it is logical to survey before reading, read before underlining, and so on. Notice that "Studying" not only explains a method but also presents a sequence. Textbook passages often convey more than one important type of knowledge or explanation: "Studying" is used as an example of a method rather than of a sequence because the *primary* purpose of the passage is to explain a method.

The following selections explain sequences. As you study "Smokers" and "Human Needs," pay particular attention to understanding the sequences these passages explain.

[4]

Smokers

Generally adolescents begin smoking and most adults continue smoking in large part because many other people smoke and because the use of nicotine and other drugs is institutionalized in society. It was only in this century, though, that the habit of smoking became firmly established among adult males in this country, and it has been a relatively few years since the smoking habit spread to large numbers of women and teenagers.

When cigarette manufacture first became a major industry at the turn of the century, the typical smoker was a middle-class working man who perhaps believed smoking made him seem more manly. For women and children, strictures against smoking were akin to moral law. Women who smoked were considered fast, loose, and capable of almost any depravity. For children, smoking was even more of a stigma: the first step toward a rotting brain and stunted growth. The cigarette was considered a "filthy weed" fraught with undertones of impending disaster.

During the 1920s, men of all professions and backgrounds turned to the cigarette. The flappers joined them; they considered smoking a fashionable mark of sophisticated decadence. It was not until the late 1930s that advertising began to build shining images for cigarettes and the people who smoked them. Smokers were the heroes of the day: fighter pilots, soldiers in the foxhole, tank drivers, doctors, and nurses.

After that, the word was trumpeted on the radio, in newspapers, and on billboards across the country. With television came visual proof that cigarette smokers were "the good guys." The smoker was a tough-skinned, handsome cowboy driving a herd of cattle across the Western plains. The right cigarette became a sexual lure, attracting bikini-clad beauties off their surfboards into the waiting arms of handsome young men. Another cigarette advertiser conferred a kind of medical certification on smoking, pointing out that more doctors smoked their cigarettes than any other leading brand.

In the 1950s and 1960s, advertising campaigns were aimed heavily at the youth market, particularly college students. Sophisticated airplane travelers received complimentary cigarettes with their meals, and children sang songs insisting that good grammar is less important than the taste of a "good" cigarette.

One cancer you can give yourself.

Horrible isn't it?

AMERICAN CANCER SOCIETY

Cigarette manufacturers pay for their advertisements, but media publishers donate space to inform the public of the dangers of smoking. (Courtesy of the American Cancer Society)

As a result of this drum-beating, more and more men, women, and children became smokers. By the fall of 1964—right after the Surgeon General's report—one-half of American men and one-third of the women smoked daily, a total of 50 to 60 million smokers. Nearly 49 percent of the young men between seventeen and twenty-four smoked, along with 34 percent of the women in that age group. Between the ages of twenty-five and thirty-four, there was a sharp upsurge to 60.7 percent of the men and 43.5 percent of women. From that age upward, considerably fewer men and women smoked.

The results of the 1975 National Study on Smoking Among Teen-Agers and Women (conducted for The American Cancer Society) shows that among teenage girls seventeen and under, 27 percent are smoking. This is a 5 percent increase from 1969 and represents a half million additional young smokers. Thirty-nine percent smoke a pack or more a day—four times the rate found by earlier surveys. Sixty percent of young teenage smokers began before the age of thirteen. Forty-nine percent of them reported the presence of smoking rooms in their schools. The majority of these smokers said that their own doctors had never said anything to them about the dangers of smoking.

[4]

Smokers

READING FOR UNDERSTANDING

Summary

_____ 1. In summary, this passage provides the **sequence** in which
     a. the body is affected by too much cigarette smoking.
     b. people develop the habit of smoking cigarettes.
     c. from 1900 to 1975, smoking became widespread in America.
     d. various types of men have become cigarette smokers.

_____ 2. The summary is best stated in the
     a. first sentence.
     b. second sentence.
     c. third sentence.
     d. fourth sentence.

Vocabulary

_____ 3. **Strictures*** are
     a. structures.
     b. closures.
     c. disciplines.
     d. restrictions.

_____ 4. If things are **akin,*** they are
     a. similar.
     b. unlike.
     c. painful.
     d. soothing.

Summary	Number right _____	X 10 =	_____
Vocabulary	Number right _____	X 10 =	_____
Comprehension	Number right	X 10 =	_____
		Total score	_____

_____   5. **Flappers*** refer to
    a. people from the best families.
    b. certain young, modern women.
    c. tight covers for the eyes.
    d. the lips while smoking.

Comprehension

_____   6. Cigarette manufacturers began to focus their advertising heavily on young people as early as the
    a. 1920s.
    b. 1930s.
    c. 1940s.
    d. 1950s.

_____   7. In 1964, people were most likely to be smokers if they were between the ages of
    a. 14 and 19.
    b. 20 and 24.
    c. 25 and 34.
    d. 35 and 44.

_____   8. The greatest increase in smokers in the 1970s was among
    a. young men.
    b. middle-aged men.
    c. young women.
    d. middle-aged women.

_____   9. Sixty percent of young teenage smokers began smoking when they were
    a. 12 or younger.
    b. 13 or younger.
    c. 14 or younger.
    d. 15 or younger.

_____   10. In the mid-1970s, smoking rooms were reported to be in schools by about
    a. 20 percent of teenage smokers.
    b. 35 percent of teenage smokers.
    c. 50 percent of teenage smokers.
    d. 65 percent of teenage smokers.

[4]

Smokers

READING FOR STUDYING

Underline the second sentence of the first paragraph. In the first sentence of the second paragraph, **circle** the words "turn of the century" and **underline** the words "middle-class working man." Then **circle** the dates in the passage ("1920s," "1930s," and so on) and **underline** the words that state the types of people who were smokers at those times. **Summarize** this information on the lines below. The dates stand out prominently to emphasize that the passage presents a sequence.

AMERICAN SMOKERS: 1900-1975

1900 *Smokers were middle-class working men. Women and children did not smoke.*

1920s _____

1930s _____

1950s _____

1964 _____

_____

_____

1975 _____

_____

_____

[5]

Human Needs

The next major study of human motivation was inspired by the need for increased production during World War II. In the 1940s, psychologist Abraham Maslow recognized that workers perform as they do in order to satisfy a wide variety of needs. He realized that these needs would have to be classified to explain motivation. As his research progressed, it became apparent that the needs were stratified, and it was possible to illustrate the relationships. The model, called Maslow's ladder, is illustrated in Figure 1. Two principles underlie this model: A human being is an animal with many needs, and only those needs not yet fully satisfied cause a person to act. When needs on a lower level are satisfied, at least in part, the rung above becomes a goal a person will strive to reach. With these principles in mind, let us now take a look at each set of needs depicted in the model (see Figure 1 on page 42).   *

PHYSIOLOGICAL NEEDS

All the basic drives that sustain life—food, clothing, and shelter—are called *physiological needs*. A person must satisfy these needs before pursuing any other objective. Most people, of course, strongly desire more than the minimum level of satisfaction required for survival: They want three meals a day instead of one and a house instead of a hut.

The physiological needs are readily satisfied in modern societies by money. Even the few pennies earned by nineteenth-century laborers were strong motivation to people who had not eaten for several days. They would suffer almost any abuse to collect them and live another day.

SAFETY NEEDS

People have a strong desire to feel protected. Usually this means protection against loss of the physical necessities, the idea of a cushion

Figure 1. Maslow's Ladder

against misfortune. The worker lucky enough to satisfy safety needs does not have to consider the possibility of being forced to scramble for survival.

Once more, money will effectively satisfy this level of need. Even today few people succeed in earning enough money to feel completely secure. This is why the classical theory of motivation held on so long.

Business now does a reasonably good job of meeting the worker's demands for safety. Wages are high enough to allow most workers to save for a rainy day. Business today frequently attempts to motivate workers by directly satisfying their need for safety. Guaranteed job security, pension plans, health insurance, life insurance, and employer contributions to Social Security are all examples of direct satisfaction of safety needs.

SOCIAL NEEDS

Humans are social animals. Their desires to associate with others and to be loved by others are nearly as strong as their will to survive. Indeed, even when the need for safety is not totally satisfied, people begin feeling social needs.

This is the first level of needs that money cannot readily satisfy. As the Hawthorne Studies clearly showed, workers' desire to be accepted by co-workers could motivate them more strongly than the desire to earn more money. Furthermore, workers need no impetus from management to seek satisfaction of their social needs. It is this drive that gives rise to the informal organization.

ESTEEM NEEDS

People need to feel *self-esteem,* a sense of personal worth derived   *
from their competence, achievement, or independence. They also need the respect of others, a respect based on a recognition of their competence rather than on friendship (a social need). The need for esteem is closely tied to the idea of status.

Status is one's rank in comparison with others in the same social group. A person with high status is one who is well regarded by friends and associates. Several factors can give a person high status in society. These include wealth, social standing, advanced education, and a prestigious occupation. The occupation held in greatest esteem by most Americans is that of physician. Note, however, that a person's status is valid only in the social group upon whose values it is based. A prominent rock musician, for example, may well have higher status than a physician in a social group made up exclusively of teen-agers.

We are all familiar with status symbols such as a Cadillac or a mansion. On a more modest level, status could be based on having this year's Buick when the neighbors drive last year's Chevrolets. Since these familiar symbols of status all cost money, it is common to mistake a striving for status as a drive to accumulate wealth. While earning a million dollars may indeed bestow status on an individual, a person motivated by esteem needs seeks the status, not the money. It has been shown that such people, if given the opportunity, will seek direct satisfaction of their esteem needs.

People in business often seek satisfaction of their esteem needs by pursuing a promotion. To some individuals, the status conferred by the title "vice-president" is more important than the salary that also comes with the job. Of course, people also manifest the need for esteem when they seek one of the occupations that our society holds in high esteem, such as physician, writer, artist, actor, university professor, lawyer, or musician.

SELF-REALIZATION NEEDS

Maslow defined the need for *self-realization* as "the desire to become more what one is, to become everything one is capable of." A person who operates on this level usually views work as something to be done in order to feel complete as a person or to fulfill a personal philosophy. It is a higher-level need than the one for esteem because the person involved *already* feels that he or his work is worthwhile and respected. Such people find their work intrinsically interesting and satisfying.   *

Jim Whittaker, the first American to climb Mt. Everest, illustrated this need when an interviewer asked him why he risked his life just to climb the highest mountain. Whittaker quickly replied, "Because it's there." He felt that meeting the challenge was ample reward in itself.

Relatively few people ever reach the stage where they are dominated by the need for self-realization. There is a tendency to think that only a Schweitzer or an Einstein is in this position. Maslow felt, however, that everyone is capable of feeling this need to some degree.

NEEDS IN REAL LIFE

Maslow's ladder is a convenient way to classify human needs. But if you see it as a simple step-at-a-time procedure, you make a serious mistake. It is not necessary for a person to satisfy each level of need completely before being motivated by a higher level. In our society, the majority of people have reached at least the fourth rung of needs. Thus, in real life nearly all needs are interacting within the individual.

A construction worker's weekly salary satisfies his basic physiological needs, but he may still want a new coat or a more comfortable house. His earnings and pension plan may satisfy his minimum safety requirements, but he still wants to save a few extra dollars "just in case." These needs may not be fully satisfied. Yet he may forego an opportunity to earn overtime pay in order to spend more time with his friends or family, a social need. He may also sacrifice a little safety by spending more money than he should on a new car so he can gain some status with his neighbors. Quite possibly, he feels his trade to be as fine as any and strives to be as good as he can at his work, fulfilling a need for self-realization. All five need levels operate in this worker, and he will actively strive to improve his position on all five rungs simultaneously.

There is another factor to be considered as needs work out in real life. As people partially satisfy each need, they tend to require more of it for full satisfaction. This is known as the phenomenon of rising expectations. It partially explains why workers today are unhappy with their earnings even though earnings have never been higher. A starving factory worker of the 1800s was overjoyed to earn enough to buy an extra potato. A factory worker today becomes angry if he cannot afford steak.

[5]

Human Needs

READING FOR UNDERSTANDING

Summary

_____ 1. In summary, this passage presents the **sequence** in which
   a. human needs are usually satisfied.
   b. people discover they have needs.
   c. Maslow discovered human needs.
   d. people satisfy the needs of others.

_____ 2. The summary is best stated in the headings and in the
   a. first part of the first paragraph.
   b. second part of the first paragraph.
   c. first part of the second paragraph.
   d. second part of the second paragraph.

Vocabulary

_____ 3. Things that are **depicted***
   a. have the points removed.
   b. have very sharp points.
   c. are drawn or painted.
   d. are presented orally.

_____ 4. If something is **derived*** it is
   a. discussed as being inferior.
   b. brought from something else.
   c. shown to have great value.
   d. removed to a distant place.

Summary	Number right _____	X 10 =	_____
Vocabulary	Number right _____	X 10 =	_____
Comprehension	Number right _____	X 10 =	_____
		Total score	_____

_____   5. That which is **intrinsically*** interesting
            a. should be very interesting.
            b. is briefly of some interest.
            c. appears to be interesting.
            d. has interest in and of itself.

Comprehension

_____   6. To have a place to live satisfies
            a. a physiological need.
            b. a safety need.
            c. a social need.
            d. an esteem need.

_____   7. How many people in this country earn enough money to feel completely
            secure?
            a. few
            b. about half
            c. more than half
            d. most

_____   8. Money cannot satisfy
            a. physiological and safety needs.
            b. social and self-realization needs.
            c. safety and social needs.
            d. safety and esteem needs.

_____   9. People try to satisfy esteem needs in business by seeking
            a. more money.
            b. more work.
            c. security.
            d. promotions.

_____   10. Of the five rungs in the ladder of needs, most people in our society reach the
            a. second rung.
            b. third rung.
            c. fourth rung.
            d. fifth rung.

[5]

Human Needs

READING FOR STUDYING

Write the word *first* in front of the heading "Physiological Needs." Then **write** the words *second, third, fourth,* and *fifth* in front of the following four headings in the passage. **Underline** the parts of the passage that best describe each need and, where possible, the parts that explain how each need is satisfied by work. **Summarize** this information on the lines below. The headings have been written to emphasize that the passage presents a sequence.

ORDER IN WHICH HUMAN NEEDS ARE SATISFIED

First: Physiological Needs

These are needs for food, clothing, and a place to live. Work provides the money for these things.

Second: Safety Needs

Third: Social Needs

_____

_____

_____

_____

_____

_____

Fourth: Esteem Needs

_____

_____

_____

_____

_____

Fifth: Self-Realization Needs

_____

_____

_____

_____

_____

_____

[FOUR]

Categories in Textbooks

In addition to presenting material on methods and sequences, textbooks also give information about categories. *Categories* are divisions created to organize facts and concepts so that they are more easily understood. For example, to study mental illness, psychologists divide the subject into two basic categories: neurosis and psychosis. Then these two categories of illness are broken down into various types. Some of the categories of psychotics are manic-depressives, schizophrenics, and paranoids.

Art history textbooks describe various types of art works; biology textbooks classify types of plants and animals; and English textbooks identify and discuss the various literary forms. All these textbooks divide their subjects into categories for discussion.

Categories are created by *analysis,* which is the act of dividing a fact or a concept into its parts so that it may be better understood. For example, to help you understand your textbooks, this book divides "information in textbooks" into various types and then discusses these categories of information. You have been introduced to three of the divisions resulting from this analysis: *methods, sequences,* and *categories.*

It is important to understand that categories generally are devised primarily to aid understanding. When scholars categorize, they usually do not consider it essential for items to be placed in one category, and one category only. Consequently, many of the classifications you will encounter in your college textbooks do not allow for clear-cut categorization. For example, you have already learned that textbook passages may present more than one of the categories of information described in this book: the first selection, entitled "Studying," (pages 11–14) explains both a method *and* a sequence. Also a psychotic person may display characteristics of two—or even all three—of the basic types of psychosis: he or she may be manic-depressive, schizophrenic, and paranoid. This overlapping is typical of many of the categories you will find explained in your college textbooks. There are times, however, when categories will not overlap. For example, when people are categorized by sex, they will all be placed in the categories of either "male" or "female."

The two selections in this part of the book categorize: their subjects are analyzed into parts so that the subjects may be more fully understood. As you read "Fitness" and "Purposes of Advertising," pay special attention to understanding the categories that are described and also to understanding why the subjects have been divided into categories.

[6]

Fitness

Movement capacity involves the development of three fitness elements: strength, suppleness, and stamina.

Strength is the basic muscular force required for movement. Normally, strength is developed by overcoming resistances, such as those supplied by parts of the body in normal daily activity; by the whole body in lifting, pulling, walking, and climbing; by another person's body as in football or wrestling; or by inanimate objects, such as grocery bags, trash cans, books, barbells, or dumbbells.

The quickest and most direct means of improving strength is through weight training. Isometric (static) exercise that develops tension may also improve strength; however, except for special circumstances and rehabilitation purposes, resistive exercise with movement is preferred because it does not inhibit blood flow or raise blood pressure to the same extent that static exercise does. Moreover, weight training seems to bring about greater strength achievement over a wider range of movement than isometric procedures, which tend to have an effect that is limited to specific angles of application.

Suppleness, or flexibility, is the quality of muscles, bones, tendons, and ligaments that permits full range of movements in a joint. One may be supple in some joints but not in others, and there may even be large differences in the same joint on either side of the body. For example, many individuals have greater range of movement in one shoulder than the other. The ability to move one's limbs and other bendable parts effectively through the full range is maintained by periodic full-range bending and stretching movements. Immobilization or restricted movement is associated with reduced suppleness, often giving rise to postural and orthopedic problems.

Stamina, or endurance, is the quality that enables an individual to mobilize energy to maintain movement over an extended period of time.... Stamina is largely a matter of developing an adequate oxygen-transport system. Normally, stamina is achieved by sustained whole-body exercise, such as that involved in running, bicycling, and swimming.

One objective of athletic programs in colleges is to help students understand the advantages of maintaining physical fitness throughout life. (Courtesy of Queensborough Community College: left photo by Hugh Rodgers, right photo by Gene Luttenberg.)

The fitness elements cannot be developed or maintained unless the specific exercise experience is reasonably intense and frequent. People who lead sedentary lives offer a marked contrast to those whose life styles provide activity of the kind, intensity, and frequency necessary for the development and maintenance of strength, suppleness, and stamina.

Compared with an untrained person, the trained individual is essentially leaner and stronger for his or her body size, has an enhanced circulatory and energy-mobilization capacity, and recovers more quickly following exercise. The untrained individual often exhibits the physical characteristics associated with early aging. Physiological middle age for the unfit may arrive before they are chronologically twenty-one years old. At the other end of the fitness spectrum, there are vigorous "youngsters" chronologically in their sixties and beyond. There is evidence to indicate that training postpones physiological aging in adulthood and enhances strength and stamina in old age. However, a declining suppleness may be one infirmity shared by the fit and unfit senior citizen, because deterioration of joints does not appear to be reversible.

[6]

Fitness

READING FOR UNDERSTANDING

Summary

_____   1. In summary, this passage presents the **categories**
a. of people who remain fit throughout life.
b. used to identify those who are unfit.
c. that make up complete physical fitness.
d. of healthfulness resulting from fitness.

_____   2. The summary is best stated in the
a. first sentence.
b. second sentence.
c. third sentence.
d. fourth sentence.

Vocabulary

_____   3. If people have **suppleness*** they have
a. softness.
b. toughness.
c. durability.
d. flexibility.

_____   4. **Orthopedic*** problems occur in the
a. cardiovascular system.
b. central nervous system.
c. joints and muscles.
d. chest and abdomen.

Summary	Number right _____	X 10 =	_____
Vocabulary	Number right _____	X 10 =	_____
Comprehension	Number right _____	X 10 =	_____
		Total score	_____

_____   5. **Sedentary*** people are
        a. stronger than most.
        b. physically inactive.
        c. settled in their ways.
        d. intellectually deficient.

Comprehension

_____   6. Compared to lifting weights, isometric exercise
        a. makes the heart beat more quickly.
        b. raises the blood pressure more.
        c. causes more problems in breathing.
        d. stimulates adrenalin flow more.

_____   7. To improve suppleness, one must
        a. lift and lower.
        b. bend and stretch.
        c. push and pull.
        d. walk and run.

_____   8. Running, bicycling, and swimming are good exercises for building
        a. muscles.
        b. strength.
        c. suppleness.
        d. endurance.

_____   9. Without physical training, people sometimes become unfit by the time they
reach the age of
        a. 20.
        b. 25.
        c. 30.
        d. 35.

_____   10. Physical training cannot improve an old person's
        a. suppleness.
        b. strength.
        c. stamina.
        d. fitness.

[6]

Fitness

READING FOR STUDYING

Underline the first sentence, **circle** the words in italic type (strength, suppleness, and stamina), and **underline** the words that best explain each type of fitness. **Summarize** this information on the lines below. The headings have been written to emphasize that the selection presents categories.

TYPES OF FITNESS

Strength

_____

_____

_____

_____

_____

_____

_____

Suppleness

_____

_____

_____

_____

_____

_____

_____

_____

Stamina

_____

_____

_____

_____

_____

_____

Purposes of Advertising

Advertising can be classified in three main categories according to its overall objectives. These are primary demand advertising, selective, or brand advertising, and institutional advertising. The three categories differ in what they try to accomplish.

Primary demand advertising tries to increase the total demand for products without distinguishing between brands. The Wool Bureau has attempted to get purchasers of apparel to select wool goods rather than synthetics. The California Prune Growers Association has tried to popularize prunes by running radio commercials extolling the virtues of "the funny fruit." Such advertising is generally sponsored by the trade association for the industry. Sometimes an industry-wide union will also advertise. For example, the Plasterers' Union, in an attempt to discourage the use of wallboard in construction, has run full-page ads calling on New Yorkers to "keep New York plastered."

Selective, or *brand, advertising* aims at getting purchasers to use a particular branded product, for example, Del Monte prunes or Hart Schaffner & Marx suits. This type of promotion accounts for the largest share of money spent on advertising. Selective advertising directed at the consumer market is generally found on TV and in newspapers and magazines. Selective advertising intended for the industrial market may be limited to trade magazines.

Institutional advertising is designed to create goodwill for a company rather than to sell specific goods. During the gasoline shortage from 1973 to 1974, oil companies spent large sums of money on newspaper and TV advertising to suggest ways to conserve gasoline. They hoped to create an image of themselves as public-spirited organizations. Other institutional advertising is even more subtle. Mobil Oil has sponsored *Masterpiece Theatre* on educational television. Xerox has financed hour-long shows on controversial issues. Local department stores sometimes run ads supporting the United Fund. In every case, the objective is to improve the company's image and to create an aura of good feeling about the company in the minds of potential customers.

Institutional advertising also has political importance, especially for privately owned public utilities. Consolidated Edison's Save-a-Watt cam-

This is for your body and your home.

The Wool Bureau, Inc., U.S. Branch of IWS, 360 Lexington Ave., New York, N.Y. 10017

Wool. It's worth more. Naturally.

This example of *primary demand advertising* attempts to increase purchases of items made of wool without promoting the sale of any specific name-brand woolen product. (The Wool Bureau, Inc.)

paign is an example. These utility companies operate under monopoly franchises that depend on public acceptance. So they must maintain a good public image in order to survive. In most foreign countries, the telephone, gas, and electric utilities are now publicly owned. The fear of such takeovers motivates many utility companies in the United States to adopt extensive institutional advertising budgets. Clearly these campaigns are directed at the public not merely as consumers, but also as voters.

[7]

Purposes of Advertising

READING FOR UNDERSTANDING

Summary

_____ 1. In summary, this passage presents **types** of advertisements according to the
a. products they attempt to promote.
b. purposes they try to accomplish.
c. institutions they attempt to serve.
d. type of media in which they appear.

_____ 2. The summary is best stated in the
a. first paragraph.
b. second paragraph.
c. third paragraph.
d. fourth paragraph.

Vocabulary

_____ 3. **Objectives*** are
a. things not affected by feelings.
b. statements of observable facts.
c. aims or goals to be reached.
d. consumers in the marketplace.

_____ 4. **Extolling*** is
a. noticing.
b. praising.
c. mentioning.
d. overlooking.

Summary	Number right_____	X 10 = _____	
Vocabulary	Number right _____	X 10 = _____	
Comprehension	Number right_____	)(10 = _____	
		Total score_____	

_____ 5. An **aura*** is
      a. an atmosphere.
      b. an ideology.
      c. a configuration.
      d. a temperature rise.

Comprehension

_____ 6. Primary demand advertising could be used to sell
      a. Wisconsin cheeses.
      b. Green Giant peas.
      c. Wrigley chewing gum.
      d. Lipton tea bags.

_____ 7. Selective advertising could be used to sell
      a. milk and eggs.
      b. cotton products.
      c. Georgia peaches.
      d. Zenith TV sets.

_____ 8. Most selective advertising is intended for
      a. magazines and newspapers.
      b. television and radio.
      c. the industrial market.
      d. the consumer market.

_____ 9. Paid television commercials for a presidential candidate are examples of
      a. selective advertising.
      b. democratic advertising.
      c. institutional advertising.
      d. primary demand advertising.

_____ 10. Which of the following is *not* an example of institutional advertising?
      a. Xerox broadcast a movie on television that was not interrupted by commercials.
      b. New York Telephone Company ran an ad telling how an operator had saved two lives.
      c. Trans World Airlines ran an ad telling about low-cost flights to Europe.
      d. Metropolitan Life Insurance Company ran an ad explaining how to stay in good health.

[7]

Purposes of Advertising

READING FOR STUDYING

Underline the first paragraph, **circle** the three types of advertising printed in italic type, and **underline** the words that best summarize the purpose of each type of advertising. **Summarize** this information on the lines below, including your own examples of what might be advertised by each type of advertising. (Your examples for selective advertising might be any brand product not mentioned in the passage, such as Timex watches, Hershey candy bars, or Exxon gasoline.) The headings have been written to emphasize that the selection presents categories.

TYPES OF ADVERTISING

Primary Demand Advertising

_____

_____

_____

_____

_____

_____

_____

Selective Advertising

_____

_____

_____

_____

_____

_____

_____

_____

Institutional Advertising

_____

_____

_____

_____

_____

_____

[F I V E]

Reasons in Textbooks

In addition to methods, sequences, and categories, textbooks also discuss reasons. *Reasons* are explanations that help us understand why things are as they are. Reasons may be given for questions that begin with the words *why* and *how*:

Why did we fight in World War II?
How did we become involved in World War II?

The answers to these questions require reasons: they require statements of the circumstances that caused us to fight in World War II.

There are two basic types of reasons: facts and theories. *Facts* are things that actually happened and that are really true. The question "Why did we fight in World War II?" can be answered by a statement of facts—actual occurrences that caused us to fight in this war. Many times, though, explanations are provided by *theories,* which are possible, but not certain, explanations. For example, we cannot be certain about how the planet earth came to be; however, scientists have offered many theories to explain its origin. Also no one knows for certain why some people become criminals, but sociologists have formulated theories to try to understand and explain antisocial behavior.

Part 5 includes two selections that are good examples of passages that give reasons: "Mate Selection" and "Marijuana." As you study these passages, pay special attention to understanding the questions they attempt to answer—and the reasons they give for their answers.

Mate Selection

A courtship system is essentially a marriage market, although different systems vary according to how much choice they permit the individual. The United States probably allows more individual freedom of choice than any other society. A parent who attempts to interfere in the choice of a son or daughter is considered meddlesome and is more likely to alienate than persuade the young lover. In our predominantly urban and anonymous society, young people—often equipped with automobiles—have an exceptional degree of privacy in their courting.

The practice of dating enables young people to find out about one another, to improve their own interpersonal skills in the market, to engage in sexual experimentation if they so wish, and finally to select a marriage partner. The metaphor of the "market" may seem a little unromantic, but in fact the participants do attempt to "sell" their assets—physical appearance, personal charms, talents and interests, and career prospects.

Who marries whom? In general, the American mate selection process is *homogamous:* individuals marry others much like themselves. Among the characteristics that seem to attract people to one another are the following:

Similar age. Married partners are usually of roughly the same age. Husbands are on average older than their wives, though rarely by more than five years, and even this difference in age is gradually declining (Parke and Glick, 1967). The 1970 census showed that the median age difference between partners was only two to four years.

Social class. Most people marry within their own social class. The reasons are obvious: we tend to live in class-segregated neighborhoods, to meet mostly people of the same class, and to share class-specific tastes and interests (Udry, 1971). Interclass marriages are relatively more common, however, among college students.

Proximity. People tend to marry people who live in the same area, even in the same neighborhood. In part this is because they are more likely to meet, in part because their common environment provides them with similar experiences and interests.

Religion. Most marriages are between people sharing the same religious faith: 93 percent of Jews, 91 percent of Catholics, and 78 percent of Protestants marry partners of the same religion (Blood, 1962). Interreligious marriages within Protestant denominations, however, are fairly common. Religious bodies generally oppose interfaith marriages, on the grounds that they may lead to personal conflicts, disagreements over the faith in which children should be raised, and an undermining of belief in a particular doctrine. Many intending spouses change their religion to that of their partner before marriage.

Education. Husbands and wives generally have a similar educational level. Since the number of years of schooling correlates strongly with social class, it is difficult to disentangle the influence of educational level from class status, but some degree of intellectual parity seems to be demanded by marital partners. The college campus is, of course, a marriage market in its own right, and college-educated people are especially likely to marry people of similar educational achievement.

Racial background. Interracial marriages are extremely rare. Several states had laws prohibiting interracial marriages until the sixties, and even today such marriages attract considerable social disapproval. Interracial marriages between blacks and whites are particularly rare; in the majority of these cases, the husband is black and the wife white.

Ethnic background. Members of the white ethnic groups are more likely to marry within their own group than outside it, but with the halt in new immigration and the steady assimilation of the ethnic groups into mainstream American society, this tendency is declining markedly.

Physical characteristics. People tend to marry partners who are physically similar to themselves in height, weight, and even in hair color, state of health, and basal metabolism (Burgess and Wallin, 1973).

Cupid's arrow, then, does not strike at random. We know very little about the personality characteristics that attract partners to one another. If a general psychological pattern exists, no researchers have yet been able to determine it with any certainty. But the social characteristics of marriage partners are much easier to establish, and all research findings point in the same direction: we tend to choose as mates people who have social characteristics similar to our own.

REFERENCES

Blood, Robert O. 1962. *Marriage.* New York: Free Press.

Burgess, Ernest W., and Paul Wallin. 1973. *Engagement and Marriage.* Philadelphia: Lippincott.

Parke, Robert, Jr., and Paul C. Glick. 1967. "Prospective changes in marriage and family." *Journal of Marriage and the Family,* 29, pp. 249–256.

Udry, J. Richard. 1971. *The Social Context of Marriage.* Philadelphia: Lippincott.

[8]

Mate Selection

READING FOR UNDERSTANDING

Summary

_____   1. In summary, this passage presents the **reasons** that
a. opposites marry each other.
b. people marry who they do.
c. teenagers should not marry.
d. many marriages do not succeed.

_____   2. The summary is best stated in the headings and in the last sentence of the
a. first paragraph.
b. second paragraph.
c. third paragraph.
d. fourth paragraph.

Vocabulary

_____   3. A **meddlesome*** person
a. destroys.
b. disrupts.
c. interferes.
d. annoys.

_____   4. To **alienate*** is to
a. divide into parts.
b. cause to withdraw.
c. travel a distance.
d. mix things together.

Summary	Number right _____	× 10 =	_____
Vocabulary	Number right _____	× 10 =	_____
Comprehension	Number right _____	× 10 =	_____
		Total score	_____

_____   5. A **homogamous*** marriage is one in which
         a. partners are the same sex.
         b. partners are much alike.
         c. there is great hostility.
         d. there is great harmony.

Comprehension

_____   6. People are most likely to marry somebody from a different social class if they
         a. are of the same religion.
         b. are older, rather than younger.
         c. have been married before.
         d. have some college education.

_____   7. People are least likely to marry someone of a different faith if they are
         a. Jewish.
         b. Catholic.
         c. Baptist.
         d. Methodist.

_____   8. Interracial marriages are
         a. extremely rare.
         b. increasingly common.
         c. generally accepted.
         d. seldom successful.

_____   9. Marriage partners are likely to be similar in
         a. their height and how much they weigh.
         b. the color of their hair and their skin.
         c. the general condition of their health.
         d. their size, coloring, and health.

_____   10. Researchers know very little about why people marry each other for reason of
         a. physical characteristics.
         b. educational characteristics.
         c. personality characteristics.
         d. social characteristics.

[8]

Mate Selection

READING FOR STUDYING

Underline the last sentence of the third paragraph and the statements under each heading that tell why people marry whom they do. **Summarize** this information on the lines below. The headings have been written to emphasize that the selection presents reasons.

REASONS PEOPLE MARRY WHOM THEY DO

Similar Age

_____

_____

_____

Social Class

_____

_____

_____

Proximity

_____

_____

_____

Religion

_____

_____

_____

Education

_____

_____

_____

Racial Background

_____

_____

_____

Ethnic Background

_____

_____

_____

Physical Characteristics

_____

_____

_____

Marijuana

How does somebody become a regular user of marijuana? Howard Becker (1953, 1963) addressed this problem at a time when marijuana smokers were still widely regarded as "dope fiends." The common sense assumption at the time was that people were motivated to use marijuana by some underlying personality disturbance. Becker's findings challenged this view, and his account of the process by which somebody becomes a marijuana user provided many insights which are now common knowledge.

Becker spent many years as a professional jazz musician, participating in a subculture in which the use of marijuana was common. He drew freely on his observations of jazz musicians for his study, and supplemented these data with in-depth interviews with individual marijuana smokers. He concluded that marijuana use is not the result of psychological disturbance on the part of the smoker, nor is it something that "just happens." Becker found that several conditions must be met before a person becomes a habitual marijuana user and that each of these conditions is fulfilled through a complex social interaction between the novice and more experienced users.

First, the novice must learn that the drug exists and that other people find its use pleasurable. Contact with experienced users increases the novice's curiosity about marijuana, and eventually he or she accepts an invitation by users to try it. But trying marijuana is not the same as getting high. The novice usually fails to perceive any effects on the first attempt to smoke the drug, and several repetitions may be necessary before he or she actually notices any symptoms. Unless the novice is willing to persevere, use of the drug is likely to be abandoned at this point. Typically, however, other users provide constant reassurance. They instruct the novice in techniques for inhaling the smoke and holding it in the lungs, and the novice's own observations of their obvious pleasure in the drug provide faith that it will eventually have an effect.

In due course the novice begins to notice physical and mental symptoms that follow inhalation of marijuana smoke. But perceiving symp-

From Ian Robertson, Sociology, pp. 127-128. Copyright © 1977 by Worth Publishers, Inc. Used by permission.

toms is not the same as getting high, either. The novice must not only consciously connect these symptoms with the fact of having smoked the drug but must also learn to experience the symptoms as pleasurable. If this interpretation is not made, marijuana usage is likely to be discontinued, on the grounds that "It does nothing for me." As Becker points out, the effects of marijuana are not automatically or necessarily pleasurable. The user's scalp may tingle; time and distance are easily misjudged; and there may be sensations of dizziness, faintness, thirst, and hunger. The novice is by no means sure that these and similar experiences are pleasant and has to learn to interpret them as enjoyable. Becker (1963) suggests that this definition "occurs, typically, in interaction with more experienced users, who, in a number of ways, teach the novice to find pleasure in this experience which is at first so frightening." Social definitions of a rather ambiguous experience predis-   * pose the new user to interpret the drug's effects as pleasant, and only at this point does the novice become a habitual user. He or she begins to secure a supply of marijuana, to develop any routines of secrecy that may be necessary, and to redefine earlier notions about the morality of marijuana use. Again, these techniques and justifications are learned in social interaction with others.

Becker (1963) concludes that marijuana use cannot be explained in terms of supposed failings in individual personality: habitual use of the drug results from resocialization through interaction with existing users:

> Instead of the deviant motives leading to the deviant behavior, it is the other way around; the deviant behavior in time produces the deviant motivations. Vague impulses and desires —in this case, probably most frequently a curiosity about the kind of experience the drug will induce—are transformed into definite patterns of action through the social interpretation of an act which is in itself ambiguous.

REFERENCES

Becker, Howard S. 1953. "Becoming a marijuana user." *American Journal of Sociology*, 59, November, pp. 235-242.
Becker, Howard S. 1963. *Outsiders: Studies in the Sociology of Deviance.* New York: Free Press.

[9]

Marijuana

READING FOR UNDERSTANDING

Summary

___ 1. In summary, this passage presents the **reasons** that
    a. marijuana is bad for health.
    b. marijuana use is increasing.
    c. people escape into marijuana use.
    d. people become marijuana users.

___ 2. The summary is best stated in the
    a. first sentence of the first paragraph.
    b. first sentence of the second paragraph.
    c. last sentence of the second paragraph.
    d. first sentence of the third paragraph.

Vocabulary

___ 3. A **novice*** is a
    a. beginner.
    b. witticism.
    c. position.
    d. notification.

___ 4. To **persevere*** is to
    a. permit.
    b. accept.
    c. receive.
    d. continue.

Summary	Number right ___	× 10 =	___
Vocabulary	Number right ___	× 10 =	___
Comprehension	Number right ___	× 10 =	___
		Total score	___

_____ 5. To **predispose*** is to
  a. prepare or make ready.
  b. rid or make not ready.
  c. put out of sight.
  d. put out on display.

Comprehension

_____ 6. Becker's account of the process by which people become marijuana users is now
  a. applied to other addictions.
  b. of great help to thousands.
  c. accepted as common knowledge.
  d. debated by marijuana experts.

_____ 7. According to Becker, to become a marijuana user one must first
  a. know an experienced marijuana user.
  b. meet a person who sells marijuana.
  c. be in need of emotional fulfillment.
  d. desire an altered state of consciousness.

_____ 8. A person who smokes marijuana for the first time will probably
  a. get high.
  b. not get high.
  c. become ill.
  d. feel guilty.

_____ 9. It was Becker who noted that to get high on marijuana one must
  a. take deep puffs and hold the smoke.
  b. learn that the symptoms are pleasurable.
  c. perceive the sensation of dizziness.
  d. drink wine or soda while smoking.

_____ 10. Becker did *not* say that people who become marijuana users will usually need to
  a. find a way to get hold of marijuana.
  b. find ways to keep their habit secret.
  c. decide that marijuana smoking is acceptable.
  d. plan that they will become hard-drug users.

[9]

Marijuana

READING FOR STUDYING

Underline the last sentence of the first paragraph and the last sentence of the second paragraph. Then **number** and **underline** the six steps that lead to marijuana use (the first step is given in the first sentence of the third paragraph; the fourth, fifth, and sixth steps are given in the next to the last sentence of the fourth paragraph). Then **summarize** the steps that lead to marijuana use on the lines below (the fourth step has been written for you). The heading emphasizes that the passage presents reasons.

HOW PEOPLE BECOME MARIJUANA USERS

1. _____

_____

_____

2. _____

_____

_____

3. _____

_____

4. *They secure a supply of marijuana.* _____

_____

_____

5. _____

    _____

    _____

6. _____

    _____

    _____

[S I X]

Points of View
in Textbooks

In addition to presenting methods, sequences, categories, and reasons, textbooks also explain points of view. *Points of view* are the positions, attitudes, opinions, or beliefs that people have. People also sometimes assume a certain point of view for the sake of argument. For example, you can discuss a movie from the perspective of what you liked about it or from the perspective of what you did not like about it.

There are often extremely different points of view on the same subject. For example, some people believe that all murderers should be put to death; others hold the opinion that no person—not even a murderer—should ever be put to death. Strong differences of opinion over important issues such as this are the bases for disagreements, disputes, and controversies.

People you know are likely to have very different points of view about the answers to these questions:

1. Should all male and female Americans be required to serve in the armed forces?
2. Should the smoking of marijuana be legalized?
3. Should all nuclear energy plants in this country be closed down?

Equally intelligent and well-educated people have widely different points of view on such questions.

Extreme points of view are often the subjects of sensational magazine and newspaper articles. A headline similar to the following appeared in a New York newspaper:

EDUCATOR SAYS THROW OUT

YOUR TV SET—IT'S MAKING

YOUR CHILDREN STUPID

This headline clearly alerts readers that somebody is expressing a controversial point of view, and its wording encourages a strong emotional reaction. However, information contained in this newspaper article also appears in an education textbook under the heading "Positive and Negative Effects of Television." The heading for the textbook passage is straightforward and appeals to reason rather than to emotion; the passage sets forth research findings indicating that television has had both good and bad effects on children. The newspaper article presents only one point of view; the textbook passage presents information to support both points of view: children benefit educationally from television *and* television hampers children's intellectual development.

It is easy to discover a point of view that is stated in an emotionally charged newspaper headline; it is more difficult to find the points of view contained in a textbook under an undramatic heading. You will need to read your textbooks carefully to find conflicting points of

view. Clues that points of view will be discussed in textbooks are
given in headings containing contrasting words such as these:

good and bad
positive and negative
yes and no
pro and con
for and against
favoring and opposing
advantages and disadvantages

Such pairs of words indicate that there are at least two ways to view a
subject. If there are two ways to view a subject, there is likely to be
more than one point of view about that subject.

As you study the following two passages, pay attention to the points
of view: "Values" examines a subject from two contrasting points of
view and "Birth Control" explores conflicting points of view.

[10]

Values

As we grew up in America, 3,000 miles from Europe, we developed a distinctive character and set of beliefs different from those of the countries our ancestors came from. Since earning a living is one of life's most important activities, many of our personal values are related to it. In the case of the United States, these values encouraged national economic growth and the accumulation of personal wealth. Unfortunately, the positive set of values that guides much of our business and personal life is matched by less attractive traits.

THE POSITIVE SIDE OF OUR VALUE SYSTEM

Generations of Americans were raised on stories about Washington's truthfulness under pressure, or Lincoln's walking seven miles a day to get an education, or Edison's trying hundreds of substances before inventing the tungsten lightbulb. These men embodied virtues that were considered important for personal happiness and success and for social health and prosperity. Americans incorporated these stories into their belief system. All our beliefs combined to make a powerful force for economic progress. These values include activism and the desire for self-improvement, pragmatism, the work ethic, thrift, material well-being, and individualism.

Activism and the desire to be better off. Americans are the most restless people in recorded history. They are descended from 35 million immigrants who took part in the greatest mass migration of people ever known. They came here seeking, among other things, personal opportunities. The value system they developed rewards active people who take chances to get ahead or to "build a better mousetrap," as Emerson put it.

Pragmatism. Faced with the real problem of staying alive in an unfamiliar land, Americans became a practical people. They quickly learned to ask such questions as "What is the problem?" "What is the solution?"

and "Will it work?" We believe that "Yankee ingenuity" deserves to be rewarded. We are instinctively the most technologically oriented people in the world.

The work ethic. Most people who came here had to believe in the *work ethic,* that work is good and necessary in and of itself. As Captain John Smith told the first settlers at Jamestown, "Those that do not work shall not eat." Many who came here were glad of the opportunity to work simply to earn a decent living. But the California and Alaska gold rushes symbolized another side of our character. Many of us dreamed that hard work, combined with skill, courage, and luck, might make a person rich.

In China, people worked very hard for centuries, while they and their country remained poor. But Americans were surrounded by examples of hard work leading to wealth. *Pluck and Luck* is the apt title of the most popular boys' book of the nineteenth century; pluck and luck epitomized the qualities required to lead a person *From Rags to Riches.*   *
The two titles in the preceding sentence are among 120 books written by Horatio Alger, whose popular stories reflected the emotions and dreams of Americans. Americans believed they were happier if their lives had work with a purpose to it. They also believed that if people were smart and lucky, and became rich, they deserved their wealth.

Thrift, sacrifice, and delayed gratification. A belief in *delayed gratification,* saving for a future good instead of spending for a present one, is essential to creating wealth in any economic or social system. If a person spends money as soon as it is earned, or a society consumes profits as soon as they are earned, there will never be savings to buy a home or build a factory. Moreover, there will never be savings to carry a person or company through hard times. The American value system reflects the Biblical story of Joseph, who persuaded Pharaoh to save during seven prosperous years for the seven lean years that were sure to come. Generations of Americans grew up believing it was right and wise to sacrifice present gains for future wealth and happiness.

Material well-being. Americans are a religious people. We believe in a divine system of rewards and punishments for our good and bad deeds. But we are not a spiritual people. The Puritans believed that God has his tasks in heaven, and that man has his tasks on earth. Americans see no inconsistency in enjoying the material things of life, in accumulating and protecting property, or in working so that they can drive Cadillacs or so that their children can afford to live in a better neighborhood.

Individualism. There was one spiritual belief that Americans did have: the belief in the individual worth of every man and woman. Americans were frequently isolated in the new land and had to learn to make their own decisions. We believe that no one is wise enough to tell us how to live our lives. Our constitution strictly limited the power of government over our lives and property. We believe that individual intelligence and effort should be encouraged and rewarded.

THE NEGATIVE SIDE OF OUR VALUE SYSTEM

The values cited above created a climate in which business could flourish and people could prosper. Although business has profited from the existence of such values, it has not always made proper use of them. In fact, some critics claim that business has distorted these values for its own ends. As a result, it has given rise to certain other attitudes that will prove unhealthy in the long run, even though their immediate impact may have been economically useful. Three major traits in this category most often singled out for criticism are wastefulness, indifference to social needs, and dishonesty.

Wastefulness. The economic boom that lasted through the early 1970s was essentially unhealthy for American life, say the social critics, because it created an economy based on waste instead of thrift. Americans were urged to buy new cars every other year. They were urged to borrow to buy household appliances or to take vacations. The world's resources were rapidly eroded in a wildly extravagant spree.

In the 1960s, at the height of the boom, many young Americans who had not experienced the Great Depression and assumed that prosperity was permanent, were appalled at the emphasis on business expansion   * and personal possessions. They associated both with waste, extravagances that much of the rest of the world, mired in poverty, could do without. The environmentalist movement, a reaction against industrial assaults on natural beauty and pollution of air and water, grew up at this time as well.

Indifference to social needs. Our belief in individualism and personal responsibility for self-advancement became distorted in our adoption of the doctrine of social Darwinism. Social Darwinism was developed by Herbert Spencer, a nineteenth-century English economist. He took Charles Darwin's biological theories of natural selection and applied them to social growth. Spencer said that the healthiest society was one that permitted "survival of the fittest" and that allowed people who could not keep up to fall by the wayside.

One aspect of this philosophy is extreme competitiveness, the feeling that you can only get ahead at the expense of someone else. Another aspect is indifference to social insurance and public benefits that cannot be measured in economic terms. We trail most other advanced nations in social insurance programs. One result is that, for such a wealthy nation, our health and life span statistics are scandalously low. (At the beginning of this decade, forty-four out of seventy countries reporting to a

United Nations agency had a lower death rate per thousand than the United States. Sixteen countries have a lower infant mortality rate.) Another result is that certain basic items are treated like business goods and services and are either expensive, such as health care, or simply inadequate, such as public transportation or middle-income housing.

Dishonesty. The result of emphasis on waste and competition, say the critics, is a continuing dishonesty in business practices. The United States has had financial scandals throughout its history. Banks have failed because deposits were used for speculation. Reputable investment houses have issued worthless stock to the public. And companies have published misleading financial statements that failed to reveal their true condition. Americans have also witnessed scandals throughout their history involving tainted foods, unsafe products, and shady claims. The American value system preaches honesty and reliability, but pressures force too many businesses to behave badly, say the critics.

[10]

Values

READING FOR UNDERSTANDING

Summary

_____   1. In summary, this passage presents **points of view** about Americans'
          a. system of values.
          b. ability to solve problems.
          c. concern for the poor.
          d. role in world leadership.

_____   2. The summary is best stated in the headings and in the
          a. first sentence of the first paragraph.
          b. last sentence of the first paragraph.
          c. first sentence of the second paragraph.
          d. last sentence of the second paragraph.

Vocabulary

_____   3. **Pragmatism*** is concerned with
          a. technological advances.
          b. philosophical theories.
          c. that which is practical.
          d. things that are practiced.

_____   4. If something is **epitomized*** it is
          a. summarized.
          b. eulogized.
          c. disturbed.
          d. disclosed.

Summary	Number right _____	× 10 =	_____
Vocabulary	Number right _____	× 10 =	_____
Comprehension	Number right _____	× 10 =	_____
		Total score	_____

_____   5. To be **appalled*** is to be
      a. shocked.
      b. stopped.
      c. upheld.
      d. thrown.

Comprehension

_____   6. Those who believe in the work ethic believe that
      a. everybody will do good work.
      b. heaven is the reward of work.
      c. work is good and necessary.
      d. everybody has the right to work.

_____   7. The creation of wealth requires that members of an economic system believe in
      a. institutional pragmatism.
      b. democratic principles.
      c. delayed gratification.
      d. individual activism.

_____   8. One of the good sides of our values is
      a. good use of raw materials.
      b. handling of social problems.
      c. successful business practices.
      d. belief in the individual.

_____   9. Critics of our value system claim that our values
      a. will be replaced by socialism.
      b. have been distorted by business.
      c. can be restored by faith in God.
      d. are collapsing, as they did in Rome.

_____   10. The major cause of our wastefulness is the
      a. stock market crash of 1929.
      b. Great Depression of the 1930s.
      c. World War of the 1940s.
      d. economic upswing of the 1960s.

[10]

Values

READING FOR STUDYING

Underline the last sentence of the first paragraph, the last sentence of the second paragraph, and the last sentence of the paragraph under the heading "The Negative Side of Our Value System." Then **underline** the words that best describe the six positive values and the three negative values. **Summarize** this information on the lines below. The headings have been written to emphasize that the passage examines our values from two points of view.

DO WE HAVE GOOD VALUES?

Yes

1. _____

_____

_____

_____

2. _____

_____

_____

_____

3. _____

_____

_____

_____

4. _____

_____

_____

_____

5. _____

_____

_____

_____

6. _____

_____

_____

_____

No

1. _____

_____

_____

_____

2. _____

_____

_____

_____

3. _____

_____

_____

_____

Birth Control

In spite of the reams that have been written on the subject, it may come as a surprise to learn that contraceptive techniques are age-old. Historical records indicate that most of our so-called modern methods, in principle at least, have been used for several thousand years. The oldest known contraceptive recipe is found on a papyrus dating from the period 1850–1550 B.C. Ancient records show quite clearly that, while many of the devices were magical in nature (the wearing of charms, the eating and drinking of ingenious concoctions), others were designed specifically for preventing the union of sperm and egg. However unwieldy and unsanitary, membranous sheaths were used to cover the male organ, and a variety of materials were employed as vaginal insertions or pessaries—gum arabic, honey, ground leaves, elephant dung, plant extracts, oils, and the like. Some of these substances—those that were gummy or acid—probably acted as a sperm deterrent, but others that were alkaline had the unlooked-for effect of increasing sperm motility!

Having but limited success with the crude contraceptive techniques that were available to them, the ancients were much more likely to resort to abortion and infanticide in an effort to keep their population within the bounds of the existing food supply. The term "contraception," however, refers to the voluntary prevention of conception and does not include abortion and infanticide. In recent years, terms such as *conception control, family planning, birth control, prevenception, fertility limitation,* and *planned parenthood* have come to be virtually synonymous with the word "contraception." Whatever the term employed, the topic itself has been a center of controversy for almost 150 years.

Areas of controversy. Birth control has not only been a controversial subject, but the *focus of argument* has shifted over the years. It will be worthwhile, therefore, to examine separately the major areas of disagreement.

Medical-legal. In the United States, the first booklet on birth control seems to have been Robert Dale Owen's *Moral Physiology,* published in 1830. Two years later, Dr. Charles Knowlton, a Massachusetts physician, published anonymously a further treatise on contraceptive methods, curiously entitled *Fruits of Philosophy.* Knowlton eventually served a term of imprisonment for his part in publishing this book, and later it was the subject of a celebrated English trial."[1] Throughout most of the nineteenth century, both in Europe and the United States, contraceptives were generally associated with prostitution and sexual immorality; in fact, the birth control movement did not begin to achieve respectability until after World War I—and even then there were many hurdles to clear.

When the late Margaret Sanger started the modern birth control movement in 1912, she was met by a torrent of abuse. Religious leaders, doctors, law-enforcement agents—and a considerable portion of the public—combined to make her early career a thorny one. But her experience as a nurse on New York's Lower East Side had convinced her that one of the greatest tragedies of the day was the fact that thousands of lower-class wives continued to bear children in the midst of squalor—because contraceptive devices were not available. So, in spite of numerous court battles and a jail sentence, Margaret Sanger persisted in her crusade to make birth control acceptable, both legally and medically.

Eventually she won the fight. Today, birth control has been accepted by both the medical profession and the public at large, with family planning centers now available in virtually every part of the country. With regard to the college population, Scarlett's survey indicated that 96 percent of the undergraduates "agreed on the desirability of limiting family size."[2]

Protestant-Catholic. As the medical-legal battle waned, the argument over birth control came to revolve around Protestant-Catholic differences. The Catholic Church has held that all forms of birth limitation, other than the rhythm method, are contrary to natural law. Granted the basic tenets of the Roman Catholic Church, this viewpoint is logical and consistent, and it is regrettable that some non-Catholic writers have been rather intolerant in their approach to the subject.

Proponents of contraception, on the other hand, have argued that birth control is an economic blessing to poorer families, that child-spacing patterns are improved, and that population growth is reduced. From a secular view, this position is also a logical one, even though certain Catholic writers have refused to accept the legitimacy of the arguments.

While it is hardly likely that Protestants and Catholics will reconcile their views on birth control completely, the argument in recent years has tended to subside. Each side has become more tolerant; in fact, it now appears that a substantial majority of Catholic wives are using some sort of birth control other than the rhythm method.

[1] Norman St. John-Stevas, "History and Legal Status of Birth Control," in Edwin Schur (ed.), *The Family and the Sexual Revolution,* Bloomington, Indiana University Press, 1964, pp. 333–348.
[2] John A. Scarlett, "Undergraduate Attitudes Toward Birth Control: New Perspectives," *Journal of Marriage and the Family,* May 1972, pp. 312–314.

[11]

Birth Control

READING FOR UNDERSTANDING

Summary

____   1. In summary, this passage presents **points of view** about
        a. the practice of birth control.
        b. the control of overpopulation.
        c. effective birth control methods.
        d. statements made by the Catholic Church.

____   2. The summary is best stated in the headings and in the
        a. first paragraph.
        b. second paragraph.
        c. third paragraph.
        d. fourth paragraph.

Vocabulary

____   3. **Infanticide*** is
        a. the killing of a baby.
        b. the removal of disease.
        c. the early years of life.
        d. a pleasant fantasy.

____   4. A **treatise*** is a
        a. type of insertion.
        b. reward for birthing.
        c. book on some subject.
        d. sperm-blocking agent.

Summary	Number right _____	X 10 =	_____
Vocabulary	Number right _____	X 10 =	_____
Comprehension	Number right _____	X 10 =	_____
		Total score	_____

_____ 5. If something **waned,** * it
    a. wound around tightly.
    b. shot out quickly.
    c. grew less gradually.
    d. reacted negatively.

Comprehension

_____ 6. The oldest written record of a birth control method was recorded about
    a. 200 years ago.
    b. 400 years ago.
    c. 2,000 years ago.
    d. 4,000 years ago.

_____ 7. The first book on birth control that was published in the United States appeared about
    a. 50 years ago.
    b. 100 years ago.
    c. 150 years ago.
    d. 200 years ago.

_____ 8. Birth control is widely accepted today largely because of a campaign that was started about
    a. 30 years ago.
    b. 50 years ago.
    c. 70 years ago.
    d. 90 years ago.

_____ 9. In holding that birth control opposes natural law, the Catholic Church is
    a. showing intolerance for suffering.
    b. being logical and consistent.
    c. denying rights to Catholic women.
    d. increasing the world's population.

_____ 10. What proportion of Catholic wives use a birth control method?
    a. very few
    b. fewer than half
    c. just about half
    d. more than half

[11]

Birth Control

READING FOR STUDYING

Underline the third paragraph and the sentences that best summarize the medical-legal and Protestant-Catholic arguments over birth control. **Summarize** this information by answering the questions listed below. The first heading has been written to emphasize that the passage presents points of view.

SHOULD BIRTH CONTROL BE PRACTICED?

Medical-legal argument

1. What opinion did most people have about birth control before World War I?

_____

_____

_____

2. What did Margaret Sanger do to help change the general opinion about birth control?

_____

_____

_____

3. What opinion do most doctors and other individuals have about birth control today?

_____

_____

_____

Protestant-Catholic argument

1. What is the opinion of the Catholic Church about birth control?

   _____

   _____

   _____

2. What is the opinion of the Protestant Church about birth control?

   _____

   _____

   _____

3. What evidence is there that members of the Catholic Church favor the Protestant opinion about birth control?

   _____

   _____

   _____

[SEVEN]

Five Types of Information
in Textbooks

In this part of the book, you will review what you have learned about five types of information that are frequently presented in textbooks:

1. *methods* of doing certain things
2. *sequences* in which things occur or appear
3. *categories* of items
4. *reasons* that things are as they are
5. *points of view*

Beginning with the selection entitled "The Wheel Theory of Love," the first Reading for Understanding questions have been written differently from the way they appeared in the first eleven passages; they have been written to give you practice in identifying what basic types of information are presented in the textbook passages. Examine the first multiple-choice question on page 101 to understand the new format for these questions.

At first you may have difficulty deciding which type of information in a passage is most important. As you know, some passages contain more than one basic type of information: "Studying," on pages 11–14, explains both a method *and* a sequence. When this is the case, you must examine a passage in its entirety and then weigh in your mind which of the types of information seems most central to the major point of a passage. Another problem you may encounter is that a passage may contain paragraphs that clearly present one type of information—a sequence, for example. However, analysis of the entire passage may reveal that the major point of the passage is to present another type of information—methods, categories, reasons, or points of view.

Consequently, in deciding about which type of information in a passage is most important, you must sometimes make a judgment or express an opinion. If you still have difficulty in making these judgments, ask your instructor for further explanation. It is not important that you agree completely with the explanations you are given; however, it is important for you to try to understand these explanations. If you understand them, you will improve your ability to analyze, read, and study your college textbooks.

The Reading for Studying exercises also have a slightly different format in this part of the book. They have been written to help you become more independent in underlining and making notes. The exercises give suggestions for underlining and making notes on the passages, but they do not give as much guidance as the earlier exercises provided. If you have carefully done the Reading for Studying exercises for passages 2 through 11, you should be ready to underline and make notes with less help.

As you answer the questions and do the exercises in this book, keep in mind that you are doing these things to acquire skills you can use in other college courses. Your skills will improve quickly only if you use in the other courses you take the things you practice here. The only way to gain the real value of the things you learn in this book is to use these skills when you read and study for your other courses.

The Wheel Theory of Love

I will begin my discussion of love with a description of the process through which love develops. My views here are based upon a study of seventy-four college students and upon many years of observation (Reiss 1960). The development of love can be conceptualized into four processes: 1) rapport, 2) self-revelation, 3) mutual dependency, 4) need fulfillment. These processes are very closely interrelated in ways that I shall describe.

When two young people meet a very quick assessment is made of felt rapport. To what extent does each of them feel at ease with the other? To what extent do they feel they "understand" the other person? To what extent do they feel free to talk to the other person? The ease of communication is the first door that must be unlocked if love is to develop. All of us seem to strive, to one degree or another, to gain rapport with those we meet—this is probably more the case for those who are in the mate-selecting process. People vary considerably in their ability to gain rapport with others and in the accuracy of their feelings about others. Some are quite good at accurately sizing up a person they have just met on a date and are able to feel at ease with a wide variety of types of people. Some are quite poor and inaccurate at understanding others and find it difficult to feel relaxed with most people. I would hypothesize that one's social and cultural background would be one key basis from which to predict the range of types of people for whom one could feel rapport. Broad factors such as religious upbringing and educational background would make one able to understand a person with similar religious and educational backgrounds, and thus make rapport more likely. The style of upbringing also affects the range of people for whom one can feel rapport. If one is brought up with a very strong "we" and "they" attitude, it would be more difficult to feel rapport for anyone who varied from the "we" type. Within some of these general-background factors, role definitions may further aid in predicting for whom one will feel rapport. For example, if two people are both relatively equalitarian about male-female rights to work after marriage, or rights to choose what to do on a date, or control over money, then one would expect such people to feel rapport for each other more easily than if one person was equalitarian and the other held to the double standard. These are some of the key factors that affect the feelings of rapport that boys and girls have for each other on their first date. To put it in extreme form: If an African Hottentot called on a girl on a blind date, the rapport level would probably be low unless the girl were an African Hottentot herself. Racial and language barriers are but one additional sign of potential social and cultural background differences. The predictions a sociologist would make would be in terms of probabilities, of course. The odds are against it, but it is conceivable that the girl might marry the Hottentot. However, the sociologist is interested in finding over-all generalizations, not in predicting each individual mating.

A feeling of rapport almost inevitably leads one to feeling relaxed and therefore revealing more about himself than he or she otherwise would. This is the second process in the love cycle, and I have labeled it simply "self-revelation." Here, too, one can see how the social and cultural backgrounds affect the way a love relationship develops. One's background is a key determinant of the sort of things he or she feels it is proper to reveal to a person at a particular stage in a relationship. For example, some groups feel that talking about one's views on religion and politics is proper even on a first date, whereas other groups advise one never to talk to a date about such topics for it will lead only to conflict and ill feelings. Males are typically brought up and socialized by parents and peers to feel that sexual intimacies are proper to reveal to one's date at an earlier point in the courtship than females are are typically trained to accept. Much of the "battle of the sexes" results from such differences in cultural timing between male and female groups. Some groups, like the upper class, may socialize youngsters to be more formal in their revelations than would be the case for youngsters socialized in middle- or lower-class groups. In short, I am asserting here that in addition to the amount of rapport felt, one other factor that is a good predictor of what one will reveal is the view on proper revelation which was present in one's socialization groups.

One tends to reveal oneself to those one feels rapport for, and in so doing, one builds up interdependent habit systems; that is, one gets used to doing things that require cooperation from both the boy and the girl to accomplish. This is the third process in the development of a love relationship, and I call it mutual dependency. One needs the other person as an audience for one's jokes, as a confidant(e) for one's fears *
and wishes, as a partner for one's sexual needs, and so forth. Thus, one develops habits of behaving which cannot be fulfilled alone, and in so doing becomes dependent on the dating partner. Here, too, social and cultural background is relevant, for clearly the type of habits which develop result from the type of revelation in the relationship; and that is dependent on one's background.

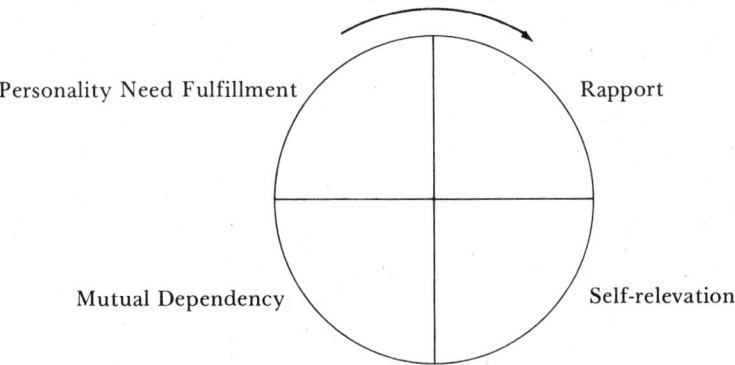

Figure 1. Graphic Presentation of the Wheel Theory
of the Development of Love.

The fourth and final process in the development of a love relationship is the one I have called personality need fulfillment. I am here referring to basic personality needs such as those Strauss (1947) used in his research, that is, the need for someone to love, the need for someone to confide in, the need for someone to stimulate ambition, and the like. These needs are of prime relevance to the important social role performances of the person. These are emotional needs related to family or occupational roles or both. By virtue of rapport, one reveals himself and becomes dependent, and in the process of carrying out the relationship one fulfills certain basic personality needs. To the extent that these needs are fulfilled, one finds a love relationship developing. In fact, one can see that the initial rapport that a person feels on first meeting someone can be presumed to be a dim awareness of the potential need fulfillment of this other person for one's own needs. If one needs sympathy and support and senses these qualities in a date, he will feel rapport more easily; reveal more; become more dependent, and if his hunch was right and the person is sympathetic, then he will also have his needs fulfilled. . . .

The basic over-all conception that love develops through the processes of rapport, revelation, dependency, and need fulfillment, I have labeled the "wheel theory." I chose this label because, as indicated in Figure 1, the processes are interdependent and a reduction in any one of them will affect the development or maintenance of a love relationship. For example, if one reduced the amount of self-revelation through an argument or by means of a competing interest, that would affect the dependency and need-fulfillment processes, which would in turn weaken the rapport process which would in turn tend to lower the revelation level even further. Thus, the processes flow into one another in one direction to develop love and can flow the other way to weaken a love relationship. The wheel analogy thus seems appropriate.

Examine the graphic presentation of the wheel theory more closely and ask yourself if it applies only to love relationships. The answer clearly is no: It seems to be an explanatory schema that would apply to the development of primary (close, intimate, face-to-face, and durable) relationships of any sort (friendship, love for parents, and so on). Thus, what I am stating here is that love is simply one type of primary relationship and develops through the same general processes as do other types of primary relationships. Courtship love in America is distinguishable from other primary relationships by its cultural dress. The norms regulating behavior in a courtship-love relationship differ sharply from those regulating behavior in a parent-child relationship. For one thing, the sexual area is defined quite differently. For another, the areas of confidence are defined differently. Relatedly, the types of needs which get fulfilled are also defined differently.

REFERENCES

Reiss, Ira L. 1960. "Toward a sociology of the heterosexual love relationship," *Marriage and Family Living* 22 (May): 139–145.
Strauss, Anselm. 1947. "Personality needs and marital choice," *Social Forces* 25 (March): 332–335.

[12]

The Wheel Theory of Love

READING FOR UNDERSTANDING

Summary

_____ 1. In summary, this passage presents
    a. the various *types* of love that exist.
    b. a *method* for finding those in love.
    c. *points of view* about love's importance.
    d. the *sequence* in which love develops.

_____ 2. The summary is best stated in the
    a. first sentence.
    b. second sentence.
    c. third sentence.
    d. fourth sentence.

Vocabulary

_____ 3. If something is **conceptualized,** it is
    a. thought of.
    b. reconsidered.
    c. developed.
    d. conducted.

_____ 4. **Rapport** between two people refers to
    a. how similar their educations are.
    b. how easily they speak when they meet.
    c. how comfortable they are together.
    d. how long they have known each other.

Summary	Number right _____ X 10 = _____	
Vocabulary	Number right _____ X 10 = _____	
Comprehension	Number right _____ X 10 = _____	
	Total score _____	

_____   5. A **confidante*** is a
         a. close, trusted female friend.
         b. close, trusted male friend.
         c. woman who keeps a secret.
         d. man who "spills the beans."

Comprehension

_____   6. Which of the following does *not* seem to be important for two people to
            develop rapport?
         a. They have a similar cultural background.
         b. They feel easy with a variety of people.
         c. They have similar educational backgrounds.
         d. They have very similar personalities.

_____   7. What we reveal of ourselves to other people seems to be determined mostly by
         a. if we feel that others can be trusted.
         b. what we have been taught is proper to reveal.
         c. if we feel we are interesting and worthwhile.
         d. how much the other people reveal to us.

_____   8. Mutual dependency develops between two people when they discover that
            they
         a. cannot survive in the world all by themselves.
         b. receive satisfaction from each other's company.
         c. have a strong physical attraction for each other.
         d. are both desperately in need of companionship.

_____   9. It seems that we tend to develop rapport with those whom we recognize
         a. reveal themselves to us.
         b. need us desperately.
         c. are from our social class.
         d. will fulfill our needs.

_____   10. The fundamental value of the "wheel theory" resides in its ability to account
            for
         a. how love gets stronger and how it weakens.
         b. what causes love relationships to dissolve.
         c. the conditions needed for love to grow.
         d. who will and will not find someone to love.

[12]

The Wheel Theory of Love

READING FOR STUDYING

Underline the parts of the passage that best summarize the information about the four processes of the development of love, and the part that explains how the four processes are interdependent. **Summarize** this information under two major headings. The first major heading should emphasize the type of explanation given in the passage and should be followed by the subheadings "Rapport," "Self-revelation," "Mutual Dependency," and "Need Fulfillment." The second major heading should be "Interrelatedness of the Processes."

Exercise

Once you know the state of your health and your level of fitness, you are well on your way to a personal fitness prescription. The dose of exercise designed to bring about safe, steady improvements in fitness can be expressed in terms of *intensity* (your training heart rate), *duration* (how many minutes or calories of exercise), and *frequency*   *
(how often you need to train).

Let's consider each factor, then summarize with ways you can prescribe your own aerobic fitness program.   *

INTENSITY

The exercise heart rate is the best indicator of exercise intensity, because it's directly related to both oxygen consumed and calories burned. As exercise becomes more intense, requiring more oxygen, heart rate increases.

Research has shown that fitness improves when you exercise at a given percentage of your maximum heart rate. Figure 1 illustrates average maximum heart rates as well as heart rate training zones for those in low, medium, and high fitness categories. The heart rate training zone tells you how intense your exercise must be to gain a training effect. Use your age and fitness level to determine your training zone—the minimum and maximum heart rates you should attain while training.

When exercising, it's simple to determine if you're in your training zone. After several minutes of exercise, stop and take your pulse for 10 seconds at wrist or throat (with a little practice pulse taking becomes easy); multiply by 6 to get the rate per minute. For example, if you get a count of 24, your rate in beats per minute is 144. You don't need to train at near maximum levels to achieve the benefits of exercise. In fact, exercising within your training zone should feel relatively comfortable. If the zone for your age and fitness level feels uncomfortably high, don't despair. Try working at the lower edge of the zone. If that is still too

From U.S. Department of Agriculture, *Fitness and Work Capacity*, by Brian J. Sharkey (Washington, D.C.: U.S. Government Printing Office, 1977), pp. 16–19.

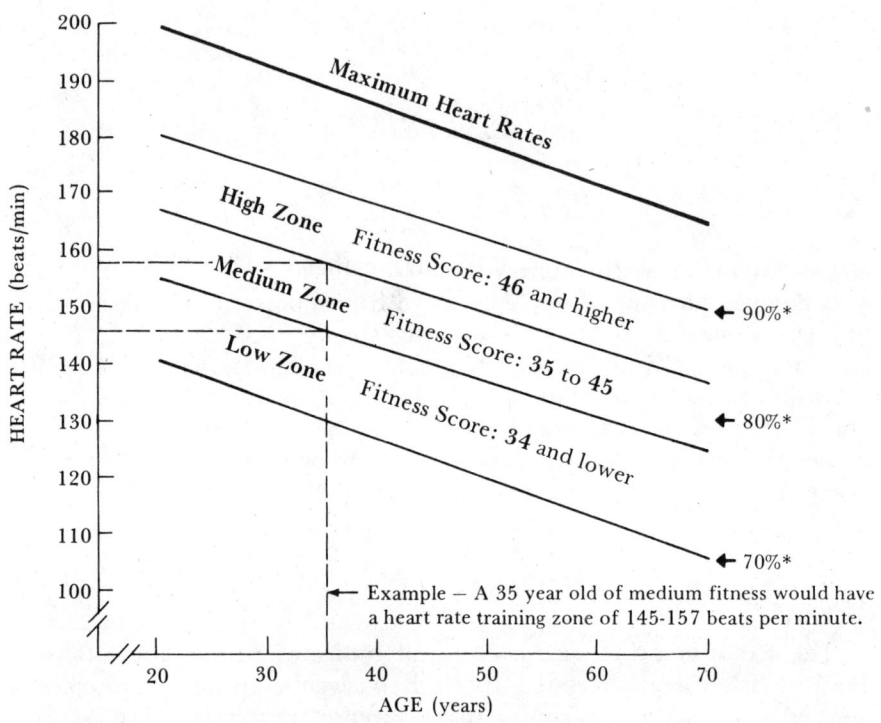

*Percent of maximum heart rate

Figure 1. Heart Rate Training Zones.

This chart illustrates average maximum heart rates as well as heart rate training zones for those in low, medium, and high fitness categories. The heart rate training zone tells you how intense your exercise must be to gain a training effect.

high, drop to a lower zone. Your maximum heart rate is probably lower than the average for your age.

The "talk test" is another good way of determining if you're in your training zone. You should be able to carry on a conversation as you exercise. With time, you won't need to check your heart rate, because you'll know how it feels to be "in the zone."

DURATION

As you'll find out, exercise duration and intensity go hand in hand, because an increase in one requires a decrease in the other. Exercise duration can be prescribed in terms of time, distance, or calories. I prefer calories. The calorie is the basic measure of energy expenditure   *

	Calories per minute*	Time taken to burn approx. 200 calories (in minutes)
Calisthenics	5.0	40
Walking (3½ mph)	5.6	36
Cycling (10 mph)	8.5	24
Swimming (crawl)	9.0	22
Skipping Rope (120/min)	10.0	20
Jogging (5 mph)	10.0	20
Running (7.5 mph)	15.0	14

*Exact calories burned depends on efficiency and body size.

Figure 2.

in work or exercise. It's the basic measure of energy intake (caloric intake from diet). So the calorie seems to be the most useful measure from an educational point of view.

I've included the caloric cost of several activities here; thus, 20 minutes of jogging burns 200 calories (20 x 10 calories); 20 minutes of walking, about 112. (See Figure 2.)

If you're in the low fitness category, your exercise should last long enough to burn *100* to *200* calories; the medium fitness category, *200* to *400* calories; and the high fitness category, more than *400* calories. It's wise to begin at the low end of the calorie scale for your fitness category. For example, if you're of medium fitness, your initial workouts should last only long enough to burn 200 calories. (See Figure 3.)

If you're overweight and wish to lose excess pounds, exercise at a lower intensity (heart rate training zone) and increase the *duration*. Exercise intensity and duration can be varied to reduce boredom. In fact nothing should be rigid about your training program.

FREQUENCY

Two or three training sessions a week are enough for those beginning a program and for those in the low fitness category. As training progresses, you can begin to exercise more; continued improvements in fitness are proportional to the frequency of training. Refer to the prescription chart (Figure 3) for information on training frequency, as well as exercise intensity and duration. The chart also includes some aerobic activities to give you an idea how long an exercise session should last to fill your exercise prescription. The aerobic exercises listed are simply suggestions. There are many more to choose from.

Fitness Category		Intensity (in beats/min)	Duration (in calories)		Frequency
			Men	Women	
High (over 45 ml/kg/min)			Over 400†	Over 300†	6 days weekly
	Age 20	164–178			
	25	162–176			
	30	160–174			
	35	157–171	—Exercise duration and frequency remain the same regardless of age— }		
	40	154–168			
	45	151–164			
	50	148–161			
	55	145–158			
	60	143–155			
Medium (35–45 ml/kg/min)			200–400	150–300	6 days weekly
	Age 20	153–164			
	25	151–162			
	30	148–159			
	35	145–157	—Exercise duration and frequency remain the same regardless of age— }		
	40	142–154			
	45	139–151			
	50	136–149			
	55	133–146			
	60	130–143			
Low (under 35 ml/kg/min)			100–200	75–150	Every other day
	Age 20	140–154			
	25	137–151			
	30	134–148			
	35	130–144	—Exercise duration and frequency remain the same regardless of age— }		
	40	126–140			
	45	122–136			
	50	118–132			
	55	114–128			
	60	110–124			

Figure 3. Aerobic Fitness Prescriptions

*Caloric expenditure is less for women, because they are smaller than men and burn fewer calories in a given activity.
† For long duration workouts (over 400 calories), training intensity may be reduced to a comfortable level.

Sample Aerobic Activities

Run		Jog		Bicycle		Swim		Walk	
Distance (miles)	Time (min)	Distance (miles)	Time (min)	Distance (miles)	Time (min)	Distance (yd)	Time (min)	Distance (miles)	Time (min)
3.4+	27+	3.4+	40+	7.8+	47+	1,600+	45+	4.2+	72+

—Distance and time remain the same regardless of age—

Run		Jog		Bicycle		Swim		Walk	
1.7–3.4	14–27	1.7–3.4	20–40	3.9–7.8	24–47	800–1,600	22–45	2.1–4.2	36–72

—Distance and time remain the same regardless of age—

Run		Jog		Bicycle		Swim		Walk	
0.8–1.7	7–14	0.8–1.7	10–20	1.9–3.9	12–24	400–800	11–22	1.0–2.1	18–36

—Distance and time remain the same regardless of age—

[13]

Exercise

READING FOR UNDERSTANDING

Summary

_____ 1. In summary, this passage presents
   a. *points of view* about the value of exercise.
   b. a *method* for planning a fitness program.
   c. *reasons* that exercise is necessary for good health.
   d. the *sequence* in which to do exercises.

_____ 2. The summary is best stated in the headings and in the
   a. first sentence.
   b. second sentence.
   c. third sentence.
   d. fourth sentence.

Vocabulary

_____ 3. A **duration*** is the
   a. length of time something lasts.
   b. freeing of energy.
   c. release of tension.
   d. building of durability.

_____ 4. **Aerobic*** fitness refers to the use of
   a. time.
   b. energy.
   c. muscles.
   d. oxygen.

Summary	Number right _____	X 10 =	_____
Vocabulary	Number right _____	X 10 =	_____
Comprehension	Number right _____	X 10 =	_____
		Total score	_____

_____ 5. A **calorie*** is a
      a. measurable unit.
      b. unit for dieting.
      c. quantity of food.
      d. measure of energy.

Comprehension

_____ 6. When exercising, the heart rate increases because
      a. activity makes it pump faster.
      b. the body is making adjustments.
      c. the body needs more oxygen.
      d. it contracts like other muscles.

_____ 7. Twenty year olds who want to achieve a high level of fitness must train with their hearts beating
      a. 190 times per minute.
      b. 170 times per minute.
      c. 150 times per minute.
      d. 130 times per minute.

_____ 8. To find your heart rate while exercising, you should take your pulse for
      a. 10 seconds and multiply by 6.
      b. 15 seconds and multiply by 4.
      c. 20 seconds and multiply by 3.
      d. 30 seconds and multiply by 2.

_____ 9. One can burn 200 calories by walking for a little longer than
      a. 30 minutes.
      b. 45 minutes.
      c. 60 minutes.
      d. 75 minutes.

_____ 10. Joggers can maintain the same fitness as runners if they jog
      a. half the distance that runners run.
      b. the same distance that runners run.
      c. half again the distance that runners run.
      d. twice the distance that runners run.

[13]

Exercise

READING FOR STUDYING

Underline the parts of the passage that state how to plan a fitness program, taking into account the three factors that must be considered. **Summarize** this information under a heading that emphasizes the type of explanation given in the passage and under the subheadings "Intensity," "Duration," and "Frequency." In your summaries, include examples of how each factor is used to plan a fitness program for a twenty-year-old man who has medium fitness. (For example, when a twenty-year-old man trains for medium fitness, intensity should be a heart training zone of 153–164 beats per minute.)

_____

_____

_____

_____

_____

_____

_____

_____

_____

_____

_____

_____

_____

Immigration

The traditional sources of new Americans in the pre–Civil War   *
period—Western and Northern Europe and Canada—continued to be the
main sources for almost thirty years. English, Germans, Irish, Scandi-
navians, and Canadians arrived in greater numbers than ever before with
the single exception of the Irish. Approximately ten million immigrants
entered the United States from 1860 to 1890, and 85 percent of them
were of the so-called "old immigration"—3 million from Germany, 1.6
million from Britain, 1.5 million from Ireland, 1 million from Scandi-
navia, and over 900,000 from Canada.

But the greatest wave of immigration was yet to come: the so-called
"new immigration" from Southern and Eastern Europe, which began
to be significant in the 1880s and by 1896 had passed the old immigration in annual size. These peoples washed onto America's shores by the
millions from 1880 until the final restrictive legislation of 1924 ended
the long unbroken tradition of open immigration. The numbers in the
new immigration were very great: 3.5 million Poles, 4.5 million Italians,
2.75 million from various parts of Russia. In the single year of 1907, 1.3
million immigrants entered the country. Not only the numbers but
the variety was far greater than ever before, as subject peoples fled from
the Russian and Austro-Hungarian Empires: Poles from Russian Poland
and Austrian Galicia; Ukrainians and Georgians from Russia; Jews from
Russia, Hungary, and Rumania; Czechs, Slovaks, Croatians, Slovenians,
Serbs, and Magyars from Austria-Hungary; Greeks, Bulgarians, Italians.
They came in what seemed a never-ending stream.

MOTIVES FOR THE NEW IMMIGRATION

Economic. Old or new, the immigrants came for the same basic reason
as their predecessors: to find a better life in the New World than they   *
faced in the Old. Economic conditions had caused severe hardships for
many. The industrialization of Western and Northern Europe brought
with it periods of chronic unemployment and low wages. The great

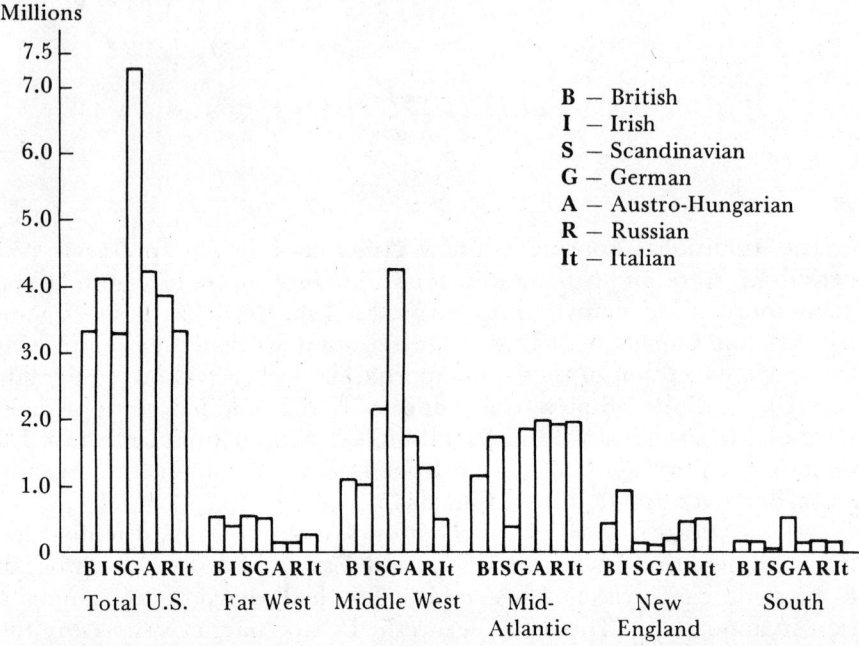

B — British
I — Irish
S — Scandinavian
G — German
A — Austro-Hungarian
R — Russian
It — Italian

Figure 1. Distribution of Immigrant Stock in the United States (1920).

expansion in population in those countries left those on the land with less and less acreage to support a family; a small plot could be divided only so often and still provide a living. America itself was in part a cause for the distress of many, since increasing supplies of cheap grain from America forced farm prices down in Europe, bringing disaster to many in the Northern and Western countries. The retarded development of industry in Southern and Eastern Europe left many economies unable to absorb in factories, mills, and mines the surplus rural population whose capacity to survive on the land was diminishing. The most primitive economic conditions in rural Russia, village Greece, and on the agricultural estates of Southern Italy and Sicily chained millions to a vicious system of poverty and degradation marked by ill health, disease, and inadequate food, clothing, and shelter.

In a pleading letter to the Emigrants Protective Society in Poland for aid in getting to America, a Polish father stated bluntly the cry of the dispossessed:

> I want to go to America, but I have no means at all because I am poor and have nothing but the ten fingers of my hands, a wife, and 9 children. I have no work at all, although I am strong and healthy and only 45 years old. I cannot earn for my family . . . and [the children] call for food and clothing

and more or less education. I wish to work, not easily only but even hard, but what can I do? I will not go to steal and I have no work. So I beg the Protective Association to accept me for this journey and not only me, but I should like to take with me two of my children, a boy 16 and a girl 18 years old. And I beg the Association. There are still other people who would readily go to America. They are also poor.

America, as it had always done, seemed a paradise to many, especially in the far reaches of Eastern Europe, who could know little or nothing of what it was really like. Some, in fact, only now heard of America for the first time, and had no idea where it was. Northern and Western Europeans may have had longer contact with America, but among common people everywhere the basic belief was the same: that the standard of living was higher in the United States than anywhere else in the world—abundant and better food, more attractive houses, more adequate clothing, medical care, education for the young. The land was fertile and rich in minerals, labor was done by machines, wages were high, there was work for all who sought it, taxes were low. It was a tantalizing picture.

"In America you get pie and puddings," wrote a British immigrant, putting it all on the most basic level. An immigrant in Nebraska wrote home that the "soil is unequalled in fertility." A Czech woman returning to her village near Prague reported that America was "rich with opportunities for people not afraid of hard work." And a Polish immigrant wrote home somewhat extravagantly: "I do very well. . . . I have very good and easy work; I can say that I don't work at all, I only stand in an iron-foundry. . . . I have 26 roubles wages weekly, counting in our country's money." A Greek immigrant wrote home to his former employer: "Here people work hard and regularly, and rest only on Sundays, but we fare well. Today, the day I write, is Sunday. I have taken my bath, I have had my milk, and I will pass the day happily. When did I know life with such order in Greece?"

Social equality. America was not only the land of economic opportunity, it was also the land of social equality. Despite the rising gap between classes and the increase in social distinctions appearing in the United States, the contrasts between American and Old World societies still seemed sharp and clear. George Jacob Holyoke, a British traveler in the United States, was struck by what he regarded as the transformation in British working-class immigrants. Whereas in England they had no social contacts with their "masters," in one American town he visited they promptly took him to meet their mayor. In 1891 a German immigrant wrote home to his brother: "And what is nicer yet is the fact that this is a free land. No one can give orders to anybody here, one is as good as another, no one takes off his hat to another as you have to do in Germany." An Italian landowner summed up the transformation

America seemed to work on its humble immigrants when he complained about the attitude of those who had been to America and who "walk through the streets as if they were our equals. . . . The worst of it is, signore, that they lose respect for us!"

The irrefutable evidence of the American paradise was the money immigrants sent back home, the letters they wrote, the pictures they posted off, and the dramatic appearance of those who had made it in America and come back home. Stoyan Christowe relates the story of the Macedonian village of Selo when a letter arrived one day from a former resident containing a money order for forty napoleons, more money than anyone in the village had ever possessed. The villagers promptly began borrowing and mortgaging to raise money for the passage to America, and this experience was repeated over and over again. Statistics reveal a close correlation between the amount of emigration and the amount of money sent home in postal money orders; a large number of emigrants were unquestionably financed in their voyages by friends or relatives already in America. Such money was also often used to improve living standards, buy an extra bit of land, pay debts, and get ahead a little. In 1907, some $85 million was sent home to Italy, an immense sum for the impoverished people of Sicily and the South where most of it went.

Pictures sent home also created an image of America as the land of wealth, opportunity, and social equality. One immigrant who was a hotel waiter stunned his village friends back home with a photograph of himself seated in an automobile and wearing a large watch chain and a ring. A Pole in Pennsylvania amazed his relatives with photographs of himself attired in a style suitable only to a member of the upper class in Poland. Immigrants who returned home permanently or for visits made a vivid impression. A simple white collar worn by a returned Italian was regarded by friends as a sign of affluence. A Hungarian woman who returned to her homeland to marry and settle down told wide-eyed villagers of her days on South Halsted Street in Chicago where she had eaten "thin bread with thick jam on it, and the land was flowing with sausages, lager beer, and chewing gum." A steelworker from Pittsburgh returned to his Yugoslav village and made an incredible impression by telling how he had actually met and shaken hands with President Theodore Roosevelt.

American persuasiveness. These were the most influential channels through which the image of America was cast as a lure before the eyes of the common people of Europe. But many Americans also had a special interest in promoting immigration and worked hard to spread the word through Europe that the chances for a better life were very good in the United States. Manufacturing and other business interests supported various companies, such as The American Emigrant Company, organized to promote emigration among Europeans in order to secure cheap labor for the United States. The great transcontinental

Figure 2. Advertisement Encouraging Emigrants
to Purchase Land in Kansas.

railroads, through federal land grants, had large quantities of land along their rights-of-way and sought settlers from abroad by heavy promotional advertising. Shipping interests sought a profit by filling their ships with passengers on the return voyage to America from European ports. Many states, especially in the West but also elsewhere, established immigration commissions to encourage settlement within their boundaries. All these interests had agents abroad flooding Europe with propaganda. They distributed brochures on American prosperity, advertised heavily in European newspapers, planted articles in the press, put up alluring posters, and even stood outside church doors, as in Italy, handing out cards with hymns praising America. Illustrations on brochures frequently showed a "typical" emigrant's progress from a sod house to a fine home. But these efforts were probably important only in providing information to the prospective emigrant on how actually to get to America, and perhaps about the geography of the country. They were rarely effective in persuading people to emigrate. Emigrants, in fact, were warned by those who had already been through the experience not to get involved with these American promoters who were more likely to fleece emigrants than to aid them. One Pole warned: "Let nobody listen to anybody but only to his relatives whom he has here, in this golden America."

There were, of course, counter-images of America spread by governments which sought to discourage emigration and publicized hard times in America. There were also returned emigrants who had failed in America and came home broken in health and spirit. But the significant fact was that for most prospective emigrants it was easier to believe in America as the land of hope—the evidence seemed so overwhelming. For those who decided to emigrate, the task of doing so was made easier than ever before by the industrial developments of the last half of the nineteenth century. Technological improvements in the steamship made the Atlantic crossing quicker and safer. Growing trade led to the rise of major steamship lines whose sharp competition drove fares down drastically. The expansion in construction of railroads in Europe made it easier and cheaper for emigrants to reach ports of embarkation. When railroads tied Eastern and Central Germany to the Baltic ports, more emigrants left for America from those regions of Germany than ever before.

And so they came, millions upon millions from all over Europe. Most became part of the American urban scene because the city was rapidly becoming the focal point of opportunity in America, although a surprising number still managed to find their way to rural areas. But it was in the city where the jobs were, and particularly the unskilled jobs, which were the only ones available to immigrants with only peasant or ancient handicraft backgrounds.

[14]

Immigration

READING FOR UNDERSTANDING

Summary

_____ 1. In summary, this passage presents the
   a. *types* of people who chose to immigrate to this country.
   b. *sequence* in which people came here from other countries.
   c. *points of view* about the effects of immigration on our economy.
   d. *reasons* people came to this country in large numbers.

_____ 2. The summary is best stated in the headings and in the first sentence of the
   a. first paragraph.
   b. second paragraph.
   c. third paragraph.
   d. fourth paragraph.

Vocabulary

_____ 3. The **pre–Civil War*** period refers to the time before
   a. 1860.
   b. 1870.
   c. 1880.
   d. 1890.

_____ 4. Our **predecessors*** are the people who
   a. will come after us.
   b. came before us.
   c. died long ago.
   d. remain with us.

Summary	Number right _____	X 10 =	_____
Vocabulary	Number right _____	X 10 =	_____
Comprehension	Number right _____	X 10 =	_____
		Total score	_____

_____   5. Those who experience **degradation**** are treated as though they
           a. cannot handle responsibility.
           b. should seek comfort in God.
           c. need more years of schooling.
           d. are of little importance.

Comprehension

_____   6. Which of the following was *not* a cause of widespread economic hardship in
           the Old World before the turn of the century?
           a. Cheap American farm products drove down prices of European farms.
           b. The railroads supplanted many previously important industries.
           c. Populations were growing at a faster rate than previously.
           d. Industrialization brought unemployment and low wages.

_____   7. By 1920, the greatest number of immigrants had come to this country from
           a. Italy.
           b. Ireland.
           c. Britain.
           d. Germany.

_____   8. Apparently, most of the immigrants who came here settled in the
           a. Far Western and Middle Western states.
           b. Middle Western and mid-Atlantic states.
           c. mid-Atlantic and New England states.
           d. New England and Southern states.

_____   9. The single greatest motivation for Italians to come to this country seemed to
           be that
           a. they received money from relatives who had come here before them.
           b. conditions in Italy were so bad that people had nothing to lose by coming.
           c. those who moved here were assured that they would be treated with respect.
           d. they wanted to have the economic security guaranteed to our citizens.

_____ 10. In the final analysis, great numbers of people came to this country during the
           last forty years of our open immigration policy probably because of
           a. the dismal degradation to which most Europeans were subjected.
           b. good, cheap railroad and steamship transportation.
           c. the immigrants' certainty of securing high-paying jobs.
           d. the immigrants' conviction that they would be respected in America.

[14]

Immigration

READING FOR STUDYING

Underline the parts of the passage that best state the reasons that large numbers of people immigrated to this country. **Summarize** this information under a heading that emphasizes the type of explanation given in the passage, and under the subheadings "Economic," "Social Equality," and "American Persuasiveness."

[15]

Packaging

Fifty years ago, "rushing the growler" was a familiar dinner-time procedure in big-city neighborhoods. A family member, usually a teen-ager, was sent running to the corner tavern with a bucket (the growler), which the proprietor filled with beer. Such simple packaging was typical of many other items consumers bought. Sugar and butter were scooped from sacks or tubs into small brown paper bags, fish was wrapped in newspapers. Since then, however, the "packaging revolution" has occurred. Almost everything we buy comes elaborately packaged, except oil that comes through pipelines, a few wheeled products like automobiles, and an occasional oddity like the daily newspaper. Businesses spend close to $25 billion a year on packaging. The blister package of screws, the aerosol can of paint, and the individually wrapped slice of cheese are typical of how goods are now packaged (or overpackaged, as some people think) for the American consumer.

THE ADVANTAGES OF PACKAGING

Packaging can serve useful purposes. It is often needed to provide physical protection for products: Plastic or cardboard egg containers fulfill this requirement. It is also designed to promote products by making them simpler for retailers to display, handle, and attract attention. The packaging of supermarket merchandise serves these functions.

Safety or convenience may also enter into the choice of a package. Plastic bottles have largely replaced glass containers for bathroom products like shampoo or mouthwash. Aerosol cans are now widely used for hairsprays and furniture polish. Some manufacturers believe that containers that can be reused offer a competitive advantage. Thus, liquor is often offered in elaborate cut-glass decanters; and margarine is sold in reusable plastic bowls.

COMPLAINTS AND SUGGESTIONS

Despite its usefulness, packaging has come under attack. Complaints about packaging emphasize the litter that it causes, the difficulty and expense of disposing of the materials, and the waste of resources. Environmentalists are particularly disturbed about the growing use of plastics because they are hard to dispose of. Many plastics are resistant to decay. Others, like polyvinyl chloride (PVC), emit poisonous gases when they are burned.

One of the most offensive forms of packaging, according to environmentalists, is the throwaway bottle or can used for 70 percent of the beer and soda sold in the United States today. Almost 65 billion of these containers are thrown away each year. Such containers represent 3,800,000 tons of glass, 2,500,000 tons of steel, and 332,500 tons of aluminum. The energy required to process these materials into the containers is an amount equal to a year's electric power needs for Washington, San Francisco, Boston, and Pittsburgh.

But people keep using throwaway bottles and cans anyway. Consumers seem willing to pay extra for the convenience of disposables. Storekeepers dislike returnable bottles because of the expense and trouble of handling them. And the producers of soft drinks and beer claim that they lose money on returnables. In our affluent society, the modest deposit fees are not enough to motivate people to return them. A bottler must average at least six round trips to pay off the higher initial cost of manufacturing a returnable bottle. Several years ago, the average soft-drink bottle made about forty trips. Today the average is only fifteen. In some cities of the Northeast, it has declined to fewer than four.

Ecologists believe that authorities must make stronger efforts to solve the problems of litter, garbage disposal, and waste associated with many forms of packaging. The state of Oregon has banned the sale of drinks in disposable containers. Some experts recommend a packaging tax: Producers would pay a sum based on the weight of the packaging material used. The tax would be used to pay all the social costs connected with the packaging, including collection and disposal.

Other concerned citizens believe that what is needed is a combination of remedies. Simple common sense should prevent certain goods, such as children's toys, from being absurdly overpackaged. Better technology, aimed at recycling, would prevent the waste now associated with one-time use of packaging materials. If technology could make recycling profitable, it would also provide the economic incentive   * required to collect and reprocess the materials.

[15]

Packaging

READING FOR UNDERSTANDING

Summary

_____   1. In summary, this passage presents
a. the long *history* of the packaging of products.
b. the various *types* of packages for consumer goods.
c. the *reasons* that product packaging is greatly needed.
d. *points of view* about the usefulness of packaging.

_____   2. The summary is best stated in the headings and in the first sentences of the
a. first and second paragraphs.
b. second and third paragraphs.
c. second and fourth paragraphs.
d. third and fourth paragraphs.

Vocabulary

_____   3. A **proprietor*** is someone who
a. dispenses liquids.
b. earns high profits.
c. conserves containers.
d. operates a business.

_____   4. **Decanters*** are
a. fancy bottles.
b. plastic bottles.
c. people who sing.
d. people who serve.

Summary	Number right _____	× 10 = _____	
Vocabulary	Number right _____	× 10 = _____	
Comprehension	Number right _____	× 10 = _____	
		Total score _____	

_____ 5. An **incentive*** is something that
   a. defines boundaries.
   b. regulates emotions.
   c. inspires confidence.
   d. stimulates action.

Comprehension

_____ 6. Sugar, butter, and beer are among products that were not put in special
   packages as recently as
   a. 30 years ago.
   b. 50 years ago.
   c. 70 years ago.
   d. 90 years ago.

_____ 7. When listing the advantages of packaging, one might *not* consider that
   packaging
   a. protects products.
   b. increases safety.
   c. attracts attention.
   d. creates employment.

_____ 8. The major complaint about throwaway bottles and cans is that
   a. we waste resources producing them and money disposing of them.
   b. they use up too much glass and metals like steel and aluminum.
   c. it takes too much electric power to produce the containers we use.
   d. they create litter on the roadsides of our beautiful country.

_____ 9. In order to recover the cost of manufacturing a returnable bottle, the bottle
   must be used
   a. three times.
   b. four times.
   c. five times.
   d. six times.

_____ 10. Apparently it has *not* been suggested seriously that overpackaging be dealt
   with by
   a. banning the use of some containers.
   b. boycotting overpackaged products.
   c. taxing containers by their weight.
   d. designing packages using common sense.

[15]

Packaging

READING FOR STUDYING

Underline and **number** (1) four advantages of packaging, (2) three complaints about packaging, and (3) four suggestions for reducing the amount of packaging now being used. **Summarize** this information under a heading that emphasizes the type of explanation given in the passage and under the subheadings "Advantages," "Complaints," and "Suggestions."

_____

_____

_____

_____

_____

_____

_____

_____

_____

_____

_____

_____

_____

_____

_____

_____

_____

[16]

Propaganda

Propaganda can be good or bad. It can serve useful purposes in persuasion. But it can also be tricky: it can fool the naive. Students * should be made aware of propaganda techniques so that they are able to evaluate persuasive arguments logically. The following types of propaganda techniques will be explained briefly: bad names, glad names, testimonial, transfer, plain folks, card stacking, and band wagon.

BAD NAMES

Bad names are those expressions whose connotations are unpleasant. The terms are employed to incite hate, to cause fear, dislike, or distress. It is not difficult to think of many bad name (sad name) expressions. Here are a few:

communist	itchy
lemon	cheap
yellow	skinny
un-American	fat

GLAD NAMES

Glad names, on the other hand, are expressions with pleasant connotations. Sometimes called "glittering generalities" or "purr words," glad names are used by advertisers to describe *their* products, though they may use sad names to describe the products of their competitors. Glad names are used by all of us to convince others of our opinions or to sway them to our point of view. Some glad names are:

marvelous	smooth
supercalifragilisticexpealidocious	economical
all-American	slim
glamorous	pleasantly plump
healthful	

From Lou E. Burmeister, *Reading Strategies for Secondary School Teachers,* pp. 207–210. Copyright © 1974 by Addison-Wesley, Reading, Massachusetts. Reprinted with permission.

131

TESTIMONIAL

A testimonial is a tribute; at its best, an affirmation or declaration of gratitude for a statement honestly recommending a person, theory, or thing. Testimonies are given by people who are grateful for their religion, their government, their university, or their favorite sportsman. Our progress in space is a testimony to our society. On the other hand, our racial problems testify to apathy or to negativism in our society, as does pollution.

In advertising, a testimonial is often rendered by a glamorous movie star, a famous athlete, a zesty barking dog or a purring cat, or possibly by a plain folk. In most cases, the testimony is well paid for.

TRANSFER

In the transfer technique, a highly regarded person, symbol, or concept is somehow related to the idea or product that is "being pushed." Many students "buy" professor's ideas if attached to the idea are the words "research proves. . . ." Or, we buy toothpaste because "dentists endorse it" or because it contains some ingredients that sound very scientific. The eagle or the American flag may be pictured on a dictionary to help increase sales. Or, a picture of a baby or a movie star may attract us to a magazine.

Careful now—not all propaganda is bad! Much is good.

PLAIN FOLKS

We are all familiar with the politician who kisses babies and parades his family in front of the public. And we have all seen pictures of candidates with holes in the soles of their shoes—a technique that may, however, backfire in time of prosperity. The affluent Stevenson was thus pictured—to play down his intellectual image. A friend of mine, a staunch Democrat, clipped this picture and pasted it to her door with the inscription: "Don't let this happen to you—vote for Ike."

The plain folks technique is gaining popularity in advertising today. Note the increasing number of ads in magazines, newspapers, and on T.V. in which average looking people, rather than the ultraglamorous, appear.

CARD STACKING

Card stacking is a technique we all use—not just advertisers, politicians, governments, etc. Not at all! What does the child who comes home with a poor report card tell his family? Does he present both sides fairly? What about the local Chamber of Commerce? And the woman whose favorite plant lost—or won—at the local floral show? What about you when you did not get that raise or that "A"?

The old art of debate forced sides to deliberately card stack. Each side presented only the best of one point of view and the worst of the other point of view. And what does a lawyer do in presenting his case? Card stacking is probably as old as man and is with us to stay. But we should be alert to it.

BAND WAGON

It is the rare person who is not anxious to "be with it," to join the crowd. Nowadays, almost everyone wants to go to college, even those who would benefit more from doing something else. We all pick up the latest slang, use it until we tire of it, and then discard it, as does the rest of our crowd—for the newer slang or jargon.

The constant plea, *everybody's doing it,* should trigger us to serious thought and careful analysis and evaluation. *Is everybody doing it? And do we wish to be one of these anonymous everybodies? Perhaps we should dare to be different.*

Everybody smokes pot. Or, all the kids smoke pot. Nonsense! Hippies don't conform. Nonsense—they conform with one another— with the other so-called "non-conformists." They are on the band wagon.

It's modern to engage in premarital sex, or extramarital sex, and, of course, we all want to be modern. We may want to be modern, but does all of this go along with it?

Where would we be if everybody did the same thing? Perhaps the prediction of Huxley's *Brave New World* would be borne out.

[16]

Propaganda

READING FOR UNDERSTANDING

Summary

_____ 1. In summary, this passage presents
  a. *methods* for making effective propaganda.
  b. several *types* of propaganda techniques.
  c. the *reasons* for propaganda effectiveness.
  d. *points of view* about propaganda's usefulness.

_____ 2. The summary is best stated in the headings and in the
  a. first sentence.
  b. second sentence.
  c. third sentence.
  d. fourth sentence.

Vocabulary

_____ 3. **Naive*** people are
  a. knowing.
  b. unwise.
  c. natives.
  d. visitors.

_____ 4. To give an **affirmation*** is to
  a. supply missing information.
  b. deny the worth of something.
  c. say something is true.
  d. present a deserved gift.

Summary	Number right _____	X 10 =	_____
Vocabulary	Number right _____	X 10 =	_____
Comprehension	Number right _____	X 10 =	_____
		Total score	_____

_____ 5. To **endorse*** is to
   a. invest.
   b. approve.
   c. sign.
   d. give.

Comprehension

_____ 6. The main purpose in learning about propaganda techniques is to become able to
   a. use it to persuade others.
   b. detect it when it is used.
   c. evaluate arguments logically.
   d. become a better educated person.

_____ 7. "Glittering generalities" is another name for the propaganda technique of
   a. transfer.
   b. testimonial.
   c. band wagon.
   d. glad names.

_____ 8. "The great religions of the world agree that those who murder should be put to death." What propaganda technique is used in this statement?
   a. card stacking
   b. band wagon
   c. testimonial
   d. transfer

_____ 9. "Thousands of average people are jogging for physical fitness—you should too." What propaganda techniques are used in this statement?
   a. glad names and transfer
   b. glad names and band wagon
   c. plain folks and card stacking
   d. plain folks and band wagon

_____ 10. In card stacking, the information presented
   a. favors only one side of an argument.
   b. considers many sides of an argument.
   c. is piled on top of other information.
   d. is given at random, as in a card game.

[16]

Propaganda

READING FOR STUDYING

Underline the parts of the passage that state the most important information about the seven types of propaganda techniques. **Summarize** this information under a heading that emphasizes the type of explanation given in the passage. Use the names of the propaganda techniques as subheadings in your notes.

_____

_____

_____

_____

_____

_____

_____

_____

_____

_____

_____

_____

_____

_____

_____

_____

[17]

Demography

A reliable method of predicting population is to look not at changes in total population size with time but at patterns of changes in **rates of growth**. For this purpose, the reader needs to understand how birth and death rates affect the size of populations and how current trends affect future patterns. Because of the uniqueness of the human pattern of growth, we shall consider it in demographic, rather than ecological, terms.

Demography is that branch of sociology or anthropology which deals   *
with the statistical characteristics of human populations, with reference to total size, density, number of deaths, diseases, and migrations, and so forth. The demographer attempts to construct a numerical profile of the population viewed as groups of people, not as individuals. For this purpose, the demographer needs to know facts concerning the size and composition of populations, such as the number of females alive at a given time or the number of infants born in a given year.

The subject may sound terribly dry to those of you who are uncomfortable with numbers and computations, but demographic data often reflect in fascinating ways the history of the country studied, the trends in medical care, and the occurrence of social changes.

In addition to studying the composition of populations, the demographer is interested in how populations change in time. This is studied by counting the number of **vital events**—births, deaths, marriages, and   *
migrations. If we knew the composition of a population at any given time and the number of vital events occurring between that time and another, we would know the composition of the population at the end of the period. For example, suppose that in 1924 the population of some village was 732. In the next two years, if there were 28 births and 15 deaths and if 4 people moved in and 1 moved out, there would be 732 + 28 − 15 + 4 − 1 = 748 people at the end of 1926.

How does a population grow? Imagine you decided to deposit $100 in a bank that offered 3 percent interest per year. Suppose you started walking to the bank carrying three dollars in change, seven $1 bills, ten $5 bills, and four $10 bills, for a total of $100. If you deposited the entire $100, you would expect to have $103 at the end of the year.

But on the way to the bank you bought an irresistible ice cream sundae for one dollar. Thus, you had only $99 to deposit when you arrived at the bank. No matter how you paid for your sundae, whether you used coins, or a dollar bill, or a bill of higher denomination and received change, your $99 would grow at a rate of 3 percent. In one year you would have $99 + $99(.03) = $101.97. This kind of growth, where the increase is proportional to the initial size, is called **geometric** or **exponential growth.**

How different a population is! Imagine a population of 100 people—3 infants, 7 children, 50 adults under 65, and 40 people at least 65 years old. Suppose that during an entire year, no one moved in or out of the population, five of the women under 65 had babies, and two of the people over 65 died. These were the only vital events. At the end of the year, the population would be 100 + 5 − 2 = 103, for an annual rate of growth of 3 percent.

Now suppose the population had contained only 99 people at the beginning of the year. What would the rate of increase have been? If the population grew in the same way that money in the bank grows, the rate of growth would be 3 percent no matter which person in the original population were no longer there. People, however, are not interchangeable like dollar bills. If the population had been missing an infant, there still would have been five births and two deaths. There would have been 99 + 5 − 2 = 102 persons at the end of the year. The annual rate of growth would have been:

$$\frac{102 - 99}{99} \times 100\% = 3.03\%$$

On the other hand, if the population had been missing one of the women who had a child, only four births would have occurred, and the rate of growth would have been

$$\frac{101 - 99}{99} \times 100\% = 2.02\%$$

If one of the elderly persons who died had been missing from the population, the population would be 99 + 5 − 1 = 103 persons at the end of a year, for an annual growth rate of

$$\frac{103 - 99}{99} \times 100\% = 4.04\%$$

This very simple example has pointed out some of the difficulties confronting the student of population size, but it also leads to three important insights that are necessary for an effective approach to the investigation of growth:

1. An overall "rate of growth" is really the difference between a rate of addition (by birth or immigration) and a rate of subtraction (by death or emigration). The rate of growth is positive only when there are more additions than subtractions.   *

     *

2. The probability of dying or of giving birth within any given year varies with age and sex.
3. The age-sex composition, or **distribution,** of the population has a profound effect upon a country's birth rate, its death rate, and hence its growth rate.

[17]

Demography

READING FOR UNDERSTANDING

Summary

_____   1. In summary, this passage presents
   a. a *method* for understanding population growth.
   b. the *categories* of anthropological demographics.
   c. the *sequence* in which populations expand.
   d. *reasons* for studying demographic statistics.

_____   2. The summary is best stated in the
   a. first sentence of the first paragraph.
   b. second sentence of the first paragraph.
   c. first sentence of the second paragraph.
   d. second sentence of the second paragraph.

Vocabulary

_____   3. **Demography*** is the statistical science concerned with the
   a. distribution of populations.
   b. growth of populations.
   c. decreases in populations.
   d. stability of populations.

_____   4. **Vital events*** include
   a. fires and floods.
   b. wars and earthquakes.
   c. births and deaths.
   d. growth and atrophy.

Summary	Number right _____ X 10 = _____
Vocabulary	Number right _____ X 10 = _____
Comprehension	Number right _____ X 10 = _____
	Total score _____

_____ 5. **Immigration*** and **cmigration*** rcfcr to
    a. leaving and coming.
    b. coming and leaving.
    c. being born and dying.
    d. dying and being born.

Comprehension

_____ 6. Which of the following is an example of exponential growth?
    a. Eleanor won $25,000 for a lottery ticket that cost her only $1.
    b. The government gives a public TV station $10 for every $10 it receives from members.
    c. Frank withdrew $100 from the bank, but the teller gave him $110 by mistake.
    d. In three months the cost of a can of tuna went from $.69, to $.79, to $.99.

_____ 7. If you deposit $500 in a bank for one year at 5 percent interest, at the end of the year you will have
    a. $505.
    b. $515.
    c. $525.
    d. $550.

_____ 8. A city of 500,000 experienced a 5 percent growth rate in a year in which 5,000 citizens died or moved away. How many births and immigrations were there during the year?
    a. 15,000
    b. 20,000
    c. 25,000
    d. 30,000

_____ 9. The population of a city increased from 150,000 to 156,000 in one year. What was its annual growth rate?
    a. 3 percent
    b. 4 percent
    c. 5 percent
    d. 6 percent

_____ 10. Communities grow fastest when they have an abundance of
    a. children and much emigration.
    b. children and much immigration.
    c. young women and much emigration.
    d. young women and much immigration.

[17]

Demography

READING FOR STUDYING

Underline the parts of the passage that (1) state the meaning of "demography," (2) state the meaning of "vital events," (3) explain how to compute the growth of money in a bank, and (4) explain how to find the annual rate of growth in a population. **Summarize** this information under appropriate headings, making it clear for items 3 and 4 exactly how you should compute the two types of growth.

_____

_____

_____

_____

_____

_____

_____

_____

_____

_____

_____

_____

_____

_____

18

Relatives

The relationships between members of a family is a complex subject that interests most people. Since the understanding of family links becomes confusing very quickly, we shall consider only the closest types of relatives: primary, secondary, and tertiary.

TYPES OF RELATIVES

Primary relatives. Many people consider an uncle or grandparent to be as close a relative as a brother or sister. The fact is, however, that our *primary relatives* are restricted to the members of our family of   * orientation (mother, father, brothers, and sisters) and our family of procreation (spouse, sons, and daughters). To understand family relationships, you must learn and remember the seven types of primary relatives.

Secondary relatives. Your secondary relatives are the primary relatives of your primary relatives, but if people are primary relatives of yours they cannot also be your secondary relatives. For example, your father is a primary relative of your mother—your mother, in other words, is a primary relative of a primary relative. But your mother is not a secondary relative of yours because she is already a primary relative. Your father's brother (your uncle), your mother's father (your grandfather), and your sister's daughter (your niece) are some of your secondary relatives.

Tertiary relatives. Now that you know the definition of secondary relatives, you should be able to guess the definition for *tertiary* (third-   * rank) relatives. They are those among the primary relatives of your secondary relatives who, of course, are not already your primary or secondary relatives. Your father's brother's wife (your aunt), your mother's father's father (your great-grandfather), and your sister's daughter's son (your great-nephew) are tertiary relatives.

From James F. Shepherd, *College Study Skills,* p. 173. Copyright © 1979 by Houghton Mifflin Company. Used by permission.

This is a *family of orientation* for the children, but a *family of procreation* for the parents. When the children marry, they will form their own families of procreation. (Photo by Ruby Mera)

BLOOD AND MARRIAGE BONDS

Family relationships are complicated by the fact that some people are related to you by blood and others only by marriage. It is for this reason that your mother's brother (your uncle) is a secondary relative, but your mother's brother's wife (your aunt) is a tertiary relative. People related to you by blood are *consanguineous relatives;* those related to you by marriage are *affinal relatives.*

*

[18]

Relatives

READING FOR UNDERSTANDING

Summary

_____ 1. In summary, this passage presents
  a. a *method* for constructing your own family tree.
  b. the various *types* of relatives a person may have.
  c. *reasons* that we feel close to our primary relatives.
  d. *points of view* about the importance of relatives.

_____ 2. The summary is best stated in the headings and in the
  a. first paragraph.
  b. second paragraph.
  c. third paragraph.
  d. fourth paragraph.

Vocabulary

_____ 3. **Family of orientation*** refers to
  a. children, parents, and grandparents.
  b. our brothers, sisters, and children.
  c. the family into which one is born.
  d. the family we form when we marry.

_____ 4. **Tertiary*** means
  a. important.
  b. unimportant.
  c. third in order.
  d. fourth in order.

Summary	Number right _____	X 10 =	_____
Vocabulary	Number right _____	X 10 –	_____
Comprehension	Number right _____	X 10 =	_____
		Total score	_____

_____ 5. **Consanguineous*** relatives are
      a. those who have died.
      b. those not yet born.
      c. related by blood.
      d. related by marriage.

Comprehension

_____ 6. Which of the following *could not be* your primary relative?
      a. your grandmother
      b. your daughter
      c. your mother
      d. your sister

_____ 7. Which of the following *could not be* your secondary relative?
      a. your father's brother
      b. your mother's aunt
      c. your brother's wife
      d. your sister's daughter

_____ 8. Which of the following *could only be* your secondary relative?
      a. a niece
      b. a grandfather
      c. an uncle
      d. an aunt

_____ 9. Which of the following *could not be* your tertiary relative?
      a. your mother's brother's son
      b. your father's sister's husband
      c. your father's mother's sister
      d. your mother's father's daughter

_____ 10. Husbands and wives are
      a. primary, affinal members of a family of procreation.
      b. primary, consanguineous members of a family of procreation.
      c. secondary, affinal members of a family of procreation.
      d. secondary, consanguineous members of a family of orientation.

[18]

Relatives

READING FOR STUDYING

Underline the parts of the passage that explain the five types of relatives. **Summarize** this information under a heading that emphasizes the type of explanation given in the passage and under appropriate subheadings. Include personal examples in your summaries: for example, when you summarize "affinal relatives," include the name of one of your affinal relatives.

_____

_____

_____

_____

_____

_____

_____

_____

_____

_____

_____

_____

_____

_____

_____

[E I G H T]

Definitions in Textbooks

In addition to the five types of information you have already studied in this book, textbooks also often present definitions of terminology. *Definitions* are statements of the meanings of words. *Terminology* (or *terms*) refers to the technical words and usages that apply to a specific field of study. The passage entitled "Fitness," on pages 51–52, states the meanings of terms, including *suppleness* and *stamina.* The selection explains that *suppleness* refers to the flexibility of the body's joints and the ability of the parts of the body to move easily. One also learns from the passage that *stamina* means endurance and the ability of the body to engage in physical activity for an extended period of time. These terms are defined in the passage because their meanings are essential to understanding fitness.

Suppleness and *stamina* are words that are also defined in dictionaries, but textbooks also often give the meanings of terms that may not be found in dictionaries. For example, the passage entitled "Purposes of Advertising," on pages 57–58, gives the meanings of terms including *institutional advertising.* You will not find the meaning of *institutional advertising* given in standard desk dictionaries.

Often textbook definitions of terminology are accompanied by examples. In the selection entitled "Purposes of Advertising," the explanations of *primary demand advertising, selective advertising,* and *institutional advertising* all include examples to help you understand the definitions that are given for these terms. Examples are given for many of the terms defined in the passages in this part of the book; some of the examples are quite long. As you study the passages, notice how the examples add to your understanding of terminology.

Almost all textbooks devote considerable attention to explaining the meanings of important terminology; one major purpose of many textbooks is to teach the vocabulary of the fields of study they discuss. It is impossible to overemphasize the value of finding and learning the meanings of words that are important to your college subjects.

However, when textbook passages give information about the meanings of words, they almost always also convey some other important type of information. For example, in addition to giving *definitions,* "Fitness" also identifies the *categories* of fitness; and "Human Needs" also explains the *sequence* in which human needs are satisfied.

The five selections in this part of *Reading Skills for College Study* all give definitions of terminology, but they also convey other important information. When the passages contain both definitions and some other type of information, the first Reading for Understanding questions ask you to identify those other types of explanations found in the passages (methods, sequences, categories, reasons, or points of view).

One of the purposes of the Reading for Studying exercises in this part of the book is to help you understand the importance of making notes to learn the meanings of important terminology in your college textbooks.

19

Self

[George Herbert] Mead (1934) discusses the emergence of the social self as a three-stage process: the preparatory stage, the play stage, and the game stage. During each of these three stages, people gain an increasing ability to view themselves objectively, as if from the standpoint of others.

During the *preparatory stage* children imitate the people around them. For example, a small boy may sit on his father's lap in a car and pretend to be driving. This imitation does not involve an understanding of the meaning of the actions in which the child engages. If the child gets tired of "driving," he can stop without serious consequences and go on to more exciting activities. The only limitations on the child's activity are his imagination and his physical capacity. Other people are not taken into consideration.

During the *play stage* the actual playing of roles occurs. The child may play mother, postman, truck driver, or cowboy. At this stage the child begins to learn that certain roles have meaning and that this meaning is in relation to other roles. The child learns to act back toward herself or himself. For example, the child may want to mail a letter. He learns during the play stage that there are certain people who are in charge of letters; these people are called postmen. The child can hand a letter over to an imaginary postman, then turn around and be the postman, take the letter from himself, and pretend to take it to the post office. It is during this stage that the child first begins to have a social self and is first able to direct activity back toward this self. This process of acting toward yourself as others act toward you is called *taking-the-role-of-the-other*. It is the essential feature in the development of the social self.

Children begin to learn to get outside of themselves at the play stage but, as yet, have no fully developed selves. A child's reference points for viewing herself or himself are particular other persons. One minute the child may be a postman; the next moment, a doctor or a fireman. Separate identities are taken to suit the child's mood of the moment. The child also passes randomly from one role to another and take roles one at a time. At this point the child has no organized and unitary view of the self. For a fully developed self to emerge, the child must enter the game stage.

In the *game stage* the child must be able not only to take a series of single roles of particular other persons but also to take several roles simultaneously. Mead uses the example of the baseball game. It is important for the person not only to know what his role is in the game but also to know the roles of each of the other players. If there is a man on first base and one out, the second baseman must be ready (in case of a ground ball to short) to receive a throw from the shortstop and then relay a throw to first for a double play. Similarly, the child who has arrived at the game stage must know not only his role but also the roles of the other people involved in the game. It is during this final stage in the development of the self that the individual comes to have an organized self.

At this point a person must do more than take the roles of particular other people; she or he must take the role of what Mead calls the *generalized other*—an objective, organized, and durable perspective on the self. By taking the role of the generalized other, a person develops a consistent standpoint from which to view himself or herself. What was during the play stage an inconsistent self that switched from moment to moment becomes in the game stage an organized self. This self reflects the individual's location in the ongoing social structure of which he or she is an integral part.   *

It is important to be able to view oneself from the perspective of the generalized other and to have a consistent self-image, for only a person with a fully developed self is able to maintain relationships over time. She or he can be expected to act in consistent ways and can expect that others will do the same. It is this consistent and durable feature of the social self that is the basis of social organization. People with organized selves can come to play organized roles.

REFERENCE

Mead, George Herbert. *Mind, Self and Society*. Chicago: University of Chicago Press, 1934.

[19]

Self

READING FOR UNDERSTANDING

Summary

_____   1. In summary, this passage presents
          a. a *method* for finding oneself.
          b. the *reasons* that a person has a self.
          c. the *types* of selves that people have.
          d. the *sequence* in which one's self develops.

_____   2. The summary is best stated in the
          a. first paragraph.
          b. second paragraph.
          c. third paragraph.
          d. fourth paragraph.

Vocabulary

_____   3. To see something **objectively*** is to see
          a. what needs improvement.
          b. the goal or aim that thing has.
          c. its various parts.
          d. it as it really is.

_____   4. **Consequences*** are
          a. questions.
          b. results.
          c. determiners.
          d. sequences.

Summary	Number right _____	× 10 =	_____
Vocabulary	Number right _____	× 10 =	_____
Comprehension	Number right _____	× 10 =	_____
		Total score	_____

_____ 5. **Integral*** parts are
   a. piercing.
   b. unwanted.
   c. necessary.
   d. proportionate.

Comprehension

_____ 6. During the preparatory stage of the development of self, children's actions are
   a. imitative.
   b. engaging.
   c. restricted.
   d. considerate.

_____ 7. The important development during the play stage of the development of self is that children
   a. begin to understand the work world.
   b. develop clear, strong imaginations.
   c. learn to play with other children.
   d. direct activity back to themselves.

_____ 8. In both the preparatory stage and the play stage of the development of self, children do a great deal of
   a. pretending.
   b. listening.
   c. socializing.
   d. verbalizing.

_____ 9. The important development during the game stage of the development of self is that children
   a. begin to play baseball and other sports.
   b. take on several roles at the same time.
   c. learn that they are developing a self.
   d. discover that life is a kind of game.

_____ 10. People who do *not* have fully developed selves
   a. maintain long, meaningful relationships.
   b. have inconsistent views of themselves.
   c. usually act in predictable ways.
   d. expect others to be considerate.

[19]

Self

READING FOR STUDYING

Underline the first paragraph. **Circle** the names of the three stages of the development of self where they are printed in italic type. **Underline** the definitions of the stages and **draw a line alongside** the examples of the stages. (For the *preparatory stage,* draw a line alongside the example of a small boy pretending to drive.) Under a heading and appropriate subheadings that emphasize the type of explanation given in the passage, **summarize** the definitions and examples.

_____

_____

_____

_____

_____

_____

_____

_____

_____

_____

_____

_____

_____

_____

_____

_____

_____

_____

[20]

The Ecosystem

An ecosystem is a portion of the total environment. It includes within its boundaries both the nonliving material, and a community of organisms that constitutes most of the food net (or food chain) of the dominant organisms of the community. Thus we speak of a forest, a field, or a swamp as an ecosystem.

One of the common ecosystems which is easily visualized is the freshwater lake, and it is with such an ecosystem we are concerned here. A lake is a convenient example because the physical boundaries are easy to identify and most people are familiar to some extent with the dominant living and nonliving aspects of a lake. The principal nonliving, or **abiotic**, components of the lake ecosystem are the air over it and the   * soil and rock which form the basin and the water contained by the basin.

It is obvious that the soil, rock, air, and water are continuous with similar materials outside of the lake basin. It is equally obvious that what happens in the lake is strongly influenced by events beyond its shores. Water running into the basin brings floating, suspended, and dissolved materials. If the lake has an outlet, materials will be exported as well as imported into the lake ecosystem. Atmospheric events, wind, sunlight, precipitation, all influence the lake. It is still reasonable to consider the lake as an ecosystem on the grounds that the great majority of the biological energy transformations involved in the "community metabolism" of the ecosystem are carried on within those limits. In most lake ecosystems the primary production, the initial fixing of energy by autotrophs, occurs in the lake itself. The exceptions would be the importation into the lake of organic material, leaves, wood, drifting organisms, and suspended debris. These imports exist and must be accounted for, but the life of the lake would go on independent of these imports. It is this *self-sufficiency* which provides a functional definition of the limits of a natural ecosystem.

The interaction of the various abiotic factors provides the basis for many diverse **habitats** within the ecosystem. The shape of the soil and   * rock basin determines the depths and contours of the various regions of

From "Life Zones in a Freshwater Lake" in *An Introduction to Biology* by Robert M. Chute, pp. 206–209 and figure here numbered Figure 1. Copyright © by Robert M. Chute. Reprinted with adaptations by permission of Harper & Row, Publishers, Inc.

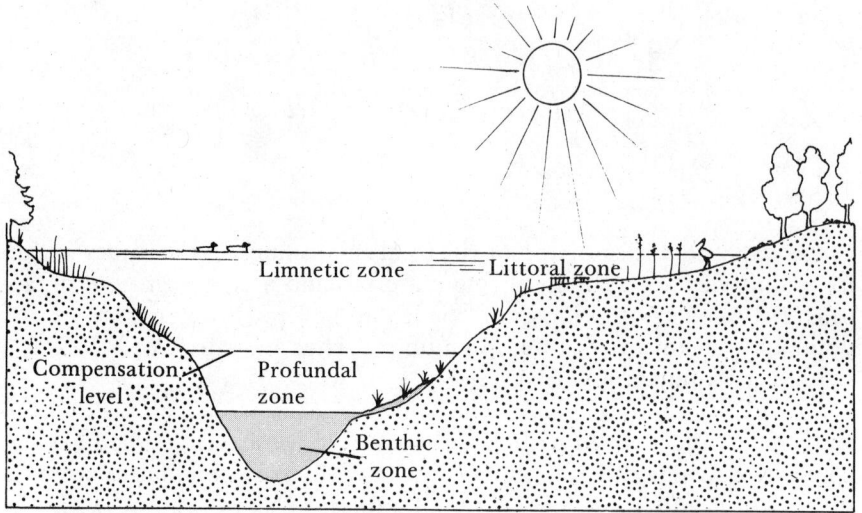

Figure 1. Life Zones in a Freshwater Lake.

The extent of the life zones is determined in part by the related factors of the depth of water and the penetration of light. Another important factor is the nature of the substrate (rock, soil, mud) underlying a zone. The littoral, limnetic, and profundal zones are, in common terms, the shallow water, open water, and deep water zones. The benthic zone comprises the bottom of the lake. Each life zone has a characteristic community of organisms. The compensation level is the point at which, due to reduction of illumination, the overall photosynthetic oxygen production is equaled by the overall respiratory carbon dioxide production.

the lake—shallows, deeps, islands, bars, and marginal marshes and swamps. Each region represents a different habitat to which different species will be adapted. The depth of the water and the nature of the bottom will determine which of the various species of rooted aquatic plants native to that area will grow in a specific region of the lake. The depth of the water, its richness in dissolved nutrients, and its temperature will determine what floating or planktonic plants can exist. The density of this phytoplankton population will usually determine the depth to which sunlight can penetrate the water and, thus, the depth at which photosynthesis can take place.

The various types of plants—emergent, floating, and submerged—provide part of the physical habitat for many animal members of the community and also for plants which live attached to other plants. The larger plants and the usually microscopic phytoplankton form the basis of the lake community food chains. Largely unseen, but critical to the survival of the more obvious producers and consumers are the decomposer organisms. Millions upon millions of bacterial and fungal cells in

the water, in sediments, on abiotic and *biotic* surfaces break down the   *
waste products and dead tissues of larger organisms and of their own
kind. The products of this decomposition add to the nutrients of the
water and to the bottom sediments.

In summary, the lake ecosystem consists of an interrelated community of many plant, animal, and microbial species. Each species is
represented by a population, the numbers of which are limited by the
interaction of specific abiotic and biotic factors. This community of
species populations is essentially self-sufficient in that the majority of the
primary production needed to support the various food chains occurs
within the lake itself.

Within a particular habitat each species would have a specific niche.
In this ecological context the word **niche** refers to the function of the
members of that species, which is the same as saying the way in which
they get their energy. The biological world contains a bewildering array
of species—so many that even the best-trained biologist can be familiar
with and know the scientific names of only a small minority. It helps us
make some sense of the confusion of organic forms to recognize that in
all ecosystems, similar functions and equivalent habitats will be represented. Thus, if we shift our attention from the lake to the sea, we find
organisms with new forms and unknown names, but they will be per-
forming familiar functions. For this reason what we learn about a lake
can, in part, be transferred to a tropical rain forest or an arctic island.

A second way in which the biologist attempts to order the larger
number of different species is to establish a system of classification
within which the organisms are grouped according to some plan (usually
their supposed evolutionary relationship) and given formal, scientific
names. Since the case history with which we are now concerned involves
not only a specific ecosystem—the fresh water lake—but also a specific
species population within that system, an outline of such a classification
system can be introduced by showing how the organism in question fits
within it. (See Figure 2 on the next page.)

Classification of the phantom midge

Phylum: Arthropoda
Subphylum: Mandibulata
Class: Insecta
Order: Diptera
Family: Culicidae
Genus: *Chaoborus*
Species: *Chaoborus astictopus**

Ten common orders in the class Insecta.†

Isoptera	the termites
Orthoptera	grasshoppers, roaches, mantids
Odonata	dragonflies, damselflies
Anoplura	sucking lice
Hemiptera	true bugs, cicadas, aphids
Coleoptera	beetles, weevils
Hymenoptera	wasps, bees, ants
Siphonaptera	fleas
Diptera	true flies, mosquitoes, midges
Lepidoptera	moths, butterflies

*The genus and species names (and subspecies designation if any) are always italicized.

†Most specialists recognize 20 to 24 orders of insects. Only the most familiar are listed here.

Figure 2. Major Categories Used in Animal Classification (Illustrated by the classification of the phantom midge, *Chaoborus astictopus,* and common order of insects).

[20]

The Ecosystem

READING FOR UNDERSTANDING

Summary

_____ 1. In summary, this passage presents
   a. a *method* for identifying ecosystems.
   b. a *definition* and an example of an ecosystem.
   c. the *types* of ecosystems to be found.
   d. the *reasons* that ecosystems sometimes die.

_____ 2. The summary is best stated in the
   a. first paragraph.
   b. second paragraph.
   c. first and second paragraphs.
   d. first, second, and third paragraphs.

Vocabulary

_____ 3. The **abiotic*** elements of an ecosystem are the ones that are *not*
   a. moving.
   b. swimming.
   c. living.
   d. walking.

_____ 4. A **habitat*** is a
   a. lake, river, stream, ocean, sea, or pond.
   b. desert, field, mountain, hill, or valley.
   c. place that is suitable for certain things to live.
   d. place that is free of environmental pollutants.

Summary	Number right _____	X 10 = _____	
Vocabulary	Number right _____	X 10 = _____	
Comprehension	Number right _____	X 10 = _____	
		Total score _____	

_____   5. A **biotic*** surface is the surface of a
         a. living organism.
         b. nonliving element.
         c. water-dwelling creature.
         d. plant that lives in water.

Comprehension

_____   6. If material such as wood, metal, and glass were *not* put into a lake, the lake
         would
         a. soon become polluted.
         b. continue without them.
         c. soon cease to exist.
         d. be free of pollutants.

_____   7. Exactly which animals and plants will thrive in a particular ecosystem is
         determined by
         a. the shape of the soil and rocks there.
         b. whether the water is shallow or deep.
         c. all possible variations in the habitat.
         d. the temperature and nutrients available.

_____   8. When kangaroos live in an ecosystem, the number of kangaroos living there
         depends on
         a. the effect living and nonliving things in the ecosystem have on each other.
         b. whether the ecosystem has suffered damage by natural disasters.
         c. the amount of annual rainfall in relation to the amount of sunshine.
         d. the extent to which kangaroos are hunted for food or display in zoos.

_____   9. About how many of the scientific names of animals and plants do well-trained
         biologists know?
         a. almost all of them
         b. almost half of them
         c. less than half of them
         d. very few of them

_____   10. Mosquitoes, termites, and roaches are from the orders
         a. diptera, coleoptera, and isoptera, respectively.
         b. isoptera, diptera, and coleoptera, respectively.
         c. diptera, isoptera, and orthoptera, respectively.
         d. isoptera, diptera, and orthoptera, respectively.

[20]

The Ecosystem

READING FOR STUDYING

Circle *ecosystem* in the first sentence, *abiotic* where it appears next to the first asterisk, *biotic* where it appears next to the third asterisk, and *habitats* and *niche* where they are printed in boldface type. **Underline** the best definitions the writer gives for each of these words. **Summarize** this information as you would to study it for a biology test, including examples where possible.

_____

_____

_____

_____

_____

_____

_____

_____

_____

_____

_____

_____

_____

_____

21

Business Games

Like life itself, business and management often are compared to a game. In recent years, several witty but serious-minded writers have described the rules for winning. Parkinson's Law, the Peter Principle, the Radovic Rule, Robert Townsend's *Up the Organization,* and other "scientific" formulations poke fun at current practices while revealing some simple truths about management in large organizations.

Parkinson's Law states that work expands to fill the time available for its completion. Bureaucratic officials, claims C. Northcote Parkinson, create work for each other, thus making sure that they always have something to do. They tend to hire inferior personnel, so that they will be surrounded by subordinates instead of rivals. They spend more time on unimportant matters than on major projects. Parkinson's central theme is that "an organization . . . will grow (if given the opportunity) irrespective of the work (if any) which has to be done."

His classic example of administrative and managerial proliferation is the British Admiralty. In 1938, Europe was on the brink of war, and in the British navy approximately four thousand dockyard officers and staff and eleven thousand admiralty officers and staff were needed to manage 308 ships. In 1967, Britain was quite peaceful and the number of ships had dropped to 114. Nevertheless, more than eight thousand dockyard officers and staff and thirty-three thousand admiralty officers and staff were being employed.

Parkinson originally observed this mushrooming in civil service organizations, but the trend is to be found at almost all levels of government and is also to be seen in business. In small firms and systems, emphasis is on work, and the productive efforts of individuals can be measured. In larger businesses, emphasis shifts to human relations and administrators' ability to maintain the organization. Rapid growth after World War II prompted social scientists to examine the phenomenon of people in larger organizations.

In 1956, William H. Whyte, Jr., coined the phrase *organization man* to describe an individual committed to a firm's goals and loyal to its ideals, perhaps at the expense of personal beliefs and feelings. In order to safeguard his position, the "organization man" tries to be what he thinks the organization wants him to be. The organization both rewards such conformity and perpetuates it. Companies decide what qualities they want their top executives to have and then seek out employees and management trainees who seem to have the desired qualities. Psychological tests are given to determine whether an individual will fit into the firm. People whose behavior, ideas, or appearance is unusual or clashes with the firm's image are not moved into top administrative positions.

In *The Pyramid Climbers,* Vance Packard pursues the concept of the "organization man." He discusses a study of corporation presidents. Seven out of ten top executives denied that there were any "organization men" in their companies. Yet in answers to other questions, they said they would be cautious about promoting people with uncommon ideas. Packard suggests that to succeed—to advance up the corporate pyramid and get to the top of the organization chart—people have to surrender some of their individuality and play the business "game" according to the company's rules. A key sentence in his chapter entitled "The Maneuvers of the Power Players" reads, "A guy doesn't move ahead accidentally."

Laurence Peter developed his well-known principle as a result of his observation of competent and incompetent business behavior. The *Peter Principle* is: In a hierarchy every employee tends to rise to her or his level of incompetence. A corollary to the Peter Principle is the proposition that in time most positions are filled by employees not capable of doing their jobs. In *The Peter Prescription,* Peter has advice for people who are good at what they do and are faced with the possibility of being promoted into a position they cannot handle: "When threatened with an unwanted promotion, pretend you are already incompetent."

Related to the Peter Principle is the Radovic Rule, laid down by Igor Radovic in the *Radovic Rule: How to Manage Your Boss.* The *Radovic Rule* is: "In any organization, the potential is much greater for the subordinate to manage his superior than for the superior to manage his subordinate." This would certainly stand to reason if the superior has reached his or her level of incompetence and both the superior and the subordinate know it. The superior would have to depend on the abilities of subordinates to maintain his or her position, and the subordinates could manage or manipulate the dependent superior.

[21]

Business Games

READING FOR UNDERSTANDING

Summary

_____ 1. In summary, this passage presents
    a. *methods* for being successful in business.
    b. a *history* of successful business practices.
    c. *reasons* that businesses should be like games.
    d. *types* of amusing practices in businesses.

_____ 2. The summary is best stated in the
    a. first sentence.
    b. second sentence.
    c. third sentence.
    d. fourth sentence.

Vocabulary

_____ 3. A **proliferation*** is a
    a. quick growth.
    b. spread of wealth.
    c. long discussion.
    d. simple organization.

_____ 4. If he **coined*** a phrase, he
    a. invented it.
    b. paid for it.
    c. reported it.
    d. looked for it.

Summary	Number right _____	× 10 =	_____
Vocabulary	Number right _____	× 10 =	_____
Comprehension	Number right _____	× 10 =	_____
		Total score	_____

_____ 5. To **perpetuate*** is to
   a. consider rationally.
   b. speak authoritatively.
   c. cause to continue.
   d. make tranquil.

Comprehension

_____ 6. It may be predicted from Parkinson's Law that when workers have eight hours in which to do work that could be done in four hours, they will complete the work in
   a. four hours.
   b. six hours.
   c. eight hours.
   d. ten hours.

_____ 7. According to Parkinson's Law, an organization
   a. will grow when work demands that it grow.
   b. will grow, even if there is no work to do.
   c. will cease, even if there is work to do.
   d. will cease when there is no work to do.

_____ 8. The "organization man" was first described by
   a. Packard.
   b. Radovic.
   c. Peter.
   d. Whyte.

_____ 9. According to the Peter Principle, employees in businesses are promoted until they arrive at a job they
   a. can do very well.
   b. cannot do well.
   c. want much to do.
   d. do not want to do.

_____ 10. According to the Radovic Rule, it is most likely that
   a. bosses will be managed by those they boss.
   b. bossy bosses will not be liked by workers.
   c. good bosses will help workers move ahead.
   d. poor bosses will get ahead most quickly.

[21]

Business Games

READING FOR STUDYING

Circle the following words where they are printed in italic type: *Parkinson's Law, organization man, Peter Principle,* and *Radovic Rule.* **Underline** the best definitions the author gives for each of these, and **draw a line alongside** examples, where they are given. **Summarize** this information under appropriate headings.

_____

_____

_____

_____

_____

_____

_____

_____

_____

_____

_____

_____

_____

_____

_____

_____

_____

_____

22

Job Hunting

It is one thing to decide on a career area. It is another to land the job you actually want. Landing a job is something like landing a fish. You must have the right equipment, the proper lure or bait. You must know where the best opportunity is and have the skill (or luck) to place your bait where it can be seen by the target. Hooking the fish can be compared to securing an interview, landing the fish to your ability to persuade a prospective employer of your abilities and qualifications.

*

THE PROPER TOOLS

A career file, a well-planned résumé, and a carefully written cover letter are the tools you need. Careful research and study will help you locate a job. Employers favorably impressed by your résumé and cover letter will ask to interview you, and eventually your career will be under way.

Career file. Starting today, keep a record of everything and anything that could be useful in your future efforts to find a job. In this "career file," keep notes on your personal goals and the results of aptitude and other tests that cast light on your job plans. Save information on occupations, industries, and business firms, so that when you actually set out to look for a job, you will have reference material.

Keep records of honors you have received, extracurricular activities, awards, recommendations, and commendations. Often you will meet people who could be of great assistance to you when you go job hunting. Keep lists of their names and addresses.

You will be telling a prospective employer that you can handle the job, but you will be much more persuasive if you can show proof of your ability. In many classes, you will be required to write a research paper or analyze a business case. Other classes may call for the solution of a real or hypothetical problem. Keep such projects, papers, and exercises as evidence of your ability to do a job. Many students take the attitude that school is all theory or that professors live in ivory towers apart from the real world. They are therefore surprised when they enter the business world and find that the very things they discussed in the classroom are the subjects discussed in planning, committee, or board meetings. The case study, the research paper, the special problem that you did in the classroom might be just the item that will help get you a desired job. Keep this material in your career file, and be prepared to take some of it along with you on a job interview.

In short, your career file should contain information that might help you attain your career goals. The file will also be of value when you begin to prepare your résumé and cover letter.

Résumé. If you plan to launch a mail campaign in search of the right   *
position, a résumé is especially important. But even if you plan to have face-to-face interviews with prospective employers, you will need a résumé. Companies keep résumés on file so that they can contact potential employees as job vacancies occur. Résumés give interviewers basic information about job applicants and serve as a conversation starter.

A résumé is a short summary about your experience, achievements, and interests. Its aim is to whet a prospective employer's interest in you.   *
The information should be brief but say enough to stimulate employment proceedings. Most companies require an applicant to fill out a detailed employment form; so your résumé need not tell your whole life history.

Your résumé should be typed and organized by categories and dates. There is not one best format. To an extent, what you decide to say will affect the appearance of the résumé. If you have trouble organizing a résumé, the placement office of your school will be able to help you. Personal information, educational background, and work experience should be mentioned. Remember that you are competing with many others for jobs. If you have special qualifications or unique interests, be sure to include them. Your résumé represents you in your absence, and it must make a good impression. (See Figure 1.)

Cover letter. Your résumé should be general, factual, and telegraphic. The cover letter, in contrast, is personal and specific. This letter accompanies your résumé when you are exploring employment possibilities by mail. In it you can fully describe the job you are interested in and the abilities that qualify you for that position. The résumé should be suitable for a multitude of opportunities; nearly every firm that you apply to will want a copy of it. The cover letter should fit the exact circumstances. It can elaborate on information given in the résumé, but it should not duplicate the résumé.

The cover letter is a sales letter, selling you. It shows a prospective employer that you are creative, able to communicate, and knowledgeable about the occupation you are interested in and about the company you are writing to. Be sincere and personal. (See Figure 2.)

```
                                                        Phone: 991-191-3402
William R. Rayburne
2622 Berry Street
Hometown, Kansas  00037

Career Objectives
    Industrial sales leading to a position in marketing management.
    Willing to relocate.

Education
    1973-1977 B.B.A., June 1977, Kansas Tech University, Alexander,
              Kansas
              Major: Marketing, with special emphasis on sales
              management
              Minor: Industrial Technology
    1969-1973 Academic course, Hometown High School, Hometown,
              Kansas

Honors
    1977      Graduation with honors
    1976      Received Kansas Tech Merit Senior Marketing Scholarship
    1974-1977 On Dean's List 6 semesters

Extracurricular Activities
    Vice President of Industrial Marketing and Management Club, in
      charge of arranging programs and field trips
    Two-year letterman on the golf team
    Senior representative on Student Council

Work Experience
    Summer 1974, 1975, 1976 Parts sales person, Watson Wholesale
                            Electrical Company, Hometown, Kansas
                            Sold over the counter and by phone
                            to contractors, builders, small
                            manufacturers, and repair firms.
                            Was responsible for inventory
                            control and reordering.
    1972-1973 Grocery clerk, Acme-Allied Stores, Hometown, Kansas
              Worked after school and on weekends bagging
              groceries and stocking shelves.

Special Qualifications
    Speak Spanish fluently; lived in Lima, Peru, for two years.
    Have third-class radio license

References
    Supplied upon request.
```

Figure 1. Example of a Typical Résumé.

```
                                        2622 Berry Street
                                        Hometown, Kansas  00037

                                        May 1, 1977


      Mr. Theodore T. Honore
      Vice President of Sales
      Home Electric Products
      3495 Ellis Street
      Vandermeer, Michigan  34298

      Dear Mr. Honore:

      Your company seems to be the kind of firm I would like to work
      for when I graduate from Kansas Tech this June. If you will be
      needing a sales person who is willing to learn the business from
      the ground up, I would appreciate the opportunity to speak with
      you about the possibility of employment.

      Although I am relatively inexperienced, I do have some knowledge
      of sales techniques and electrical products. My major at Kansas
      Tech is marketing, and I am familiar with many of your products
      as the result of some sales experience with the Watson Wholesale
      Electrical Company in Hometown, Kansas. Your products are always
      of fine quality, and I know that Mr. Watson thinks highly of the
      way you do business.

      I have enclosed a copy of my resume, and I will be happy to supply
      additional information or references. I am very interested in
      working for Home Electric Products. I would welcome the chance to
      prove that my enthusiasm coupled with hard work will be profitable
      for both of us. I would be glad to come to Vandermeer for an in-
      terview any time after June 10.

                                        Sincerely,



                                        William R. Rayburne

      Enclosure
```

Figure 2. Example of a Cover Letter.

[22]

Job Hunting

READING FOR UNDERSTANDING

Summary

_____   1. In summary, this passage presents
           a. the *reasons* résumés are needed.
           b. some *types* of job opportunities.
           c. a *sequence* for writing résumés.
           d. *methods* for finding employment.

_____   2. The summary is best stated in the headings and in the
           a. first paragraph.
           b. second paragraph.
           c. third paragraph.
           d. fourth paragraph.

Vocabulary

_____   3. A **prospective*** employer is
           a. one found by much searching.
           b. one who pays high salaries.
           c. a possible future employer.
           d. an employer who advertises.

_____   4. A **campaign*** is
           a. a method of distributing mail.
           b. a planned, organized approach.
           c. another word that means résumé.
           d. a struggle to find employment.

Summary	Number right _____	× 10 =	_____
Vocabulary	Number right _____	× 10 =	_____
Comprehension	Number right _____	× 10 =	_____
		Total score	_____

_____ 5. To **whet*** interest is to
    a. stimulate it.
    b. cut it off.
    c. disregard it.
    d. need it badly.

Comprehension

_____ 6. A list of people who will speak well of you to an employer should be contained in a
    a. résumé.
    b. career file.
    c. cover letter.
    d. personnel office.

_____ 7. Résumés are especially important when
    a. one has a very long work history.
    b. one has just graduated from college.
    c. jobs are applied for through the mail.
    d. there is much competition for jobs.

_____ 8. The most important goal of your résumé is to
    a. deemphasize why you should not be hired.
    b. provide your complete personal history.
    c. summarize your important work history.
    d. arouse employers' interest in hiring you.

_____ 9. A primary difference between résumés and cover letters is that cover letters are more
    a. formal.
    b. elaborate.
    c. specific.
    d. general.

_____ 10. The most important characteristic that a résumé and cover letter share is that they both
    a. try to sell the job applicant.
    b. summarize one's work history.
    c. are sincere and personal in tone.
    d. are very neatly typewritten.

[22]

Job Hunting

READING FOR STUDYING

Underline the first sentence following the heading "The Proper Tools"; also underline the best definitions that the author gives for *career file, résumé*, and *cover letter*. **Summarize** these definitions. Then **study** the example of a résumé and, under an appropriate heading, **list** the categories you would include in a résumé you might prepare to seek employment.

_____

_____

_____

_____

_____

_____

_____

_____

_____

_____

_____

_____

_____

_____

_____

_____

23

Mass Hysteria

Mass hysteria is a form of collective behavior involving widespread and contagious anxiety, usually caused by some unfounded belief. In extreme cases mass hysteria can result in panic, particularly if the source of the anxiety is believed to be sufficiently close or threatening. The medieval witch-hunts . . . are an example of mass hysteria, created in this instance by the illusory belief that many of the problems of late medieval society were caused by witches. McCarthyism, the secular witch-hunt of the fifties which aimed at finding communists in influential positions in American society, also had many of the characteristics of mass hysteria.

Let us look briefly at two instances of mass hysteria that have been closely studied by sociologists.

THE MARTIAN INVASION OF EARTH

In 1938 a radio dramatization of the *War of the Worlds* was broadcast in the New York area. The result was mass hysteria and even outright panic, involving perhaps as many as 1 million of the 6 million people who heard the broadcast.

Although an announcer made the nature of the program clear at the outset, many people tuned in later and did not realize that they were listening to a play. The dramatization itself started innocently enough, with what purported to be a music concert. The music was interrupted with an announcement of strange atmospheric disturbances, followed by an interview with an expert who assured listeners that this could not possibly be the start of an invasion from Mars. The music continued, only to be interrupted again by an eye-witness account of a strange meteorite that had landed near New York (quoted in Cantril, 1940):

> Just a minute! Something's happening! Ladies and gentlemen, this is terrific! . . . The thing must be hollow! . . . Good heavens, something's wriggling out. . . . There, I can see the thing's body. It's large as a bear and glistens like wet leather.

From Ian Robertson, *Sociology*, pp. 521-523. Copyright © 1977 by Worth Publishers, Inc. Used by permission.

But that face. It . . . it's indescribable. I can hardly force myself to keep looking at it. The eyes are black and gleam like a serpent. The mouth is V-shaped with saliva dripping from its rimless lips that seem to quiver and pulsate. The crowd falls back. . . . What's that? There's a jet of flame . . . and it leaps right at the advancing men. . . . Good Lord, they're turning to flame!

This "on-the-spot" transmission ended abruptly, and various "experts," "public officials," and "scientists" then took turns at commenting on the invasion. The listeners were eventually told (quoted in Cantril, 1940):

Ladies and gentlemen, I have a grave announcement to make. Incredible as it may seem, both the observations of science and the evidence of our eyes lead to the inescapable assumption that those strange beings who landed in the Jersey farmlands tonight are the vanguard of an invading army from the planet Mars. The battle which took place tonight at Govers Mill has ended in one of the most startling defeats ever suffered by an army in modern times; seven thousand men armed with rifles and machine guns pitted against a single fighting machine of the invaders from Mars. One hundred and twenty known survivors.

A very large number of people accepted this broadcast as fact, not fiction. Some of them hid in cellars. Others bundled their children into their cars and drove as fast as they could from the scene of the supposed invasion. Others telephoned their relatives to give them the terrible news and to say farewell. Others simply prayed and waited for the inevitable end. Crowds gathered excitedly in public places, and fresh rumors about the invasion were generated.

Why did such an improbable tale of invasion from outer space have such a devastating effect? One reason was undoubtedly the skill of the dramatists, who used an unusual and imaginative form of presentation. The use of the "bulletin" format, with comments from supposed scientific experts and public officials, gave a certain credibility to the events. Equally important, however, was the fact that in this pretelevision age people relied heavily on the radio for up-to-the-minute news. Much of the news at the time dealt with the growing tensions in Europe, which in 1938 stood on the brink of World War II. Listeners were glued to their radio sets as never before, had learned to expect interruptions of their scheduled programs, and expected that these interruptions might deal with conflict and warfare (Cantril, 1940). In addition, knowledge of other planets was far less extensive than it is today. Observations of Mars had led some astronomers to the mistaken conclusion that its surface was criss-crossed by "canals," presumably constructed by highly intelligent Martians. Belief in the possibility of advanced life forms on Mars was quite widespread among the ordinary public. . . .

THE SEATTLE WINDSHIELD-PITTING EPIDEMIC

In late March 1954, Seattle newspapers carried occasional reports of damage to automobile windshields in a city eighty miles to the north—damage that the police suspected was caused by vandals. On the morning of April 14, newspapers reported windshield damage in a town only sixty-five miles away, and later that day similar incidents were reported only forty-five miles from the city limits. On the same evening, the mysterious windshield-pitting agent struck Seattle itself: between April 14 and April 15, over 15,000 people called the Seattle police department to complain about damage to their windshields.

The windshield damage usually consisted of small pitting marks, which often grew into bubbles about the size of a thumbnail. Many people tried to protect their windshields by covering them with cardboard or by garaging their cars, but even these tactics did not guarantee immunity. Clearly, vandals could not be responsible. The most popular culprit was the H-bomb, which had recently been tested in the Pacific. On the evening of April 15, the Mayor of Seattle dramatically announced that the pitting was "no longer a police matter" and called on the state governor and the president of the United States for help. Yet the epidemic ended almost as soon as it had started. Newspapers suggested on April 16 that mass hysteria, not radioactive fallout, was the cause of the problem. On that day the police received only forty-six complaints; on April 17, only ten; and thereafter, none at all.

Careful scientific analysis of the pitted windshields revealed that the amount of pitting increased with the age and mileage of the car in question, and that there was no evidence of pitting that could not be explained by ordinary road damage. What had happened was that the residents of Seattle, for the first time, had started to look *at* their windshields instead of *through* them.

In a study of the epidemic, Nahum Medalia and Otto Larsen (1958) found that for two months before the epidemic, Seattle newspapers had been printing reports about H-bomb tests and fallout, "hinting darkly at doom and disaster." The epidemic, they suggest, may have served to relieve the tensions that had been built up, if only by focusing these diffuse anxieties on a very narrow area of experience, automobile windshields.

REFERENCES

Cantril, Hadley. 1940. *The Invasion from Mars.* Princeton, N.J.: Princeton University Press.

Medalia, Nahum Z., and Otto N. Larsen. 1958. "Diffusion and belief in a collective delusion: The Seattle windshield pitting epidemic." *American Sociological Review*, 23, pp. 221–232.

[23]

Mass Hysteria

READING FOR UNDERSTANDING

Summary

_____ 1. In summary, this passage presents
a. the *reasons* that masses become hysterical.
b. the *types* of mass hysteria that exist.
c. the *history* of mass hysterical behavior.
d. a *method* for identifying mass hysteria.

_____ 2. The summary is best stated in the
a. first sentence.
b. second sentence.
c. third sentence.
d. fourth sentence.

Vocabulary

_____ 3. An **illusory*** belief is
a. a realistic belief.
b. a widely held belief.
c. an incorrect belief.
d. an understandable belief.

_____ 4. "**Purported*** to be a music concert" means that it
a. really was a music concert.
b. claimed to be a concert, but wasn't.
c. was in no way a music concert.
d. did not claim to be a music concert.

Summary	Number right _____	X 10 =	_____
Vocabulary	Number right _____	X 10 =	_____
Comprehension	Number right _____	X 10 =	_____
		Total score	_____

_____ 5. Those at the **vanguard*** are
    a. at the highest pinnacle.
    b. among the most intelligent.
    c. of the upper social class.
    d. in the leading position.

Comprehension

_____ 6. It seems that people become hysterical because they
    a. panic and become overly anxious.
    b. believe something that isn't true.
    c. have primitive patterns of thought.
    d. fear a take-over by the communists.

_____ 7. Which of the following is *not* a reason that the 1938 radio broadcast created mass hysteria?
    a. It was dramatized with great skill as news.
    b. At that time people relied on radio, not TV, for news.
    c. Belief in life on Mars was widespread.
    d. Well-known personalities gave the report.

_____ 8. When Seattle newspapers suggested that reports of windshield pitting was induced by mass hysteria, reports on windshield pitting
    a. increased for two days.
    b. increased for two weeks.
    c. stopped within two days.
    d. stopped within two weeks.

_____ 9. Analysis revealed that cars had more windshield pits when they were
    a. from the suburbs rather than downtown.
    b. from downtown rather than the suburbs.
    c. owned by workers, not professionals.
    d. older models with more miles on them.

_____ 10. The basic reason that Seattle residents saw pits in their windshields was that reports of windshield pitting caused them to
    a. become anxious and tense.
    b. see things that weren't there.
    c. look at their windshields.
    d. displace worry over disaster.

[23]

Mass Hysteria

READING FOR STUDYING

This passage demonstrates how long examples may be used to ensure understanding. **Underline** the definition of *mass hysteria* in the first two sentences of the passage, and the parts of the two examples that best illustrate this definition. **Summarize** the definition and examples as you would to prepare for a test on this information.

_____

_____

_____

_____

_____

_____

_____

_____

_____

_____

_____

_____

_____

_____

_____

_____

[NINE]

Comparisons in Textbooks

This part of the book introduces comparisons, the seventh type of information frequently found in textbooks. *Comparisons* are explanations of the ways in which two or more persons, places, or things are alike or different in two or more ways. The following passage describes five stages of development that Sigmund Freud proposed; it explains two ways in which each of the five stages is different from the other stages.

THE PSYCHOSEXUAL STAGES, ACCORDING TO FREUD

Sigmund Freud proposed that there are five stages in people's psychosexual development. He believed that the success with which individuals deal with the problems of each stage is related to their personality development.

The first stage, which lasts from birth until about one year of age, he called the *oral stage*. During this time the infant's pleasure centers around the mouth in eating, biting, chewing, and sucking. The *anal stage,* which lasts from age one year to age three, is the time when the young child finds pleasure in holding and letting go of waste matter from the body. This is the important time of toilet training. The *phallic stage* begins at age three and continues until age six. It is during this time that the child, male or female, derives pleasure from primary sex organs to a great degree. Beginning at age six and continuing until about age eleven, the child passes through what Freud called the *latency period*. During this time the child denies affection and attraction for the parent of the opposite sex and identifies strongly with the parent of the same sex. Adolescence marks the beginning of the *genital stage,* which is the awakening of sexuality and the desire for heterosexual love. (From James F. Shepherd, *College Study Skills,* p. 188. Copyright © 1979 by Houghton Mifflin Company. Used by permission.)

Figure 1 shows the information about the psychosexual stages summarized in a *comparison chart* under headings that emphasize the two ways in which the stages differ from each other: "Age" and "Characteristics." Notice that the comparison chart not only points out the differences among the stages, but it also gives importance to the sequence in which the stages occur. Comparisons, like definitions, usually appear in textbook passages that also convey some other important type of information.

The five passages in Part 9 all contain comparisons, but they all *also* convey some other important type of information. Therefore, the first

The Psychosexual Stages, According to Freud

	Age	Characteristics
Oral Stage	Birth to 1 year	Gets pleasure from mouth by sucking, eating, biting and chewing.
Anal Stage	1 year to 3 years	Gets pleasure from holding and letting go of body waste.
Phallic Stage	3 years to 6 years	The child derives pleasure from his or her own primary sex organs.
Latency Period	6 years to about 11 years	Child denies attraction for parent of opposite sex and identifies with parent of the same sex.
Genital Stage	Adolescence	Awakening of sexuality and desire for heterosexual love.

Figure 1. An Example of a Comparison Chart.

Reading for Understanding questions for the passages ask you to identify the *other* type of explanations found in the passages (methods, sequences, categories, reasons, or points of view).

The Reading for Studying exercises will give you practice in making comparison charts of the type illustrated in Figure 1. You are probably familiar with charts of this kind; they appear in many textbooks. However, you may not have considered the value of making such charts yourself to study things you need to learn in your college courses.

If you ever have difficulty learning the information you have put into notes, ask yourself this question: "Does this information explain how two or more persons, places, or things are alike or different in two or more ways?" If the answer to this question is yes, you will find that the information is easier to learn if you organize it in a comparison chart. The Reading for Studying exercises will give you practice in making comparison charts.

24

Social Class

The pioneering work in social class was done by W. Lloyd Warner and his colleagues in their studies of American communities. Richard   *
Coleman, one of Warner's associates, characterized the six social classes:

1. *Upper-Upper.* This is the smallest of the classes, with less than 1 percent of the population of a community. It is comprised of   * families who have been prominent in the town or city for two or three generations and who are concerned with "living graciously, upholding the family reputation, reflecting the excellence of one's breeding, and displaying a sense of community responsibility."

2. *Lower-Upper.* Approximately 2 percent of a community is comprised of people who have acquired wealth recently. They are likely to be founders of large businesses, executives of important companies, and newly rich doctors and lawyers. Their goals are to live graciously and pursue success.   *

3. *Upper-Middle.* The 10 percent of a community in this class is likely to be college educated. They tend to be "moderately-successful professional men and women, owners of medium-sized businesses, and 'organization men' at the managerial level." They are concerned with having successful careers and reflecting this success in their homes and social relationships. The major difference between the Upper-Middle and Lower-Upper class is the degree of success they have achieved and the extent to which they reflect this in their lifestyles.

4. *Lower-Middle.* Somewhere between 30 and 35 percent of a community may be described as being "at the top of the 'Average Man's World'." They are likely to be white-collar workers, small businessmen, and high-status blue-collar workers. Respectability and striving characterize the members of this class. They live in comfortable homes in the "right" part of town, shop in "good" stores, plan for the college education of their children, and are active in clubs and churches.

Reprinted, with adaptations, from Richard Coleman, "The Significance of Social Stratification in Selling," in *Marketing: A Mature Discipline,* edited by Martin Bell, 1961, published by the American Marketing Association. Used by permission.

People from different social classes share many common experiences. Here two men from different classes enjoy listening to music in a park. (Photo by Joan Dufault)

5. *Upper-Lower.* With nearly 40 percent of a community, this is the largest of the six classes. These are the semiskilled workers on assembly lines and at thousands of other essential jobs. Though they may make good money, they are more interested in "getting by" and in "enjoying life" than they are with respectability and planning for the future.
6. *Lower-Lower.* The remaining 15 percent of a community is comprised of the unskilled and underemployed. Opportunity is limited for these people. Their outlook on life is that they cannot change their condition and there is no reason for attempting to do so.

[24]

Social Class

READING FOR UNDERSTANDING

Summary

_____ 1. In summary, this passage presents
   a. *methods* for finding the class to which we belong.
   b. the *categories* of social classes in this country.
   c. the *reasons* that we have only six social classes.
   d. *points of view* about the need for social classes.

_____ 2. The summary is best stated in the headings and in the
   a. first paragraph.
   b. second paragraph.
   c. third paragraph.
   d. fourth paragraph.

Vocabulary

_____ 3. **Colleagues*** are
   a. types of classes.
   b. types of schools.
   c. fellow workers.
   d. social scientists.

_____ 4. **Comprised*** means
   a. decided.
   b. thought.
   c. made up of.
   d. brought out of.

Summary	Number right _____	× 10 =	_____
Vocabulary	Number right _____	× 10 =	_____
Comprehension	Number right _____	× 10 =	_____
		Total score	_____

_____   5. To **pursue*** success is to
           a. need it.
           b. chase it.
           c. want it.
           d. have it.

Comprehension

_____   6. The two classes that are most similar are the
           a. upper-upper and lower-upper.
           b. lower-upper and upper-middle.
           c. upper-middle and lower-middle.
           d. lower-middle and upper-lower.

_____   7. The owner of a neighborhood dry-cleaning shop is probably a member of the
           a. lower-upper class.
           b. upper-middle class.
           c. lower-middle class.
           d. upper-lower class.

_____   8. The people most interested in enjoying life belong to the
           a. upper-upper class.
           b. lower-upper class.
           c. lower-middle class.
           d. upper-lower class.

_____   9. The people least likely to move from their present class to the next higher
           class are those in the
           a. lower-lower class.
           b. upper-lower class.
           c. lower-middle class.
           d. upper-middle class.

_____ 10. There are almost as many people in the top three classes combined as there
           are in the
           a. bottom three classes combined.
           b. lower-middle class, by itself.
           c. upper-lower class, by itself.
           d. lower-lower class, by itself.

[24]

Social Class

READING FOR STUDYING

The passage discusses six social classes, describing how they differ with regard to (1) the percentage of people in each class; (2) the types of people in each class; and (3) the goals of the people in each class. **Summarize** this information in the "comparison chart" that follows. Use these headings across the top of the chart: *Percentages, Types of People,* and *Goals.* List the names of the classes down the left side of the chart, beginning with *Upper-Upper* at the top and ending with *Lower-Lower* at the bottom.

Figure 1. A Comparison Chart.

25

Intelligence

As we turn from physical to mental development, we find that psychologists' views concerning thinking in children have been profoundly influenced by the work of one man, a Swiss psychologist named Jean Piaget. Through extensive observations of his own three children and others and a program of research at various institutes in Geneva, Piaget has developed a description of four stages of intellectual growth beginning in the second year of life. The child's behavior prior to this time is essentially sensory-motor activity.

STAGES OF DEVELOPMENT

Preconceptual stage. At approximately eighteen months of age, the child's behavior begins to include symbolic activity, which is the use of signs or symbols to represent such things as external objects, situations, and relationships. The use of words is one example of symbolic activity. "Doggie" may mean "Where is the doggie?" or "I want the doggie," or it may have still another meaning, but in each instance the word stands for something other than itself. This stage, which lasts until approximately four years of age, is called *preconceptual* thinking. The child has learned to symbolize and attach labels to some things in his environment, but he has not yet mastered the abstracting and generalizing processes that are required in conceptual thinking.

Intuitive stage. Among the most widely cited of Piaget's investigations are those referred to as "conservation" experiments. The principal idea here is to discover whether or not the child recognizes that an amount is not increased or decreased when only its appearance is changed. When two identically shaped jars contain equal amounts of liquid, and the contents of one are poured into a third jar which is low and wide, its volume is not changed—it is conserved. The child in the *intuitive* stage, as the second period is called, recognizes that the two volumes are equal when the two tall jars are used but not when the

Figure 1. Equipment for the Conservation Experiment
Using Marbles Instead of Liquid.

contents of one are transferred to the wider vessel. The child's thinking
is determined by the most prominent features of what he observes, and
therefore he indicates that the taller jar contains more liquid. This type
of thinking—of which this conservation experiment is but one illustration—is described by Piaget as pre-operational. The child "reasons" in
terms of the dominant perceptual experience, rather than the operations or processes involved (Figure 1). This stage occurs approximately
between four and seven years.

Concrete operations stage. Recognition of the conservation principle is
a characteristic aspect of the transition to the third stage, *concrete
operations.* In fact, Piaget has written that the child at this stage "no
longer needs to reflect, he decides, he even looks surprised that the
question is asked, he is certain of the conservation" (1950, p. 140). The
child is beginning to understand the operations of classification, relations, number, temporal and spatial order, and so forth. For example,
"When a child aged 7 has arranged a series of manikins in order of size,
he will be able to make a series of sticks or bags correspond to them,
and he will be able to identify which element in one series corresponds
to which in another even when they are all jumbled . . ." (Piaget, 1950,

p. 143). In the stage from seven to eleven years, the child's thinking is described as operational because the child has mastered many of the processes (operations) required in solving problems where there are concrete materials.

Formal operations stage. At the stage of *formal operations,* extending approximately from eleven to fifteen years, the child's capacity for thinking has developed to the extent that he can reason apart from concrete situations. He engages in abstract reasoning comparable to but with less sophistication than that observed in adults. In the previous stage the child was able to classify, serialize, enumerate, and place objects and events in time and space. At this stage he can imagine the possibilities inherent in a problem; he can deduce what should occur if a given possibility is true; he can perform useful experiments to test his deductions; he can draw valid conclusions from the experiments; and he can think about these conclusions in a practical way.

REFERENCE

Piaget, J. (1950). *The Psychology of Intelligence.* New York: Harcourt, Brace.

[25]

Intelligence

READING FOR UNDERSTANDING

Summary

_____   1. In summary, this passage presents
          a. a *method* for measuring intelligent behavior.
          b. the *reasons* that some people are very intelligent.
          c. *points of view* about testing for intelligence.
          d. the *sequence* of the stages of intelligence.

_____   2. The summary is best stated in the headings and in the
          a. first sentence.
          b. second sentence.
          c. third sentence.
          d. fourth sentence.

Vocabulary

_____   3. The classic example of **symbolic*** activity is
          a. drawing.
          b. dancing.
          c. playing.
          d. speaking.

_____   4. **Conservation*** experiments test a child's ability to notice that an amount of
          liquid or marbles
          a. has not increased or decreased.
          b. has been moved to a different jar.
          c. was saved for others to examine.
          d. was put aside for use in the future.

Summary	Number right _____ X 10 = _____	
Vocabulary	Number right _____ X 10 = _____	
Comprehension	Number right _____ X 10 = _____	
	Total score _____	

_____ 5. To **deduce*** is to
   a. cause to increase.
   b. cause to decrease.
   c. conclude logically.
   d. infer illogically.

Comprehension

_____ 6. Children start speaking when they are about
   a. 15 months old.
   b. 18 months old.
   c. 21 months old.
   d. 24 months old.

_____ 7. When young children see liquid poured from a tall, thin container into a low, wide container they think that the low, wide container contains less liquid because they
   a. do not know the meaning of conservation.
   b. look at the containers, not the pouring.
   c. are intuitive in their thinking processes.
   d. have not learned about mass displacement.

_____ 8. The major accomplishment for children during the first five years of school is learning to
   a. solve problems.
   b. be imaginative.
   c. be intuitive.
   d. classify objects.

_____ 9. People are usually older than fifteen years before they can
   a. imagine possibilities of problems.
   b. test important experiments.
   c. draw valid conclusions.
   d. reason the way adults do.

_____ 10. Piaget found that there are major changes in the development of intelligence at ages
   a. two, four, and ten.
   b. two, seven, and twelve.
   c. four, seven, and eleven.
   d. four, nine, and twelve.

[25]

Intelligence

READING FOR STUDYING

The passage describes four stages of intellectual development, examining (1) the ages of the children in each stage and (2) the intellectual developments during each stage. **Summarize** this information in the comparison chart that follows. Write the headings *Ages* and *Intellectual Development* at the top of the chart and insert the names of the four stages of development as headings down the left side of the chart.

Figure 2. A Comparison Chart.

26

Effects of Advertising

Does advertising raise costs? One of the chief complaints about advertising is that it adds to the cost of the products and services. Table 1 shows advertising cost as a percentage of sales for a selected group of companies. The table indicates, for example, that Alberto-Culver spent $.34 out of $1 it took in from the sales of its hair-care products on advertising. Some critics suggest that if such advertising expenditures were reduced, companies could afford to sell their products to the public at lower prices. Other critics emphasize another way in which advertising increases costs. Expensive nationwide advertising campaigns, when successful, can develop such brand loyalty for a few brands that it becomes impossible for newcomers to enter the field, especially if they are smaller companies. As a result, a few large companies can continue to dominate the market, charging higher prices than they could in a more competitive siuation. In 1971 the Federal Trade Commission issued a complaint against the four largest cereal manufacturers on exactly these grounds, accusing them of cornering the cereal market through huge advertising outlays and thus realizing monopoly profits.

Many experts believe that these criticisms are unjustified. They claim that advertising stimulates demand so that higher levels of production are possible. As a result, the unit cost is reduced. For example, advertisements informed potential customers of the availability and advantages of pocket-sized calculators. Without this promotion, the demand would have remained very limited. Manufacturers would then have been unable to set up large-scale, efficient production methods that allowed them to cut the cost of the calculators in half since they were first introduced. In brief, this argument holds that even though spending for advertising may increase the price in the short run, it has the opposite effect in the long run because of its impact on production costs.

Does advertising inform? Almost everyone agrees that advertising performs useful informational functions. By advertising, a seller can inform a potential buyer of his existence, line of goods, and prices. Such advertising can reduce the time and effort spent by consumers in seeking out goods and services. It lets them know in advance what is available and where it can be bought. Clearly, most classified advertising and much local newspaper advertising is overwhelmingly informational in nature. Certainly some national advertising is too.

There is a side benefit related to the informational nature of advertising: The dollars spent by advertisers are used to subsidize the media. One estimate is that 60 percent of the cost of periodicals, 70 percent of the cost of newspapers, and 100 percent of the cost of commercial radio and TV broadcasting are paid for by advertising. Without advertising, the information and entertainment provided by these media would have to be financed by other sources.

Is advertising wasteful? It is obvious that not all advertising is informational, designed to help consumers find the products they need. Nor does it always serve to increase total demand. Instead, many advertisements are tug-of-war efforts. What they really do is to shift sales among firms. Another complaint is that some advertisements do indeed create additional demand, but it is undesirable demand. Do we need electric bean pots or heated shaving lather? Demands for such products are fulfilled at the expense of greater social needs. The result is that our society's resources are misallocated.

Again there is disagreement. The defenders of advertising claim that such judgments are based on the subjective values of those who make them. In a democratic society, they say, consumers should be left to decide for themselves what is good and what they should buy.

Is advertising truthful? In 1929 one issue of the best-selling *Liberty* magazine carried nineteen different product endorsements from a leading actress of the day, Mabel Normand. Could anybody believe that the

Table 1. Advertising as Percent of Sales in 1973

Company	Advertising	Sales	Percent
Alberto-Culver	$ 63,000,000	$ 184,420,140	34.2
Carter-Wallace	33,800,000	148,694,000	22.7
Miles Laboratories	47,000,000	245,092,000	19.2
Seven-Up	27,358,000		18.6
S. C. Johnson	49,600,000	270,000,000	18.4
Sterling Drug	95,000,000	534,246,000	17.8
Warner-Lambert	141,723,000	973,777,000	14.6
Hanes	40,000,000	275,883,000	14.5
Bristol-Myers	132,000,000	1,036,995,000	12.7
Lever Brothers	70,000,000	566,000,000	12.4

Reprinted with permission from the August, 1974, issue of *Advertising Age*. Copyright © 1974 by Crain Communications, Inc.

lady honestly meant her praise for all these different brands of merchandise? Today many people argue that much advertising involves similar untruths or half-truths. One airline has advertised that it is the fastest to New Orleans. Investigation showed that it is the only line flying that route. Thus, the advertisement was true, as far as it went.

Advertising people attempt to distinguish between untruths and *puffery*. They define the latter as legitimate artistic license, which, they claim, is accepted by the public as such. Nobody really believes, they say, that the "friendly skies of United" are any different from the skies where TWA or American fly. Nobody honestly imagines that the "Pepsi generation" consists of soda drinkers who are inherently more lively and more charming than those who drink different brands. But are all consumers this sophisticated? Advertisements for children's toys and dry cereals are probably accepted quite literally by many young viewers. It is possible, too, that a generation of homemakers has accepted, consciously or unconsciously, the industry's verdict that "ring-around-the-collar" can break up an otherwise satisfactory marriage.

[26]

Effects of Advertising

READING FOR UNDERSTANDING

Summary

_____ 1. In summary, this passage presents
   a. *methods* for improving advertising.
   b. the *types* of advertising that there are.
   c. *reasons* that some advertising is successful.
   d. *points of view* about the value of advertising.

_____ 2. The summary is best stated in the
   a. first paragraph.
   b. second paragraph.
   c. third paragraph.
   d. four headings.

Vocabulary

_____ 3. **Expenditures*** are
   a. information given as news.
   b. amounts of money spent.
   c. distasteful advertisements.
   d. people who take but don't give.

_____ 4. If money is **misallocated***, it is
   a. counted incorrectly.
   b. not allowed for use.
   c. put to the wrong use.
   d. difficult to locate.

Summary	Number right _____	X 10 =	_____
Vocabulary	Number right _____	X 10 =	_____
Comprehension	Number right _____	X 10 =	_____
		Total score	_____

_____ 5. If people are **sophisticated***, they are
    a. very knowledgeable.
    b. beautifully dressed.
    c. bright and witty.
    d. socially well trained.

Comprehension

_____ 6. If you spend a dollar on a product that is widely advertised by a large company, the company will probably use about
    a. 11 cents of your dollar for advertising.
    b. 17 cents of your dollar for advertising.
    c. 28 cents of your dollar for advertising.
    d. 35 cents of your dollar for advertising.

_____ 7. Advertisers claim that if a great deal is spent on advertising,
    a. products cost only a little more.
    b. more people can enjoy the products.
    c. the standard of living is increased.
    d. products can be sold for much less.

_____ 8. It seems quite clear that advertising
    a. provides information.
    b. is usually truthful.
    c. makes products cheaper.
    d. does not create waste.

_____ 9. The main way in which advertising creates wastefulness is that it encourages people to
    a. consider unnecessary purchases.
    b. spend their money improperly.
    c. want things they cannot pay for.
    d. change their good buying habits.

_____ 10. Advertisers claim that people
    a. need to become sophisticated consumers.
    b. know when advertisements exaggerate.
    c. believe their advertisements are true.
    d. are not influenced by advertisements.

[26]

Effects of Advertising

READING FOR STUDYING

The passage presents four questions about advertising and tells how they have been answered "yes" and "no." **Summarize** the disagreements in the comparison chart that follows. Write *Yes* and *No* as headings at the top of the chart and place the four questions as headings down the left side of the chart.

Figure 1. A Comparison Chart.

27

Marry?

In earlier times it was unlikely that young people paused to ask themselves the question, "Why do I want to marry?" since the alternative—bachelorhood or spinsterhood—was a rather grim one. Today the question has real meaning, and most young people are aware of that fact. For several years the writer has routinely raised the question ("Why marry?") for class discussion. From the students' view, the reasons mentioned most often include love, companionship, economic security, sexual gratification, the stigma attached to the unmarried, and a desire for children. To make things interesting, the writer tries, half in jest, to refute the arguments or reasons for marriage. For what they are worth, the usually proposed reasons—and the "refutations"—follow. The specific question is: "Why do you want to marry?"   *

Love. If there is such a thing as a prime motivating factor in American marriage, romantic love must be it. As one student put it, "Well, you fall in love and marry. It's as simple as that." Whether or not falling in love is a simple matter can be debated; nevertheless, there is no denying the fact, as married couples will attest, that the romantic love experienced before marriage is, by its very nature, not the kind that lasts very long after marriage. Romantic love is an emotion, and like all emotions it is difficult, if not impossible, to sustain. Married love may be more satisfying than premarital romance, but the former seems to be an all-encompassing term, involving companionship, security, sex, and so on, and these points must be defended on their own merits. As far as romantic love is concerned—as more than one writer has pointed out—marriage is likely to bring it to a fairly abrupt end.   *

Companionship. Admittedly, many husbands and wives are companions in a very meaningful sense, but it is also common observation that many are not. Despite the fact that sex roles are—fortunately—less rigid than they used to be, they have not entirely disappeared. There are still some conversational spheres that tend to interest females, while others are "male-oriented." The decline in sex-role stereotyping is of fairly recent origin, and there is probably some distance to go before companionship in marriage can be said to be the norm.

Economic security. It may well be, in today's society, that marriage *lessens* economic security. At a yearly salary of $12,000 to $20,000, a single man can lead a reasonably comfortable life. With a wife, two or three children, and a home, this same man could hardly be characterized as free from economic worries. The same is true for a woman. An unmarried woman with a salary in the $12,000 to $20,000 range can live rather well. But if she were to marry and bear children, either she would have to work or her husband would have to earn more than twice that amount to provide the level of living to which she was accustomed. In either case, "economic security" would be hard to substantiate as a rationale for marriage.

Sexual gratification. Although most men and women do have sexual needs, is it really necessary in this day and age to *marry* in order to achieve this need-gratification? As a matter of fact, could it not be argued that marriage is a rather expensive method of attaining sexual satisfaction? Some individuals, furthermore, would prefer a variety of partners, a practice that is neatly blocked by monogamous marriage.   *

Stigma attached to the unmarried. At one time, no doubt, the unmarried were looked upon somewhat askance, especially in the case of women. But cultural norms have changed markedly. Today, social

(Photo by Rick Smolen from Stock/Boston)

stigma attaches neither to the unmarried nor to the divorced. Indeed, with more and more wives entering the labor market—many in responsible positions—one could argue that the unmarried career woman is being emulated rather than stigmatized!

Children. Most people want children, true, but they seem to be wanting them in smaller and smaller numbers. This is hardly surprising when one considers that, according to government figures, it costs around $45,000 to raise a child from birth through college. The same figures also show that, by having one or more children, the "mother who might have worked" lost even more income than the net cost of the offspring.

Expense notwithstanding, how much do children contribute to overall marital adjustment? In the review of a decade's research literature, Hicks and Platt found that—blow of blows—"Perhaps the single most surprising finding to emerge from research is that children tend to detract from, rather than contribute to, marital happiness!"[1]

When confronted with the "refutations" listed above, most college students are somewhat taken aback. Their attitude is one of good-natured disbelief in the instructor's arguments. "What's the catch?" they want to know. "You've poked fun at our answers, but now tell us, *what is* the reason for marriage?" But there is no catch, really. The refutations are oversimplified and somewhat exaggerated, but, taken piecemeal, each of them contains more than a germ of truth.

The reason that "anti-marriage" arguments prove disconcerting is that many students have never had occasion to think along such lines. Conditioned as they are to envision matrimony in terms of personal happiness, students sometimes fail to realize that there are two sides to the picture, i.e., that, along with personal pleasures, there are also displeasures and responsibilities. Maintaining a house, raising children, dealing with in-laws—such things call for an infinite amount of patience on the part of both husband and wife. Understandably, society tries to "sell" marriage to its young people, for if a substantial number of persons did not marry and reproduce, society itself would be threatened. The catch seems to be that some young people are oversold.

REFERENCE

1. Mary W. Hicks and Marilyn Platt, "Marital Happiness and Stability: A Review of Research in the Sixties," *Journal of Marriage and the Family*, November, 1970, p. 569.

[27]

Marry?

READING FOR UNDERSTANDING

Summary

_____ 1. In summary, this passage presents
　　a. *methods* for selecting a marriage partner.
　　b. the *types* of people who should not marry.
　　c. *reasons* that people have unsuccessful marriages.
　　d. *points of view* about reasons for marrying.

_____ 2. The summary of the passage is best stated in the headings and in the
　　a. first sentence of the first paragraph.
　　b. second sentence of the first paragraph.
　　c. first sentence of the last paragraph.
　　d. second sentence of the last paragraph.

Vocabulary

_____ 3. **Refutations*** prove something
　　a. to be false.
　　b. to be true.
　　c. in a clear way.
　　d. in an unclear way.

_____ 4. To **attest*** is to
　　a. request good proof.
　　b. say with clarity.
　　c. prove to be wrong.
　　d. state to be true.

Summary	Number right _____ X 10 = _____	
Vocabulary	Number right _____ X 10 = _____	
Comprehension	Number right _____ X 10 = _____	
	Total score _____	

_____   5. A **monogamous*** marriage is
        a. one with only one child.
        b. a marriage to one person.
        c. a one-sided marriage.
        d. one that has no chance.

Comprehension

_____   6. People who marry can expect romantic love to last
        a. throughout marriage.
        b. until middle age.
        c. about four years.
        d. a very short time.

_____   7. Husbands and wives often do *not* make the best companions because
        a. living closely together breeds contempt.
        b. men and women have different interests.
        c. women demand too much attention from men.
        d. men expect wives to be like their mothers.

_____   8. Those who want to be free from money worries will probably
        a. not find this freedom by getting married.
        b. need a marriage with two incomes.
        c. need at least $20,000 in income a year.
        d. marry somebody who has a good job.

_____   9. Research has shown that children
        a. make for much happiness in marriages.
        b. create an unnecessary financial burden.
        c. do not tend to make marriages happier.
        d. prevent people from getting divorces.

_____   10. The author of this passage wants people to
        a. not get married and bring up children.
        b. live together without getting married.
        c. understand their reasons for marrying.
        d. destroy all our traditions of marriage.

[27]

Marry?

READING FOR STUDYING

The passage gives six reasons that people marry and presents arguments for and against marrying for these reasons. **Summarize** the disagreements in the comparison chart that follows. The chart has been started for you.

	Arguments **For**	Arguments **Against**
Love	It is the main motivation in American marriages.	
Companionship		
Economic Security		

Figure 1. A Comparison Chart.

[28]

Education

Education and training in America involve large numbers of people, programs, settings, and purposes. It is possible to get either a general education or a special education for an occupation, sometimes at the same place. The purpose of this section is to present the ways of extending your education beyond a year or two at college.

APPRENTICESHIP PROGRAMS

The use of apprenticeships for passing on knowledge and skills to new workers dates back to the Middle Ages. Various guilds, or groups of skilled craftsmen, developed a system of indenture in which young workers were bound to serve master craftsmen. The period of indenture was often seven years. The worker who successfully completed the program was accepted by the guild as a journeyman, or independent craftsman. Even today a person who successfully completes an apprenticeship is known as a journeyman. The experience of Benjamin Franklin, who was an apprentice printer under his older brother, is an example of this practice in our colonial history.

Apprentices become highly skilled craftsmen—bricklayers, for example, cement masons, electricians, plumbers, pipefitters, sheet metal workers, tool and die workers, or carpenters. They do so in a formal training program that combines classroom instruction and paid on-the-job experience under supervision. An apprenticeship program, by federal regulation, must contain at least two years of work experience (not less than 4,000 hours) and 144 hours per year of related classroom instruction. An apprenticeship program is one way to enter some 350 skilled occupations in this country. About 79,000 new apprentices—including a record 12,000 from minority groups—were admitted to registered programs during 1971. This pushed the total number in training in 1971 to a new high of 274,024.

Apprenticeship programs are not for men only. Women are or have been apprentices in more than 60 of the 350 programs. Most women have been in programs that prepare cosmetologists, bookbinders, cooks, printers, computer programmers, dental and medical technicians, drafting technicians, electronic technicians, engravers, machinists, optical laboratory technicians, upholsterers, and watchmakers.

An apprentice must be at least sixteen years of age. He or she works under a written agreement registered with a state apprenticeship council. For a young worker entering employment, apprenticeship has these advantages: (1) the opportunity to develop highly prized skills, (2) further training and education with pay, (3) assurance of wages with regular increases, (4) opportunity for employment and advancement, and (5) recognition and prestige as a skilled artisan. Disadvantages are: (1) some apprenticeship programs are very inflexible, (2) some have unrealistic entry standards, (3) some require long periods to complete them, and (4) the demand for apprentices is related to business cycles; when business is good, demand for apprentices is high, but in poorer times, employers are reluctant to employ apprentices.

Apprenticeship Information Centers have been established in some 100 major cities. These centers provide information on apprenticeship opportunities and requirements. In 1963, locally sponsored programs were established to recruit apprentices among minorities and help them in passing entry tests.

BUSINESS, INDUSTRY AND UNION ON-THE-JOB TRAINING

Today many business, union, and industrial organizations conduct educational and training programs. Those provided by Ford, General Motors, and Chrysler are well known. The main purpose of most industry schools is to train workers in special skills required by the particular company. It is fairly difficult to gain admission to these established, long training programs, but once you get in and complete the course, you are almost sure of a job.

Some independent training programs are offered in cooperation with other agencies like the public schools or the state employment and training service. These training programs are designed to provide job orientation, instruction in additional skills for job advancement or job transfer, supervisory training, and management development.

Some companies have training programs for new employees (initial training). Others have established training programs for potential employees (pre-employment training) when they need workers for specific occupations. As their needs are satisfied, these training programs may be discontinued. Those who enroll in initial training programs are usually paid either a trainee rate or the hiring rate for their job. Those in pre-employment courses are seldom paid, but neither are they charged any costs.

The following are examples of formal training programs established by employers to provide skills and knowledge needed for specific occupations:

1. An eighty-hour course plus ten weeks of on-the-job training for electronic assemblers, offered by an aircraft manufacturer.
2. Training in programming, machine operation, and system design work provided by an electronic equipment manufacturer.
3. An airline school for stewardesses providing six weeks' training at no cost to trainees.

COLLEGES AND UNIVERSITIES

In its more than 350 years of existence, higher education in the United States has experienced remarkable expansion in numbers, size, and variety. Higher education today includes small and large public and private liberal arts colleges, universities, technological schools, and two-year colleges. Approximately 40 percent of the population between the ages of eighteen and twenty-four enter college, and the proportion of youth who do so continues upward each year. Great variety exists in American schools of higher education—in standards and objectives, curricula, organization, financing, administration, and size and composition of student body.

Today's two-year college student has the option of transferring to any of several accredited colleges and universities. The college or university that accepts transfer students expects the two-year college to offer freshman and sophomore courses that are parallel to its own offerings. Currently, the college to which a person seeks to transfer is likely to examine the student's transcript to determine whether the coursework is similar in content and quality to that required of its own students. If a student has taken courses for which the university offers no parallel, he may not be given full credit for them. If the transfer student has failed to complete a specific course required in the first two years at the receiving institution, junior standing may be refused until the course is successfully completed.

Students should know that among many two-year colleges and universities some ill-feeling exists about the matter of transfer. On the one hand, many universities have been critical of the course work at the two-year colleges—what was and was not taken and its content and quality. On the other hand, many two-year college authorities have expressed dissatisfaction because they believe that the universities dictate their curriculum by approving or denying transfer applications.

The ill-feeling and dissatisfaction have led many two-year colleges to negotiate agreements with the institutions to which many of their students seek admission, permitting transfer with a full junior standing. Such agreements are, without doubt, in the students' best interests, for all too often it is they who have to pay for any "differences" between the two institutions. If you are a student who plans to transfer, you should find out what the host institution requires and you should discuss your plans, well before the time of the transfer, with your counselor or academic advisor.

GOVERNMENT TRAINING PROGRAMS

Most training programs are designed for people who find it difficult to get and hold employment. These programs offer such services as vocational testing and counseling, medical services, transportation assistance, remedial education, and job placement. Many are financed for the most part by the federal government, and training stipends or money allowances are paid to those who satisfy certain requirements. On-the-job trainees receive wages from their employers. In many parts of the country, skill centers and work experiences are provided in more than one occupation.

HOME-STUDY COURSES

Home-study courses are another way to obtain further schooling. These courses are particularly useful to people living in small towns and rural areas, to women who must stay at home with small children, and to individuals who must work while they learn. The correspondence plan provides course work needed for many commercial and service occupations and even for some professions. Registration, assignments, and examinations are handled by mail.

Here is a small sample of the many correspondence courses that are offered:

Accounting	Photography
Bookkeeping	Real estate
Clothes designing	Shorthand
Drafting	Tailoring
Hotel training	Typing

Home-study courses offer opportunities to learn skills not taught locally, but the self-discipline needed to complete them make home study the hardest way to get further schooling. Students who take them must exercise initiative in the learning process and progress at their own rate of speed. Anyone who hopes to qualify for a particular type of job by completing a home-study course is strongly urged to check with local employers about the merits of any course and consult the *Home*

Study Blue Book, which lists approved schools. Students should discuss plans for a correspondence course with a college counselor.

MILITARY SERVICE TRAINING

For some young people, the best educational opportunities are in the military services. Many young men and women volunteer for service in order to get the special schooling they want. Obviously, the curriculum and training provided by the military are designed to develop skills needed by a particular branch of service. However, many military career fields have some relationship to civilian occupations. The degree to which transfer of training from military to civilian work is possible varies from almost complete carry-over in some fields to relatively little carry-over in other fields. No doubt, the degree of usefulness is probably less than that pictured by eager recruiting officers or hoped for by uninformed enlistees. However, the quality of training in some military career fields equals or exceeds any available in civilian life.

In addition to its specialty schools and on-the-job training, the military encourages its members to study voluntarily in off-duty hours. The services operate some thirty correspondence-school centers, which offer more than two hundred courses that have been taken by more than one million servicemen and servicewomen. They also hold contracts with about fifty colleges and universities for 6,000 additional correspondence courses. Moreover, the United States Armed Forces Institute (USAFI) is available to all persons in service. This agency, offering courses through correspondence, self-teaching, or group study, does not grant credit for work completed. It does, however, help service personnel get credit by sending to high schools, state boards of education, colleges, or employers official reports of work completed.

VOCATIONAL AND TECHNICAL SCHOOLS

The history of vocational education stretches back to early colonial days, but 1917 was the first year that the federal government acted to support vocational education. It is only recently that as much attention has been given to vocational and technical education as has been given to preparing students for college.

In its broadest sense, vocational education includes any experiences or activities designed to help people become more efficient in occupational pursuits. More narrowly defined, it is preparation for any occupation except those designated as professional or those that require a college degree.

In 1975 about 14 million people were enrolled in vocational and technical education programs. At one time vocational and technical schools served a relatively narrow group, but now they are attended by individuals who vary widely in ability, age, and educational background. The variety will be even greater in the future.

People served by vocational and technical education programs include students who leave or graduate from high school without a marketable skill, unemployed or underemployed adults, workers whose skills or knowledge must be increased or updated, older workers whose work skills are no longer saleable, apprentices in skilled trades and technical occupations, foremen and supervisors who need leadership training, and workers with physical and emotional handicaps.

The major purpose of vocational education is to enable its students to enter and keep themselves in gainful employment. This means more than obtaining the skills or the technical competence required for entry-level jobs. It includes mastery of technical, social, and thinking skills that enable the individual to profit from on-the-job learning and to grow and mature as a worker and a person. Some people still think of vocational education as inferior programs for inferior students, less valuable than college. But college has little meaning or reality for thousands of young people who are in no way inferior but who have no desire, interest, or need to engage in college study. Attitudes toward vocational education have changed and are changing, and it is moving away from its step-child status.

[28]

Education

READING FOR UNDERSTANDING

Summary

_____ 1. In summary, this passage presents the
   a. *types* of education available to us.
   b. *methods* for selecting a good school.
   c. *history* of education in this country.
   d. *reasons* for getting a good education.

_____ 2. The summary is best stated in the headings and in the
   a. first sentence.
   b. second sentence.
   c. third sentence.
   d. fourth sentence.

Vocabulary

_____ 3. **Indentures*** are
   a. binding contracts of service.
   b. a certain number of years.
   c. courses for journeymen.
   d. apprenticeship procedures.

_____ 4. An **orientation*** is
   a. a breaking down of unsuccessful habits.
   b. an explanation of college requirements.
   c. a time of introduction and adaptation.
   d. a type of relaxation and meditation.

Summary	Number right _____	× 10 =	_____
Vocabulary	Number right _____	× 10 =	_____
Comprehension	Number right _____	× 10 =	_____
		Total score	_____

_____   5. **Transcripts*** are
           a. signatures on important papers.
           b. letters of recommendation.
           c. recordings of important programs.
           d. records of college courses taken.

Comprehension

_____   6. The efficient way to learn about apprenticeships is to consult
           a. various local labor unions.
           b. an Apprenticeship Information Center.
           c. professional employment offices.
           d. reference books in college libraries.

_____   7. Most people who continue education after high school do so in
           a. apprenticeship programs.
           b. colleges and universities.
           c. military service training.
           d. vocational education schools.

_____   8. The most difficult way to get further education is in
           a. union on-the-job training.
           b. trade and technical schools.
           c. government training programs.
           d. home-study courses.

_____   9. The quality of education in the military service is considered to be
           a. very good.
           b. satisfactory.
           c. unsatisfactory.
           d. very poor.

_____   10. Preparation for occupations that are not professional or that do not require a
             college education is called
             a. on-the-job training.
             b. vocational education.
             c. career job training.
             d. apprenticeship courses.

[28]

Education

READING FOR STUDYING

The passage discusses seven ways to get an education; it emphasizes (1) what can be learned in each type of education; (2) the advantages of some of the types of education; and (3) the disadvantages of some of the types of education. **Summarize** this information in the comparison chart that follows. Write the names of the seven types of education as headings across the top of the chart and put the following three headings down the left side of the chart: *What Can Be Learned, Advantages,* and *Disadvantages.*

Figure 1. A Comparison Chart

(TEN)

Preparing for Essay Tests

When you answer the multiple-choice Reading for Understanding comprehension questions, you are practicing for taking multiple-choice tests in college. However, not all college instructors give multiple-choice tests. Some give *essay tests,* for which students prepare long, written answers to certain questions. For example, in a business course an instructor might use the following essay question to test students' understanding of information they have read:

> *Summarize what you know about Parkinson's Law,*
> *the Peter Principle, and the Radovic Rule.*

In Figure 1, there is an example of a good answer for this question. Notice how well organized the answer is and how efficiently it summarizes information in the passage entitled "Business Games" on pages 169–170. Good answers for essay questions have the following characteristics:

> Parkinson's Law, the Peter Principle, and the Radovic Rule all point out some amusing facts about big businesses.
>
> Parkinson's Law states that organizations grow, even if there is no work to do. As a result, the number of employees in an organization will increase even when work decreases, and employees will make work expand to fill the time available. For example, if a manager has one week to write a report that can be written in one day, it will take him or her one week to write the report.
>
> The Peter Principle claims that employees are promoted until they reach a job they cannot do well. This results in many people having important jobs they do poorly.
>
> The Radovic Rule states that employees manage those who supervise them, rather than the other way around. This is because supervisors hold jobs they cannot do well and need subordinates to help them stay in their supervisory positions.

Figure 1. Sample Answer for an Essay Question.

1. They are well organized, and the major points stand out clearly.
2. They contain informative details and examples.
3. They begin with a short introduction that summarizes the answer.
4. They give exactly the kind of answer requested by the question.

Study the sample essay answer in Figure 1 and observe how it reflects all these characteristics. In doing the Reading for Understanding exercises, you have practised writing (1) well-organized answers with (2) informative details and examples; however, you may increase your skills by reading the following fuller explanations of the third and fourth characteristics of good essay answers.

Whenever possible, begin your answer with a short introduction that summarizes your answer. Read the following essay question and the two possible introductions:

   Do you believe sales tax should be abolished? Explain.

Students who agree that the sales tax should be abolished might begin their essays in this way:

Yes, I believe sales tax should be abolished because it places too great a burden on the poor and too small a burden on the rich.

Students who want to argue for the necessity of sales tax might begin their essays in this manner:

No, sales tax must not be abolished because it provides the funds for vital services.

These introductory statements make it absolutely clear what the answers will be; they help students write well-organized answers.

To give exactly the kind of answer requested by a question requires (1) understanding the meanings of direction words and (2) responding to all parts of a question. The direction words are underlined in the following question:

   Identify the three basic types of advertising and describe how each might be used by a large, well-established department store.

Identify, in this context, means to "state the characteristics of"; *describe* means "make it possible to visualize." To identify the characteristics of primary demand advertising, selective advertising, and institutional advertising, you must give definitions for each type; to describe how a department store might use each of the types of advertising, you must make it possible for your instructor to visualize the appearance of advertisements the store might use. For primary demand advertising, you might describe an advertisement that promotes the store's jewelry department without featuring any specific piece of jewelry at a specific price. For selective advertising, you might describe an advertisement for a specific piece of furniture that sells for $699.00. For institutional advertising, you might describe an advertisement saluting employees who have given many years of service to the store.

Answers for essay questions are inadequate unless they are exactly the kind of answers that were requested.

The Reading for Understanding questions in Part 10 contain essay questions that you may use either to practice preparing for taking essay tests or to practice writing answers for essay questions. Either method will help you write better answers to essay test questions.

If you wish to practice working with more thought-provoking questions than those in the Reading for Understanding exercises, try some of the questions in Part 11, Reading with a Critical Eye.

Norms

When Captain Cook asked the chiefs in Tahiti why they always ate apart and alone, they replied, "Because it is right" (Linton, 1945). If we ask Americans why they eat with knives and forks, or why their men wear pants instead of skirts, or why they may be married to only one person at a time, we are likely to get similar and very uninformative answers: "Because it's right." "Because that's the way it's done." "Because it's the custom." Or even "I don't know."

The reason for these and countless other patterns of social behavior is that they are controlled by social *norms*—shared rules or guidelines that prescribe the behavior that is appropriate in a given situation. Norms define how people "ought" to behave under particular circumstances in a particular society. We conform to norms so readily that we are hardly aware they exist. In fact, we are much more likely to notice departures from norms than conformity to them. You would not be surprised if a stranger tried to shake hands when you were introduced, but you might be a little startled if he or she bowed, curtsied, started to stroke you, or kissed you on both cheeks. Yet each of these other forms of greeting is appropriate in other parts of the world. When we visit another society whose norms are different, we quickly become aware that we do things *this* way, they do them *that* way.

Some norms apply to every member of society. In the United States, for example, nobody is permitted to marry more than one person at the same time. Other norms apply to some people but not to others. There is a very strong norm in American society against the taking of human life, but this norm does not apply to policemen in shootouts, soldiers in combat, or innocent people acting in self-defense against armed attackers. Other norms are even more specific and prescribe the appropriate behavior for people in particular situations, such as college students in lecture rooms, shop clerks serving the public, or marijuana smokers rolling and sharing a joint.

FOLKWAYS AND MORES

Norms ensure that social life proceeds smoothly, for they give us guidelines for our own behavior and reliable expectations for the behavior of others. This social function of norms is so important that there is always strong social pressure on people to conform. But although most of us conform to most norms most of the time, all of us tend to violate some norms occasionally. In the case of certain norms, the folkways, a fair amount of nonconformity may be tolerated, but in the case of certain other norms, the mores, very little leeway is permitted (Sumner, 1906).

Folkways. The *folkways* are the ordinary usages and conventions of everyday life; they are, quite literally, the "ways of the folk." Conformity to folkways is expected but is not absolutely insisted upon. We expect people to keep their lawns mowed, to refrain from picking their noses in public, to turn up on time for appointments, and to wear a

Do *mores* prohibit marijuana smoking, or has marijuana smoking become a *folkway*? (Photo by Nicole Toutounji Takla)

matching pair of shoes. Those who do not conform to these and similar folkways are considered peculiar and eccentric, particularly if they consistently violate a number of folkways. But they are not considered immoral or depraved, nor are they treated as criminals. People are not   *
deeply outraged by violations of folkways and on the whole are tolerant of a certain amount of nonconformity to them.

Mores. The *mores* (pronounced "mor-ays") are much stronger norms. People attach a moral significance to them and treat violations of them much more seriously. (The word "mores" was a Latin term for the ancient Romans' most respected and even sacred customs.) A man who walks down a street wearing nothing on the upper half of his body is violating a folkway; a man who walks down the street wearing nothing on the lower half of his body is violating one of our most important mores, the requirement that people cover their genitals and buttocks in public. Theft, drug abuse, murder, rape, desecration of the American   *
flag, or contemptuous use of religious symbols all excite a strong social reaction. People believe that their mores are crucial for the maintenance of a decent and orderly society, and the offender may be strongly criticized, punched, imprisoned, committed to a mental asylum, or even lynched. Some violations of mores are made almost unthinkable by *taboos*—powerful social beliefs that the acts concerned are utterly loathsome. In the United States, for example, there is a very strong taboo against eating human flesh, a taboo so effective that most of our states do not even bother to have laws prohibiting the practice.

Not all norms can be neatly categorized as either folkways or mores. In practice, norms fall at various points on a continuum, depending on how seriously they are taken by society. There is also a constant shift in the importance attached to some norms. The fashion of short hair for men was apparently regarded by many Americans as one of our mores for most of this century. Youths who grew their hair long in the early sixties were sometimes insulted, attacked, and even shot at. In the 1970s, however, long hair on young males has almost become a folkway. In many parts of the country a youth with a crewcut might draw curious glances, at least from his own age group.

Some norms, particularly mores, are encoded in law. A *law* is simply a rule that has been formally enacted by a political authority and is backed by the power of the state. The law usually codifies important norms that already exist, but sometimes political authorities attempt to introduce new norms by enacting appropriate laws. Civil rights legislation in the United States, for example, was aimed at destroying some traditional norms of race relations and replacing them with new ones. Attempts to introduce new norms in this way are not always successful, as the American attempt to legislate the prohibition of liquor proved. Laws that run counter to cultural norms, particularly in the area of personal morality, are often ineffectual and tend to fall into disuse. For example, many of our drug laws and laws prohibiting sports and entertainments on Sunday are now widely disregarded.

REFERENCES

Linton, Ralph. 1945. *The Cultural Background of Personality*. New York: Free Press.
Sumner, William Graham. 1906. *Folkways*. Boston: Ginn.

[29]

Norms

READING FOR UNDERSTANDING

Summary

_____ 1. In summary, this passage presents
      a. a *method* for establishing new norms.
      b. the *sequence* in which norms develop.
      c. the basic *types* of norms that societies have.
      d. the *reasons* that norms differ in societies.

_____ 2. The summary is best stated in the headings and in the first two sentences of the
      a. first paragraph.
      b. second paragraph.
      c. third paragraph.
      d. fourth paragraph.

Vocabulary

_____ 3. **Norms*** are
      a. forms of expression.
      b. degrees of difference.
      c. sociological categories.
      d. guidelines for behavior. ·

_____ 4. **Depraved*** actions are
      a. evil.
      b. joyous.
      c. approved.
      d. different.

Summary	Number right _____	X 10 = _____
Vocabulary	Number right _____	X 10 = _____
Comprehension	Number right _____	X 10 = _____
		Total score_____

_____ 5. **Desecration*** is the act of treating something as though it is
   a. sacred.
   b. not sacred.
   c. legal.
   d. not legal.

Comprehension

_____ 6. A norm is a behavior that
   a. is always expected of all people in a society.
   b. applies only to certain people, like teachers.
   c. does not apply to certain people, like soldiers.
   d. may be expected of some people and not of others.

_____ 7. The basic importance of norms is that they
   a. predict how people will behave.
   b. define what good manners are.
   c. provide standards for behavior.
   d. encourage mutual understanding.

_____ 8. In some societies people sit on chairs, and in others they sit on the floor; societies have different
   a. habits.
   b. customs.
   c. mores.
   d. folkways.

_____ 9. Behaviors that are completely forbidden and disgusting to a society are called
   a. norms.
   b. folkways.
   c. taboos.
   d. laws.

_____ 10. There is most likely to be a law forbidding a behavior if that behavior is classified as a
   a. more.
   b. norm.
   c. folkway.
   d. custom.

[29]

Norms

READING FOR STUDYING

This essay question tests whether students understand norms and the various types of norms:

Define the following words: *norms, folkways, mores,* and *taboos.*

Define means "give the meaning of," and, as you have seen, examples also help in understanding the meanings of words. A good answer to the question will include the meanings of the four words as well as examples of each meaning. **Underline** the parts of the passage needed to answer the question. Then either **summarize** this information under a heading and four subheadings or **write** an answer to the question.

_____

_____

_____

_____

_____

_____

_____

_____

_____

_____

_____

_____

_____

_____

Spellings

The first English-speaking settlers in North America were bound by few absolute rules of orthography. The spelling of the language was often dictated by whimsy. There were few dictionaries in those days that could serve as authoritative lexicons, and people tended to spell words as they pronounced them. Although the first printing press in North America (set up in Cambridge, Massachusetts, in 1638) helped to initiate a movement toward some kind of uniformity in spelling, printers in the New World, like those in Europe, were notoriously independent when it came to deciding how a word should be spelled. For example, the word *mosquito* was spelled *mosquito* or *musquito; both* was spelled *both* or *bothe.*

    *

    *

DR. SAMUEL JOHNSON'S DICTIONARY

However, the publication in England of Dr. Samuel Johnson's *A Dictionary of the English Language* (1755) was a monumental accomplishment which contributed to the stabilization of the English orthography both in England and in America. By the end of the 18th century, spelling was virtually standardized.

AMERICAN DICTIONARIES AND THEIR INFLUENCE

By this time, about 20 percent of the English-speaking people of the world lived in the United States, and they were determined to establish a system of education that would prepare a literate citizenry. The need for a school dictionary became evident. In 1798, Samuel Johnson, Jr. (an American clergyman and educator, and not related to Dr. Johnson) published *A School Dictionary,* the first English-language dictionary compiled by an American.

Johnson continued his efforts by collaborating with John Elliott to produce *A Selected and Pronouncing and Accented Dictionary* (1800), an expanded and revised edition of his earlier dictionary, which contained about 10,000 words, including many that were borrowed from

From Paul R. Hanna et al., *Spelling: Structure and Strategies,* pp. 53–55. Copyright © 1971 by Houghton Mifflin Company. Used by permission.

American Indian languages and were therefore peculiar to America (*tomahawk, tepee, wampum,* etc.).

The Columbian Dictionary by Caleb Alexander of Massachusetts, containing about 32,000 entries, was also published in 1800 and also included a few American-usage words. Some of them were *Yankee, dime, Congress, Congressional, minute-man, dollar, elector,* and *lengthy.* Alexander employed such American spellings as *honor* (for British *honour*), *troop* (for *troup*), *color* (for *colour*), and *favor* (for *favour*); but he did allow a choice between *screen* and British *skreen, sponge* and *spunge, checker* and *chequer,* and *calendar* and *kalendar.*

NOAH WEBSTER (1758–1843)

Noah Webster did as much as any one man to advance the cause of literacy in America. He had a great many interests (law, education, politics), but his great passion was language, and particularly the American language. He worked mightily to overcome what he felt to be an unwarranted and slavish bowing to the dictates of British English. He was influenced in this attitude by Benjamin Franklin, who, in 1768, published *A Scheme for a New Alphabet and a Reformed Mode of Spelling.*

Although Franklin's plan of adding six new characters to the alphabet to simplify spelling was too extreme a proposal even for Webster, Webster did propose an overhaul of the English language to make its orthography completely consistent. Had he been given the support he needed, we might today be spelling the word *head* as *hed, friend* as *frend, give* as *giv, thumb* as *thum, bought* as *bot,* and *calf* as *kaf.*

In 1806, Webster published a small school dictionary called *A Compendious Dictionary of the English Language.* This was a dictionary of the American-English language for Americans, and as such it omitted many British-English words that Webster considered useless or inappropriate for American life. It also included words not found in Dr. Johnson's British dictionary, and even new meanings for old words.

New American words arose because the struggle to make a living in an undeveloped country produced new tools and new experiences. These words were not usually included in British dictionaries for two reasons: they were unacceptably crude by British standards, and they held meaning only for former colonists. For example, the colonists added many Indian words to their vocabularies, and these words were adapted to American-English pronunciation and standardized in terms of English orthography: the Algonquin words *segongw* and *moos* became *skunk* and *moose;* from Cree, *otchock* became *woodchuck.* Nevertheless, these words, like others having to do with frontier life in America, were foreign to people in England. Such words as *hominy, possum,* and *spinning-bee* would eventually find their way into the great English dictionaries, but in the meantime they needed to be included in a recognized American authority.

Webster's school dictionary gave a great boost to the development of literacy in the United States. And his revised and enlarged two-volume edition called *An American Dictionary of the English Language,* which he completed in his seventy-first year, was considered superior to Dr. Johnson's British dictionary in the following respects:

1. Dr. Johnson's definitions were gleaned primarily from literary sources; Webster's were based on current usage.
2. As compared with Dr. Johnson, Webster included many more scientific and technical terms.
3. Webster's etymological entries were more extensive and more accurate than Dr. Johnson's.

[30]

Spellings

READING FOR UNDERSTANDING

Summary

_____   1. In summary, this passage presents
        a. some *methods* for improving spelling.
        b. the *reasons* for our illogical spellings.
        c. *points of view* about preferable spellings.
        d. the *history* of spelling standardization.

_____   2. The summary is best stated in the headings and in the
        a. first paragraph.
        b. second paragraph.
        c. third paragraph.
        d. fourth paragraph.

Vocabulary

_____   3. **Orthography*** is another word for
        a. handwriting.
        b. composing.
        c. printing.
        d. spelling.

_____   4. **Lexicons*** are
        a. writers.
        b. compilers.
        c. English books.
        d. dictionaries.

Summary	Number right _____	× 10 =	_____
Vocabulary	Number right _____	× 10 =	_____
Comprehension	Number right _____	× 10 =	_____
		Total score	_____

_____   5. That which is **gleaned*** is
            a. collected.
            b. polished.
            c. understood.
            d. distributed.

Comprehension

_____   6. English spellings were almost completely standardized by the year
            a. 1749.
            b. 1799.
            c. 1849.
            d. 1899.

_____   7. The first book to have a great impact on the standardization of English spelling
            was written by
            a. Caleb Alexander.
            b. Noah Webster.
            c. Dr. Samuel Johnson.
            d. Samuel Johnson, Jr.

_____   8. The American spelling *color* (for the English spelling *colour*) was introduced
            by
            a. Noah Webster.
            b. Benjamin Franklin.
            c. Caleb Alexander.
            d. Samuel Johnson, Jr.

_____   9. Noah Webster's book on spelling was influenced most directly by
            a. Benjamin Franklin.
            b. Caleb Alexander.
            c. Samuel Johnson, Jr.
            d. Dr. Samuel Johnson.

_____   10. Webster's dictionary was considered superior to Dr. Johnson's dictionary in
            several ways, but *not* because it
            a. included more scientific terms.
            b. contained more accurate spellings.
            c. gave more etymological information.
            d. based definitions on current usages.

[30]

Spellings

READING FOR STUDYING

This essay question tests whether students understand the history of the standardization of American spellings:

Summarize the events that contributed to the standardization of American spellings.

Summarize means "briefly tell." You are to briefly tell the events that contributed to the standardization of American spellings. **Underline** the parts of the passage needed to answer the question. Then either **summarize** those parts under a heading, or **write** an answer to the question. Make the dates stand out clearly; the first two dates will be 1755 and 1798.

[31]

Long Life

Although there is no consensus as to which, if any, theory of aging is *
correct, certain factors are generally agreed to play a role in determining how long a person can expect to live. These include environment, eating habits, activity level, social roles and social environment, marital status, and attitude toward aging.

The twentieth-century gift of technology is a primary factor in determining longevity. In general, the more technologically advanced a society is, the longer the life expectancy at birth is. However, technology simply makes it possible for people to live longer and does not increase the life span appreciably. Thus, life expectancy for today's adults has not increased much since the turn of the century. An American who was sixty-five in 1900 could expect to live for thirteen more years. Today's life expectancy for sixty-five-year-olds is fifteen years, only an additional two years.

Heredity is another primary factor in determining how long an individual can expect to live. Longevity tends to run in families, and children of long-lived parents are more likely to live longer than children of short-lived parents.

There also is a marked difference between the life expectancies of men and women. Generally, women outlive men in societies where they no longer perform hard physical labor, where their chances of dying in childbirth are small, and where sanitation is adequate. In American society, although more boy babies are born than girl babies, girls begin to outnumber boys after age eighteen. In the later adulthood years, there are 135 women for every 100 men. . . .

In this country, one's ethnic background also affects the length of time that one can expect to live. Black men and women have a lower life expectancy than white men and women. . . . A Mexican-American has a typical life span of around 56.7 years. In comparison to American Indians, however, Mexican-Americans do well. The average American Indian can expect to live for forty-four years. Obviously, poverty, poor housing, and lack of medical care and education have profound effects not only on the physical and intellectual development of blacks, Mexican-Americans, and American Indians, but also on their life expectancy.

Extreme longevity is customary in three communities in the world, and it is common to live beyond the age of 100 in these places: Vilacabamba in Ecuador, Hunza in Kashmir, and Abkhazia in the Soviet Republic of Georgia. By looking at these groups of long-lived people, one can see that environmental factors are closely related to their longevity. Their diets have much in common. All three areas are predominantly agrarian, and the people's diets contain almost no saturated   *
fats, which are generally found in meat and dairy products. This absence of saturated fat is likely to delay the progress of atherosclerosis and the incidence of cardiovascular disease . . . People in these communities also eat less than Americans do, and reduced caloric intake is known to be related to longevity.

Although all of these people may have uninteresting diets by some American standards, other aspects of their lives are far from bland. For example, these older people continue to be interested in sex. One 110-year-old man from the Caucasus said that he thought that youth meant engaging in sexual activity and then admitted that he had considered himself a youth until he was 98. The majority of these long-lived people were married, and those women who had borne many children tended to live longer. Several women had borne more than twenty children.

Another common element of life in these societies is that the people are used to prolonged physical labor, and they remain very active throughout life. People over 100 continue to tend flocks, clean house, and care for grandchildren. In these societies there is no such thing as retirement. In addition to being highly active, these long-lived people retain their social roles and responsibilities throughout life, thus facing few of the stressful transition points characteristic of American life. In their societies there is little demand or need to be highly adaptive because there are few changes to adapt to. An additional factor that may contribute to their longevity is their joy for living and their emphasis on the importance of a worry-free and calm state of mind. Also, these people *expect* to live a long time, and, perhaps as a result, they generally do.

In the United States, a number of characteristics that appear to be common among people who live long and well recall the life style of these people from Ecuador, Kashmir, and the Soviet Union. Findings from interviews with individuals between the ages of 87 and 103 indicate that these people have parents who lived a long time, that they are happily married, and that they are sexually active.

Another characteristic of long-lived Americans is that their physical abilities and reaction times tend to remain above those considered normal for the later years; so do their intellectual skills and abilities. These people are physically and socially active. They refuse to give in to social or physical change. They take long walks and get plenty of exercise. In general, long-lived Americans also are unlikely to be anxious, have always been independent, and have a joy for living. They are religious but not extremely orthodox. They tend to be moderate eaters. Some   *

This couple, shown with their grandson, exhibit typical characteristics of long-lived Americans: marriage, physical activity, and a rewarding family life. (Photo by Joan Dufault)

drink, and some never have. Some smoke occasionally. Unlike the non-Americans who live to be centenarians, long-lived Americans by necessity tend to be highly adaptable. They prefer to live in the present, with all its problems, rather than in the past.

[31]

Long Life

READING FOR UNDERSTANDING

Summary

_____   1. In summary, this passage presents
            a. *methods* for enjoying a long lifetime.
            b. *histories* of people who have lived long.
            c. *reasons* some people live a long time.
            d. *points of view* about lengthening life spans.

_____   2. The summary is best stated in the
            a. first paragraph.
            b. second paragraph.
            c. third paragraph.
            d. fourth paragraph.

Vocabulary

_____   3. A **consensus*** is a
            a. counting of people.
            b. general agreement.
            c. long-lived person.
            d. collection of data.

_____   4. In **agrarian*** areas there is much
            a. industry.
            b. farming.
            c. culture.
            d. learning.

Summary	Number right _____	× 10 =	_____
Vocabulary	Number right _____	× 10 =	_____
Comprehension	Number right _____	× 10 =	_____
		Total score	_____

_____ 5. **Orthodox*** people
    a. wear unusual clothing.
    b. attend very few religious services.
    c. show kindness and love for others.
    d. follow their religions strictly.

Comprehension

_____ 6. Since 1900, the life expectancy for sixty-five-year-old people in the United States has increased
    a. two years.
    b. four years.
    c. thirteen years.
    d. fifteen years.

_____ 7. The people with the shortest life expectancy in this country are
    a. Afro-Americans.
    b. Italian-Americans.
    c. American Indians.
    d. Mexican-Americans.

_____ 8. People from areas in which the age of 100 is common do *not* have
    a. much work to do.
    b. active sex lives.
    c. interesting diets.
    d. very many children.

_____ 9. Which of the following characteristics apparently does *not* contribute to long life?
    a. religion
    b. heredity
    c. technology
    d. retirement

_____ 10. People who live a long time
    a. don't eat much.
    b. don't drink alcohol.
    c. have few children.
    d. worry actively.

[31]

Long Life

READING FOR STUDYING

This essay question tests whether students understand the reasons that some people live a long time:

Identify the factors that contribute to long life.

Identify means "state or point out." You are to state or point out the factors that contribute to long life. **Underline** the parts of the passage needed to answer the question. Then either **summarize** this information under a heading or **write** an answer to the question. **Number** the factors.

32

Defenses

In response to stress, individuals react not only in subdued, aggressive, and repetitive ways, but also in ways unknown to them. Actually, it is not quite correct to say that the behaviors to which we now turn are unknown to the individual producing them, but at least the *reasons* for the behavior are *presumably* unknown. Such reactions are called *defense mechanisms,* a term used by Freud to describe the unconscious * process by which an individual protects himself from anxiety.

Repression. Repression refers to the exclusion of unpleasant experiences from awareness; they are somehow forgotten. Earlier, we discussed repression in connection with memory and noted several examples, including the frustrated suitor who constantly forgot the name of his rival. Charles Darwin was so aware of the tendency to forget the unpleasant and so intellectually honest that he made a point of jotting down immediately any observation which failed to support his views. Observations confirming them needed no special attention.

Repression was considered by Freud to be the primary defense mechanism. In fact, he viewed repression of hostile and sexual impulses as virtually universal in nineteenth-century Western society. Equally important, repression presumably serves as a basis for other defense mechanisms.

Rationalization. Aesop's fable, "The Fox and the Grapes," is a frequently quoted illustration of rationalization. When the fox couldn't obtain some delicious-looking grapes, he decided that they were sour anyway. In *rationalization,* "good" but false reasons are substituted for real reasons. Hence, we hear the expression "sour grapes."

A three-year-old child did not want a neighborhood boy to visit him because this child monopolized his toy fire engine. When told he must invite the other child to have a ride, he said that the other boy might be having his nap. When told that the other boy was up, he said the sky looked as if it might rain. When he was told that it would not rain, he said that the boy's mother might not want him to come. The same boy, in conflict between his desire to take his teddy bear to school, on the one hand, and being thought of as a "big boy" on the other, finally decided not to take the bear. His reason was that the bear might catch a cold.

In our society, which places much value on rational thought, it is often difficult to determine whether or not someone is rationalizing. The distinction sometimes can be made by observing the individual's willingness to examine his thinking. If he becomes upset, *perhaps* the real reasons are not being acknowledged and he becomes anxious because they may be brought closer to his awareness.

Reaction formation. A bombardier reported that he was eager to return to combat after a narrow escape from death during one of his missions, but he fainted following each of his next two missions. During an interview he laughed at the interviewer's questions, stated he never experienced fear while flying, and declared that in fact he had never feared anything. Later, following administration of sodium pentothal, a drug that influences recall of underlying feelings, he declared: ". . . the plane suddenly shook . . . down we fell . . . I was scared. Me scared! I didn't think I'd ever be scared—didn't think any man could scare me . . ." (White, 1964, p. 64).

Apparently the flyer adopted the attitude of bravado and jocularity as a means of coping with the unwanted thought. *Reaction formation* involves repression and the adoption of conscious attitudes and behavior exactly *opposite* of those judged unacceptable. The latter, it is hypothesized, serve to aid repression.

Parental *over*protection perhaps is a form of reaction formation. The father or mother may feel that he should love the child but finds child rearing a burdensome task. Hence, he may try to conceal his resentment, even from himself, by being overly solicitous of the child's welfare. Persons who crusade against the use of alcohol in any form whatsoever or against any form of sexual expression perhaps are struggling to control their own desires for engaging in such activities. An overly "sweet" woman indicated what she did when she became angry with other people: "I kill 'em with kindness."

Projection. In a general sense, whenever an individual inaccurately attributes his own personal feelings or characteristics to others, he is projecting. Children frequently project their thoughts and feelings, believing that others feel just as they feel. When a child is sad, he may say that his friend is sad too. In the present context, however, projection has a more restricted meaning. It refers to unknowingly attributing one's *unwanted* traits to others. Again, there are two aspects: repression of the unacceptable thoughts and ascribing them to others.

In a study of projection, college men rated themselves and each other on four socially undesirable traits: stinginess, obstinacy, disorderliness, and bashfulness. Some subjects demonstrated an awareness of their undesirable traits by giving themselves high ratings where they also received high ratings from their friends. Others gave themselves low ratings on traits for which they received high ratings by others, thus demonstrating little recognition of their undesirable traits. Furthermore, they rated others higher on these same traits than did the rest of the group. They apparently lacked insight into their own undesirable traits and projected them onto others (Sears, 1936).

Projection also may involve wish fulfillment. A girl who becomes frustrated in attracting the interest of men may imagine that men have a special interest in her. A woman known to one of the writers complained that men chased her through a park, but investigation revealed that no such events had occurred. An extreme reaction of this type is dramatically depicted in Faulkner's short story "Dry September" (1950).

The reactions we have just considered do not represent a complete list of defense mechanisms; our aim has been to illustrate their general nature.

REFERENCES

Faulkner, W. 1950. "Dry September." In *Collected Stories of William Faulkner,* New York: Random House.

Sears, R. R. 1936. Experimental studies of projection. I. Attribution of traits. *J. soc. psychol.,* 7, 151-163.

White, R. W. 1964. *The Abnormal Personality.* New York: Ronald Press.

[32]

Defenses

READING FOR UNDERSTANDING

Summary

_____   1. In summary, this passage presents
           a. a *method* for identifying defense mechanisms.
           b. four *types* of common defense mechanisms.
           c. the *sequence* for studying defense mechanisms.
           d. the *reasons* that people need defense mechanisms.

_____   2. The summary is best stated in the headings and in the
           a. first paragraph.
           b. second paragraph.
           c. third paragraph.
           d. fourth paragraph.

Vocabulary

_____   3. **Defense mechanisms*** are ways to
           a. fight off negative influences.
           b. defend against hurtful criticism.
           c. shield ourselves from the world.
           d. protect ourselves from anxiety.

_____   4. A **solicitous*** person shows
           a. contempt and indifference.
           b. solidarity and firmness.
           c. certainty and sureness.
           d. attention and concern.

Summary	Number right _____ × 10 = _____	
Vocabulary	Number right _____ × 10 = _____	
Comprehension	Number right _____ × 10 = _____	
	Total score_____	

_____   5. **Ascribing*** thoughts to others means
           a. writing about others' thoughts.
           b. speaking about the thoughts of others
           c. stating that others have the thoughts.
           d. identifying what others' thoughts are.

Comprehension

_____   6. According to Sigmund Freud, the defense mechanism that is the basis for all
            the others is
            a. repression.
            b. regression.
            c. projection.
            d. rationalization.

_____   7. A grocer failed in business because he did not have good business sense, but
            he claimed that he failed because of unfair competition. The grocer used the
            defense mechanism of
            a. repression.
            b. projection.
            c. rationalization.
            d. reaction formation.

_____   8. A psychologist theorized that a patient was using rationalization, because
            when the psychologist asked the patient to examine his thinking the patient
            a. examined his thinking.
            b. seemed to be irrational.
            c. became extremely relaxed.
            d. became extremely upset.

_____   9. To "kill with kindness" those who anger us is to use
            a. rejection.
            b. projection.
            c. defense mechanisms.
            d. reaction formation.

_____   10. When people incorrectly find their own characteristics or feelings in others,
            they are using
            a. reaction formation.
            b. rationalization.
            c. projection.
            d. repression.

[32]

Defenses

READING FOR STUDYING

The following essay question tests whether students understand the similarities and differences among defense mechanisms:

Compare the defense mechanisms of repression, rationalization, and projection.

Compare means to "show how they are alike and different." To compare satisfactorily, you should define the terms, give examples of them, and also show how they are similar and dissimilar. **Underline** the parts of the passage needed to answer the question. Then either **summarize** this information under an appropriate heading and subheadings or **write** an answer to the question.

33

Buying

Psychology is the behavioral science that most directly helps market researchers define the needs and wants of consumers. These needs and wants can be converted into *motives for buying,* the reasons people make purchases.

Psychologists interested in marketing have defined two major kinds of motives that affect what people buy; these are rational motives and emotional motives. They have also isolated a category of motives that affect where people buy; these are patronage motives. Since all of these factors are important in understanding buying habits, we will discuss them in some detail.

RATIONAL MOTIVES

Imagine that you are standing at a store counter buying a wool scarf. If a stranger armed with a notebook and pencil approached you and asked you why you were buying it, you would probably answer that you needed something to keep your neck warm in cold weather. This would be a *rational motive,* that is, one prompted by reason and what might be called good sense. Marketers often appeal to rational motives in selling goods. Such motives are largely related to cost, dependability, and usefulness.

Cost frequently determines what product consumers buy. If a 1-pound can of Hills Brothers coffee is on sale . . . and Maxwell House costs [fifty cents more], you might try the can of Hills Brothers. If you already drink Hills Brothers, you might take advantage of the sale to buy several cans. The cost-conscious customer also buys in quantities when such quantities lead to lower unit costs. Retail stores cut their prices at the end of a season, selling Christmas cards in January and bathing suits in September. The stores want to clear their shelves for new merchandise, and many cost-conscious customers wait for those sales.

Dependability determines what product consumers choose. This motive is most frequently used by upper-middle-class customers who can afford to pay more for a product that will work better and last longer.

Maytag washing machines are more expensive than any competitor's, but they are successfully sold on the basis of dependability. Zenith can charge high prices for its television sets because its reputation has convinced customers that "the quality goes in before the name goes on."

Usefulness is the motive of customers who buy a product because they need it for a particular job. (Your wool scarf is an example.) Skilled marketers frequently help the sales of a product by finding new uses for it. For example, sales of Arm & Hammer baking soda had gone down because fewer people were doing their own baking. The market manager discovered new uses for baking soda, and the company is now successfully selling it as a household deodorant and cleanser.

EMOTIONAL MOTIVES

Now imagine that you are at a counter buying some expensive cologne. If the inquisitive stranger approached you at this point and asked your reason for buying, you might have trouble answering. It could well be that you are acting from an *emotional motive,* that is, one having to do with your feelings, such as pride or emulation. Emotions are used most often to market products such as cigarettes or deodorants. The consumer has no rational basis for his choice. Emotional motives include satisfaction of the senses, fear, pride, sociability, and emulation.

The most basic of emotional motives is satisfaction of the senses: taste, touch, smell, sight, and hearing. (Your cologne would fit into this category.) Attractive men and women arouse and satisfy the senses of other men and women. Thus, advertisements use attractive models to sell a wide range of consumer products. Advertisers urge you to "taste and compare" Winston cigarettes or to use Pond's cold cream for "the skin you love to touch."

Fear is the emotion arising from the instinct of self-preservation. It is a useful emotion because it helps people to avoid unnecessary risks and to take care of themselves. Marketers use it to help sell life and health insurance, fire and theft insurance, health foods, and safety devices for cars and homes. Following commercial marketers' lead, the American Heart Association has sponsored an anti-cigarette campaign that appeals to this same emotion.

Pride in position in life, home, family, or good looks can be used to sell a wide range of products to enhance personal appearance or to confirm wealth and good taste. Rolls-Royce automobiles and Ambassador twenty-five-year-old Scotch appeal to pride of ownership.

Sociability is the desire to be with other people in an attractive setting. Pepsi-Cola is sold to "the Pepsi generation," often depicted as a group of people at a beach party. Beer, soft drinks, restaurants, resorts, and trips on cruise ships are sold to individual customers as items that will make them part of attractive groups of people.

Emulation is a widely used emotional marketing tactic. It is based on the fact that most people want to follow leaders or imitate movie stars. Athletes help sell "Wheaties, the breakfast of champions." J. Paul Getty, the oil millionaire, appears in television ads for his brokerage house.

OVERLAPPING MOTIVES

In listing all these rational and emotional motives, it should be remembered that motives can overlap. A consumer frequently has more than one motive for selecting a given brand. Your scarf may not only keep you warm, but also appeal to your senses of touch and seeing. A college student may buy a Volkswagen because of its economy (the cost motive), because it is expected to last longer and need fewer repairs (the dependability motive), because Billie Jean King drives one (the emulation motive), or because it is attractive (satisfying the sense of sight). A market manager knows how to orchestrate these various motives to persuade a consumer to choose one product over another.

PATRONAGE MOTIVES

Rational and emotional motives influence what consumers buy. *Patronage motives* influence where they buy, the sellers they patronize, once they have decided to make a purchase. The most important patronage motives are reputation, convenience, service, and the variety of products offered.

Reputation for integrity and quality is an especially strong patronage motive for purchasing nonbrand goods like fresh food or jewelry. If A&P reputedly has the best meat counter in the neighborhood, consumers are likely to buy meat there. Tiffany sells its reputation rather than a brand of diamond or gold jewelry. A firm's reputation is, of course, most important when the firm controls the product or service being supplied. An auto repair shop eventually succeeds or fails depending on the reputation it builds up in the community over the years.

Convenience is an important patronage motive. Customers frequently shop at, and pay a few cents more for products at, a store that is located nearby or that is open on Sundays or late at night. The 7–11 stores appeal to this motive.

Good service, including competent and courteous salespeople, charge accounts, free delivery, and baby-sitting for shoppers, is another motive for patronizing a particular store. Special services have become a feature of some large department stores. For example, Marshall Field has a reputation for offering almost unlimited exchanges or refunds (it once refunded money on a pair of fifty-year-old, but unworn, high-button shoes).

Variety of product availability is another strong patronage motive. Macy's attracts customers because of its reputation as "the world's largest store." It offers a huge variety of both name brands and house brands in every price range. Shopping centers succeed because they provide a wide variety of services within an easy walk from a parked car.

[33]

Buying

READING FOR UNDERSTANDING

Summary

_____ 1. In summary, this passage presents
   a. *methods* for making wise purchases.
   b. the *types* of purchases we make.
   c. the *reasons* we make our purchases.
   d. a *sequence* for making wise purchases.

_____ 2. The summary is best stated in the headings and in the
   a. first sentence of the first paragraph.
   b. last sentence of the first paragraph.
   c. first sentence of the second paragraph.
   d. last sentence of the second paragraph.

Vocabulary

_____ 3. To **enhance*** appearance is to
   a. improve it.
   b. enlarge it.
   c. destroy it.
   d. enclose it.

_____ 4. **Emulation*** is the
   a. lowering of prices.
   b. appeal to emotions.
   c. imitation of others.
   d. creation of desire.

Summary	Number right _____	× 10 =	_____
Vocabulary	Number right _____	× 10 =	_____
Comprehension	Number right _____	× 10 =	_____
		Total score	_____

_____ 5. If a store **reputedly*** has good products it
  a. continually has very good products.
  b. has a reputation for good products.
  c. intentionally stocks good products.
  d. does not really have good products.

Comprehension

_____ 6. The basic characteristic of a rational motive for buying is that it reflects
  a. consideration of price.
  b. consideration of usefulness.
  c. a search for dependability.
  d. thought and good sense.

_____ 7. Which of the following is most likely to be purchased for rational reasons?
  a. soft drinks
  b. laundry soap
  c. organic fruit
  d. potato chips

_____ 8. Which of the following is most likely to be purchased for emotional reasons?
  a. television sets
  b. denim pants
  c. shoe polish
  d. mouthwash

_____ 9. Rational and emotional motives influence
  a. where you buy.
  b. when you buy.
  c. whether you buy.
  d. what you buy.

_____ 10. People are most likely to spend more for their purchases than they need to if they make purchases *only* at stores that
  a. are conveniently located.
  b. have good reputations.
  c. offer good services.
  d. offer much variety.

[33]

Buying

READING FOR STUDYING

This essay question tests whether students understand the reasons that people make purchases.

Contrast rational motives and emotional motives for buying.

Contrast means "to show or emphasize differences." Show how rational motives for buying differ from emotional motives for buying. **Underline** the parts of the passage needed to answer the question. Then either **summarize** this information under appropriate headings or **write** an answer to the question.

[34]

Marriage

Numerous factors contribute to the success or failure of a marriage. Experts cite statistics showing that couples are more likely to stay married if they are of similar age, race, and religion and share the same education, social background, and socioeconomic status. These characteristics are certainly important, but a marriage that defies the statistics can still be successful.

PERSONALITY DIFFERENCES

It is important to the success of a marriage that partners create a mutually gratifying life style, based on awareness of each other's differences in personality and abilities rather than on traditional sex-role expectations. In one study of personality and marriage, researchers differentiated a group of college women on the basis of varying degrees of autonomy and conflict. The more autonomous women chose men   * who allowed them to develop as persons and who made demands of them that they could fulfill without interfering with the primary task of developing their own talents and interests. One woman writer, for example, married another writer and they both shared a single teaching position. Both had strong interests in being parents, and sharing a half-time job enabled them to enjoy their children and writing. Their arrangement was designed to gratify mutual needs for autonomy as well as creativity.

The college women in the study who were described as less autonomous wanted traditional marriages in which they could play supportive roles and could be protected from the complexities and shortcomings of the world outside the home. They viewed the traditional roles of wife, mother, and community leader as the only ones that interested them. They needed a man to make this life style possible, and they were eager and willing to manage households and care for their husbands and children in exchange.

In both groups, those who came from "happy" homes moved into marriage with relatively little conflict and approached their life tasks

Children provide parents with opportunities to become mature, caring people. (UNICEF photo by Tom Marotta)

with vigor and optimism. Unfortunately, those who came from conflict-filled homes frequently selected partners who tended to continue the process of conflict.

MONEY

When marriages are new, partners may minimize the importance of money for stability. Yet problems involving money often cause misery and divorce in many families. In American society, controlling money means different things to different people. To some, it means freedom of choice; to others, power over people. The way a family handles financial decisions reveals much about the relationship between husband and wife and the relative positions of the partners. Do they budget and decide cooperatively? Do partners take responsibilities on the basis of sex role or on the basis of talent in spending and saving? Is money used to enrich a mutual relationship, or is it used to define a power situation?

Handling money in a fair way to achieve short- and long-term objectives is a challenging task, especially as family finances change for better or worse. All financial decisions have meaning; they relate crucially to issues of autonomy, cooperation, and dominance. Whether funds are spent as a result of joint decision making or as primarily the privilege or responsibility of one partner indicates an assumption about adult responsibility of husband and wife. The reservation of some money for free, unaccounted use by each partner indicates an attitude respecting the individuality of each partner.

SEX

When wives were pregnant every year or so and fear of pregnancy was a familiar part of marital sex relations, the sexual needs of men were frequently frustrated within marriage. In addition to the fact that pregnancies made the wife less available for sexual purposes, the sexual mores of Victorian times discouraged men and women from comfortably exploring their own sexuality in the service of greater gratification. In the United States in the not too distant past, and in some cultures today, it was and is considered somewhat "lady-like" to view sex as one of the duties and trials of marriage rather than one of its pleasures. Now, with the current emphasis on enjoyment of sex, both husband and wife are free to experiment, admit to sexual pleasure, and seek verification of their efforts to please each other.

In stable marriages, individuals have the opportunity to work through sexual changes. Just as adulthood is not an even, placid, unchanging period, neither is the sexuality of individuals a steady, monotonous experience. Sex between developing adults is constantly changing, provides variety, and calls for sensitivity. At one time or another, each partner may have to use long-time knowledge of the other person's responsiveness in order to be helpful and understanding.

THE EFFECT OF CHILDREN

Research indicates that childless marriages, when they survive, appear to be healthier than marriages with children. . . . There are fewer demands on the couple, and the husband and wife appear to be happier with each other. Research further indicates that fathers find marriage to be more restrictive and more full of problems than do childless husbands. Fathers describe themselves as feeling more inadequate and dissatisfied with themselves than do husbands without children.

Child rearing is a responsibility that may bring both financial and psychological conflicts, and not every couple finds the pleasures of parenthood equal to the demands and problems involved. Parents may have differing ideas about child rearing and different reactions to the needs of the children. Problems of infancy and the twenty-four-hour demands of the baby can be very wearing and upsetting for the couple. The problems of the school-age child also raise difficulties for some parents, and the teenage period is rarely described as a source of pleasure or delight to parents. . . .

Paul Rosencranz has commented that although children may be the cement that holds traditional marriages together, they are disruptive to egalitarian marriages. Small children's needs are urgent and unpredict-   *
able, and egalitarian couples often resent the inconvenience, time, and effort required to give a child a good start in life.

The current trend is toward small families, with one or two children. There is still little research about the two-child family, so we can only speculate, but it is likely that children in such families are treasured by parents as an opportunity to enhance their own development and help themselves become mature, caring people.

[34]

Marriage

READING FOR UNDERSTANDING

Summary

_____ 1. In summary, this passage presents
   a. *reasons* that marriages are successful or not.
   b. *methods* for having a successful marriage.
   c. *points of view* about what a good marriage is.
   d. *types* of people who have unhappy marriages.

_____ 2. The summary is best stated in the headings and in the
   a. first sentence.
   b. second sentence.
   c. third sentence.
   d. fourth sentence.

Vocabulary

_____ 3. **Autonomous*** people
   a. respond automatically—like machines.
   b. are loving and filled with good will.
   c. function well without supervision.
   d. need much supervision to function well.

_____ 4. To work with **vigor*** is to work
   a. in bad temper.
   b. without stopping.
   c. with much energy.
   d. with little energy.

Summary	Number right _____	× 10 =	_____
Vocabulary	Number right _____	× 10 =	_____
Comprehension	Number right _____	× 10 =	_____
		Total score	_____

_____ 5. **Egalitarian*** people value
a. the demands of parenthood.
b. their freedom and rights.
c. beautiful possessions.
d. living in large cities.

Comprehension

_____ 6. Unhappy marriages most often exist when marriage partners
a. develop their own interests.
b. assume untraditional roles.
c. have very little education.
d. come from unhappy homes.

_____ 7. If each marriage partner keeps aside some money to spend without accounting for its use, this indicates that both partners
a. hide things from each other.
b. have not learned to share.
c. respect individuality.
d. have an unhappy marriage.

_____ 8. Sex between people who have long, stable marriages
a. gets worse with time.
b. changes constantly.
c. stays much the same.
d. stops after forty years.

_____ 9. Apparently, marriages are healthier when there
a. are no children.
b. is only one child.
c. are two or three children.
d. are four or more children.

_____ 10. Children are least likely to give pleasure to parents when they are
a. one through three years old.
b. four through seven years old.
c. eight through twelve years old.
d. thirteen through nineteen years old.

[34]

Marriage

READING FOR STUDYING

This essay question tests whether students understand why some marriages fail:

Discuss how personality, money, sex, and children can contribute to an unsuccessful marriage.

Discuss means "give as much information as you can." Give as much information as you can about how personality, money, sex, and children can contribute to an unsuccessful marriage. **Underline** the parts of the passage needed to answer the question. Then either **summarize** the information under a heading and the four subheadings indicated in the question or **write** an answer to the question.

_____

_____

_____

_____

_____

_____

_____

_____

_____

_____

_____

_____

_____

[35]

Grades

Perhaps even more controversial than testing is the question of grades or marks, whether on assignments, examinations, or courses. (Sometimes in the following material we will use the words "grades" and "marks" interchangeably; however, in education the word "mark" often is applied to grades recorded for courses, rather than to "grades" on examinations and assignments.) In general, there are three viewpoints: (1) grading by comparison, (2) grading by achievement of individual potential, (3) abolition of grades.

Supporters of grading by comparison believe that pupils should be graded or ranked on assignments, examinations, or courses in comparison with other pupils. Implicit in this assumption is the belief that some *   kind of standard should be established and that those who achieve beyond this standard should receive marks above the average while those who achieve below the presumed standard should receive lower than average marks. Yet proponents of this view sometimes have difficulty in defining exactly what the chosen standard actually is.

Since the standard must be in relationship to the performance of some other group, the question arises as to which of several groups to use as a standard.

1. Should a national group of a given grade or age be used as a standard for grading performance? If a national standard were used in the United States, the vast majority of students in the slums would be graded somewhere between failure and below average, whereas the majority of students in suburban areas would be graded somewhere between success and above average.

2. Should the mark be based on some smaller unit for comparison, such as community or the school itself? But schools differ as to social class and local factors within a community. If the grade level of a given school is the unit used, problems arise when there are several classes at the same grade level or in the same subject area. What should be done about groups which are sectioned in terms of ability? Should all "fast" sections have a heavy preponderance of high grades *   and all "slow" sections have a heavy preponderance of low grades

From William Van Til, *Education: A Beginning*, 2nd ed., pp. 539–541. Copyright © 1974 by Houghton Mifflin Company. Used by permission.

and failure? What happens then to the motivation of less able students who are constantly deprived of opportunities for success as measured by grades? If an honors group must demonstrate extremely high accomplishment to receive a high grade, does this penalize such students and reduce their motivation to enroll in an honors group?

3. So a third proposal is to judge the comparative performance of the individual in his own class. The teacher assumes that he knows what a desirable standard or average for his class is and he grades accordingly. Some students receive high grades and some lower grades, depending on academic achievement alone. No consideration is given to the individual's effort or potential. Some criticize this approach as unfair and inhumane.

4. Another possibility in judging performance is to depend on the teacher's idea of what is, in general, typical for the age level or grade or subject. But estimations of what is typical in general vary widely from teacher to teacher. No clear reference group is involved because individual teachers' standards are vague and undefined.

An alternative to grading based on the comparison of the individual with some group, whether national, school-wide, class, or "typical" of children and youth everywhere, is grading the student on the basis of his own achievement of his potential. In this system of grading the student who proceeds at his maximum capacity receives the better marks. The student who is achieving less than he is capable of achieving receives lower than average marks. The student who is proceeding normally presumably receives an average mark.

The approach to grading on the achievement of potential is defended as opening up the possibility for success to each student. After all, the student is not being graded on someone else's ability—he is being graded on the basis of his own achievement in relationship to his potential. But opponents of this form of grading ask how is the teacher to know whether the student is living up to his potential? Can the teacher really assess this? Some point out that there is a danger that students will be marked high if they are docile, compliant, dutiful, and industrious, and marked low if they are unruly and skeptical, or perhaps creative and original! Still other critics point out that the world is essentially competitive and that grading on the basis of individual achievement might be socially misleading to pupils, and thus in the long run no help to them at all. The academically weak student who tries hard might discover that only the school, not the competitive world, regards him as "A." The brilliant student who does not live up to his potential might be cheated or handicapped by "C's" interpreted as evidence of low ability by college and graduate school admissions officers.

[35]

Grades

READING FOR UNDERSTANDING

Summary

_____ 1. In summary, this passage presents
    a. *sequences* for grading students.
    b. *points of view* about how to grade.
    c. *reasons* that grading is necessary.
    d. *types* of grades that students prefer.

_____ 2. The summary is best stated in the
    a. first paragraph.
    b. second paragraph.
    c. first and second paragraphs.
    d. first and last paragraphs.

Vocabulary

_____ 3. If something is **implicit***, it is
    a. understood but not directly stated.
    b. completely obvious and clear.
    c. exactly what should be expected.
    d. contrary to our expectations.

_____ 4. A **preponderance*** is a
    a. boring subject for discussion.
    b. position of great importance.
    c. good solution to a problem.
    d. great amount of something.

Summary	Number right _____	X 10 =	_____
Vocabulary	Number right _____	X 10 =	_____
Comprehension	Number right _____	X 10 =	_____
		Total score	_____

_____   5. **Docile*** people are
             a. not too smart.
             b. easily managed.
             c. not very strong.
             d. very well liked.

Comprehension

_____   6. The basic problem in grading by comparing students seems to be
             a. that teachers do not like to compare students.
             b. that it is not possible to make such comparisons.
             c. in deciding what group to compare them to.
             d. that tests cannot be used for comparisons.

_____   7. If students in "fast" and "slow" classes are graded by comparing them to all
             the students in a school, students in
             a. "fast" classes will get too low grades.
             b. "slow" classes will get too high grades.
             c. "fast" classes will seldom do well.
             d. "slow" classes will seldom do well.

_____   8. The basic problem with grading by comparing students to members of their
             classes is that it does not account for students'
             a. previous test scores.
             b. work in other classes.
             c. effort or potential.
             d. need to be successful.

_____   9. The basic problem with teachers' grading by what they judge is typical for a
             grade is that
             a. teachers disagree on what is typical.
             b. law courts have ruled against this method.
             c. it gives teachers too much power.
             d. it makes students distrust teachers.

_____   10. The basic problem with grading students in relation to their ability is that it
             gives students the wrong understanding of
             a. the type of life work they should do.
             b. subjects that they should and should not study.
             c. how the rest of the world will judge them.
             d. whether or not they have used their potential.

[35]

Grades

READING FOR STUDYING

This essay question tests whether students understand the problems in grading:

> *Explain* the problems in (1) grading students by comparing them to other students and (2) grading students on the basis of their own achievement.

Explain means "give reasons." Give the reasons for problems in using the two grading procedures. **Underline** the parts of the passage needed to answer the question. Then either **summarize** this information under a heading and the two subheadings indicated in the question or **write** an answer to the question.

_____

_____

_____

_____

_____

_____

_____

_____

_____

_____

_____

_____

_____

Decisions

This goal of human behavior may serve as an explanation of how decisions are made. The simplest explanation of decision making is that people choose the alternative that leads to the greatest amount of positive as opposed to negative utility. Other things being equal and given a choice among alternatives, you choose the one with the positive utility * or the greatest worth.

However, it is not possible to jump immediately from this general principle to making excellent decisions. You cannot say, "I prefer pleasure over pain; therefore, I choose to be a bookkeeper rather than a salesman." There are several steps in making sound, satisfying decisions, and you are likely to go through all of them, either consciously or unconsciously. Very briefly, these steps are:

D Determine the difficulty.
E Explore the difficulty.
C Collect information.
I Interpret the information.
D Decide what to do.
E Examine your decision later.

DETERMINE THE DIFFICULTY

The first step in decision making can be very hard—or just the opposite. Usually it is easy to know when you have a problem that needs to be solved. For example, if you need to declare your curriculum preference by next Wednesday, raise your grades, or increase your income, you are quite aware that you have a problem. You have what some psychologists call a *felt difficulty.*

No one can begin to make any headway against a problem without first recognizing that the difficulty exists. Some students may be spending so much time on campus activities that their classwork is beginning to suffer. But they may be unaware of this fact—and thus be unable to do anything about it—until an instructor comments on their poor work or until they begin to get poor grades.

Sometimes it is harder than this to become aware of a problem. A person may have a vague sense of dissatisfaction with life, or even feel extremely worried, sad, or upset without being able to put a name to any specific problem. But even then, as soon as the person can say, "I am not happy; maybe I can change myself or my environment to make things better," the solution of the problem is under way. Psychologists agree that the necessary first step in any kind of personal problem solving is to acknowledge that a problem exists and to believe that change is possible.

EXPLORE THE DIFFICULTY

In many cases, the felt difficulty is clear enough, but the student cannot do anything about it without exploring the problem and narrowing it down. For instance, a student may need to improve his or her grades, but until the cause of the poor grades is located, it is impossible to make sensible plans for changing them. They could be the result of too heavy an academic load, ill health, family problems, poor study habits, or a host of other causes. Merely deciding to "try harder" is not likely to produce satisfactory results.

The simple process of talking your problem over with someone may help you see it more objectively. Don't overlook family, friends, and instructors when you need a friendly ear. Occasionally, a student needs professional psychological help in exploring underlying causes in order to see the problems clearly enough to begin to cope with them.

"Exploring" difficulty, however, does not always involve a search for underlying causes. Very often all that is necessary is to define the problem a little more narrowly. If a student feels "I need more money," it takes only a little thought to figure out whether it is needed for necessities, luxuries, or debts. Is a steady income for the next three years needed, or would an extra $50 for the next four months be enough?

Analyzing the problem, finding its causes, and narrowing it down to manageable size help you know what kind of information you need to solve the problem, what kind of solution you should be looking for.

COLLECT INFORMATION

The next step in decision making is gathering all the information you can that may have a part in the final plan. In making personal decisions, two kinds of information are essential.

First is information about yourself. The better you understand yourself, the more you know about your likes and dislikes, your strengths, and weaknesses, the more likely you are to make decisions that will be right for you.

It is neither possible nor desirable to be cold-bloodedly objective about yourself. But it is possible to isolate a few characteristics that have a bearing on the particular decision that needs to be made. For example, Barbara is offered two part-time jobs, one in the college library and the other at a fast-food restaurant. Which one should she take? She knows that she likes a quiet atmosphere, enjoys reading, and has good verbal skills. She also has good manual dexterity, likes to cook and handle food, and enjoys people. These qualities by no means describe everything there is to know about Barbara. But they are a few of the characteristics that she thinks may have a bearing on which job she should choose. Other aspects of her self-understanding may be important, too, but Barbara does not think of them until later in the decision process. That is quite all right. The important thing now is that she recognizes that her own personal characteristics are an essential ingredient in deciding which job to take. *

The other essential kind of information is objective facts about the situation. What kind of work would Barbara be doing at the library? Would it involve working with office machines, talking with students at the circulation desk, reshelving books, typing catalog cards, or what? What do the two jobs pay? How far away is the restaurant? Would transportation be a problem? What are the hours for each job? What are the supervisors like? Barbara should be extremely careful to get the facts right. She should not assume, for instance, that because the restaurant manager is friendly the hours will be convenient.

Also, in collecting information at this stage, you should not try to evaluate or eliminate any possibilities. Sometimes students make the mistake of closing their options too soon. If your need is for a quiet place to study, do not rule out "far-fetched" ideas like an empty classroom, a park bench, your car, or the boiler room in your dormitory. These may turn out to be terrible ideas: the places may be noisy, unavailable when you need them, or physically uncomfortable. But don't let fears about the impracticality of a solution stop you from considering it.

This is the creative stage in decision making. Use your imagination, your experience, your reading, your friends, to list every possible solution to your problem. Then go ahead and get the facts about each one. Criticism comes later.

Barbara, who is trying to decide between two jobs, may find still another solution to her problem. From what was said earlier, we can guess that her "problem" is not to choose between the two jobs but to solve some felt difficulty that she has narrowed down to a need for a part-time job. In Barbara's case, the need is for greater independence. She feels too sheltered by her parents and wants to show that she can take care of herself in the real world. Perhaps regular volunteer work in a hospital would satisfy her need just as well as a part-time job. Perhaps she could be business manager of the college newspaper, a tutor for children with arithmetic problems, or a political activist. The point is that if she considers a wide range of solutions, she is more likely to make a good decision.

Of course, it is not entirely possible to keep from weighing alternatives and judging solutions as soon as you think of them. No human mind is that compartmentalized. But you can refrain from making snap decisions at this stage. Let your mind think of all the solutions that seem remotely possible, and then collect information about them—and about yourself—that will help you weigh the evidence.

INTERPRET THE INFORMATION

Perhaps the most important part of decision making—unfortunately the most neglected—is sorting and weighing information about the various alternatives. Scientists tell us that the human brain can deal with up to ten ideas per second. However, most of us do not use our brains to full capacity to process the information we acquire.

Most decisions involve more than immediate consequences, and most have more than two alternatives. Usually several possibilities are available, and the important consequences of each one are often difficult to figure out. For many of us, our experience has poorly prepared us to sort and interpret the large amounts of information that have to be handled to arrive at a decision. Also, we sometimes do not foresee the consequences of our actions even when information is available. When undesirable consequences do occur, we wonder why we chose as we did.

You may choose any one of several ways to think through the information about alternatives and their expected outcomes. First, you may try to sort your way through a lot of information by using a *strategy* that reduces the number of facts you are considering at any one time. You ease your load by thinking about only a few factors at a time and ignoring the rest.

Second, you may rank the advantages of the alternatives in order of decreasing importance. If one alternative is clearly the best answer to your felt difficulty, as defined and narrowed, you may stop and make your decision right there. If other alternatives would also bring this main advantage, you try to see which alternative would be most likely to produce a second advantage. Eventually, you choose the alternative that will result in the most advantages. This may be called a *sequential strategy*.

Third, you may tend to separate all consequences into "good versus bad." After a choice based on good versus bad has been made and time has gone by, however, the decision maker sometimes realizes that the choice was not the best one, even by subjective standards. This might happen to you. The reason may have been your inability to weigh all the characteristics of the various alternatives against each other. That is, although you could evaluate each alternative separately with respect to good versus bad, you may have had trouble evaluating all of them simultaneously.

Quite apart from the method used to rank the alternatives is the *utility* of each one. The utility of an alternative will depend upon each individual's evaluation of its attractiveness. That which is considered worthwhile by one person may not be considered so attractive by another. Now is the time to weigh personal characteristics. In interpreting the evidence about the library job, should Barbara give more weight to her love of books or to her love of cooking? Which job will give her a greater feeling of independence?

Besides utility, there is a second factor that enters into decision making. It is called *probability*. An example may help to explain it. Ramon, a first-semester college student, feels that he would like to take trigonometry instead of algebra. However, his faculty adviser shows him that students whose high school mathematics grades were like his did not do as well in trigonometry as they did in algebra. The student changes his mind and decides to take algebra because he has a better chance, or *probability,* of getting a higher grade. His expectation of success is greater for algebra than for trigonometry, and on this basis algebra has more positive utility for him.

Knowing the probability of success of a course of action is not in itself a satisfactory basis for decision making. Statements about probabilities, or odds, are based on facts for groups of people. Ramon may differ from the group with whom he is being matched in all other characteristics except the one being considered. These differences may enable him to beat the odds and do better in trigonometry. Moreover, it should be remembered that the evaluation of the utility of a choice is different for each person.

DECIDE WHAT TO DO

After all this problem defining, information collecting, and alternative weighing, it might seem that making the actual decision would be relatively easy. Most people, however, have trouble making choices. When one alternative is clearly better than another in all ways, there is, of course, no conflict in deciding between them. Often, however, one alternative is better in some ways and another alternative (or alternatives) is better in other ways. Because of this, you experience *conflict* in choosing among the alternatives. In such cases, the utility and probability of each alternative must be re-evaluated.

Similarly, you are often faced with a decision in which no alternative is better than any other. In those situations, you will probably depend on your "state of mind" or on what you assume (without evidence) to

be the advantages of one course of action. In some cases, to avoid unpleasant uncertainty, you may convince yourself that one alternative is
better than another even though there is no clear-cut advantage.

Most decisions contain an element of risk, for no one can know pre-
cisely what will result from the choice of any given alternative. The
problem is to choose the alternative that offers the best positive utility
or payoff and the highest probability that the payoff will take place.

In life, decisions often occur in sequence. Information available for
later decisions is likely to depend on the nature and consequences of
earlier ones. This suggests that a single decision has some relationship
not only to decisions that were made before it but also to decisions that
have to be made after it. This interdependence makes present decisions
more important and, in a sense, more risky, because you cannot know
all the ways in which a decision may affect your future range of choices.

It may be encouraging, when thinking about risks, to recall that most
famous and successful people have not become so by avoiding risks.
Thomas Edison and the Wright brothers, to name only two examples,
took reasonable chances and kept going despite repeated failures. Risk
taking is a part of every decision and every meaningful life.

No doubt you have been told many times to be *objective* when making a decision. Those who tell you this mean that your judgment should
be unaffected by your feelings. They hope that your choice will be
made on the basis of what will be best for you in the long run. Unfortunately, few if any guidelines can be suggested to help you become
objective. So-called objectivity can never be free from subjective or
emotional elements. No matter how objective you try to be, there are
elements in every decision that are subjective. Your personal characteristics, needs, and drives definitely influence the choices you make. For
example, in some individuals the drive to achieve success is greater than
that to avoid failure. In other individuals the reverse is true. Undoubtedly, their ideas of what they are like have much to do with the choices
they make. . . .

EXAMINE YOUR DECISION LATER

It is never too late to change the course of your life. Although certain
options may be closed out because of earlier decisions, there is always
something that can be done to improve a bad situation.

For this reason, examining the consequences of a decision makes a
lot of sense. The sooner the consequences can be evaluated the more
likely it is that you can get back on the right track, if you find you are
not on it. And, just as in correcting the course of a rocket ship, minor
adjustments made early can make a big difference in the final results.

[36]

Decisions

READING FOR UNDERSTANDING

Summary

_____   1. In summary, this passage presents
             a. *types* of decisions we must make.
             b. *reasons* for making good decisions.
             c. a *method* for making decisions.
             d. *points of view* about how to make decisions.

_____   2. The summary is best stated in the headings and in the
             a. first paragraph.
             b. second paragraph.
             c. third paragraph.
             d. fourth paragraph.

Vocabulary

_____   3. **Utility*** refers to
             a. usefulness.
             b. electricity.
             c. requirements.
             d. organization.

_____   4. If something is **vague***, it is
             a. in style.
             b. not clear.
             c. valuable.
             d. very small.

Summary	Number right _____ × 10 = _____
Vocabulary	Number right _____ × 10 = _____
Comprehension	Number right _____ × 10 = _____
	Total score _____

_____   5. Good **manual dexterity*** is good
           a. skill with the hands.
           b. manners with customers.
           c. ability with reading.
           d. thinking and planning.

Comprehension

_____   6. Decisions should be explored by
           a. use of introspection.
           b. reading biographies.
           c. formulating hypotheses.
           d. talking with somebody.

_____   7. When you collect information needed to make a decision about taking a job,
           it is *most* important that you
           a. collect information about yourself.
           b. collect information about the job.
           c. eliminate irrelevant possibilities.
           d. consider all available information.

_____   8. Of the following steps in decision making, the most important one is to
           a. explore the difficulty.
           b. determine the difficulty.
           c. interpret the information.
           d. collect the information.

_____   9. When interpreting the information collected for making a decision, it is *not*
           advised that one
           a. ignore unfavorable or negative consequences.
           b. reduce the total number of facts considered.
           c. arrange alternatives in order of importance.
           d. consider the chance that a plan has for success.

_____ 10. Famous and successful decision makers seem to be those who
           a. know exactly what they want.
           b. are willing to take risks.
           c. possess only relevant facts.
           d. develop a strong intuition.

[36]

Decisions

READING FOR STUDYING

This question tests whether students understand how to make wise decisions:

> *Apply* the steps for making decisions to an important decision you (or a friend) must make.

Apply means "use." Use the steps given in the passage to make a decision. **Underline** the parts of the passage that explain the method for making decisions. Then either **summarize** this information or **write** an answer to the question. Begin your notes or your answer by stating the important decision that you are making for yourself or for a friend (for example, taking a new job, moving from home, getting married, breaking up a friendship). Organize your answer under the headings given in the passage.

[37]

Unwed Mothers

The choices open to a girl or woman who unintentionally becomes premaritally pregnant (as opposed to someone who wants a child but not marriage) are limited. She may get married before the baby's birth; she may remain unmarried and have her baby; or she may seek an abortion.

If the girl marries before the birth of her baby, she makes the child legitimate. The prospects of success in such marriages, however, are notoriously poor; the divorce rate is about twice as high among those *
marriages in which conception occurs before the wedding as it is among those in which conception occurs afterwards (Christensen & Meissner 1953). One or both partners may enter such a marriage with extreme reluctance, thereby producing unconscious—if not conscious—hostility. Furthermore, forced marriage may curtail education and impose finan- *
cial hardship on the young couple, adding further strain on an already shaky relationship.

The girl who remains unmarried yet has her baby has the choice of keeping the infant and rearing it; or placing the child for adoption through an official agency, an attorney, doctor, or the black market. Or she may turn the baby over to her own or the father's parents or relatives to rear. In a society such as ours, which still holds in disgrace the child born out of marriage and harshly criticizes its mother, considerable pressure exists to conceal the illegitimacy (Kenkel 1966).

If a prospective mother chooses to have an abortion, there are ethical, psychological, legal, religious, and social considerations that she must face. The mother, perhaps even more than the child, pays—and pays, and pays—for the sexual misadventure that results in an illegitimate child.

Despite changing sexual attitudes, society still applies the traditional double standard of judgment to illegitimate mothers and illegitimate fathers. A woman continues to be judged more harshly than a man for any form of nonmarital sexual behavior. She is judged especially severely for the ultimate in sexual missteps—having a child outside marriage. The unwed mother has obviously had "illicit sex" and is often seen as a threat by those women who may doubt their own sexual desirability or whose marriages are shaky.

Because middle-class people tend to see illegitimacy as a problem of the lower class, they frequently make no effort to try to understand the causes of illegitimacy, and content themselves with viewing the issue as a moral one.... The causes of illegitimacy among the lower classes lie primarily in the basic problems of "second-class citizenship." But they are also related to the considerably greater family and marital instability that appears to exist in lower-class groups (DeBurger 1967). Relationships between the sexes in the lower-class group are much more casual, suggesting a willingness to engage in sexual activity even when there is no strong emotional attachment between the partners (Rodman 1965). The less emotionally involved a man is with a woman, the less concern he shows for her welfare, and the less likely he is to protect her from pregnancy (Kirkendall 1961; Udry 1966). But the fact is important that, although there are more unwed mothers in the lowest socioeconomic class than in any other, premarital pregnancies occur at all levels. The upper levels are simply better able to hide the pregnancy or to end it through abortion (Beigel 1961).

Educational factors are also related to the incidence of illegitimacy. One study revealed that, of those unmarried girls who became pregnant, the majority had ended their education with grammar school. Of those girls who had had some high-school education, 7 percent became pregnant before they were twenty years old, while less than half this number of college girls twenty years of age suffered the same mishap (Beigel 1961).

It has been estimated that, when a boy and girl who are still in high school marry, the chances are as high as 80 percent that the marriage was precipitated by a premarital pregnancy (Udry 1966). As a matter of fact, 33 percent of *all* firstborn children in the United States are conceived out of wedlock ("In the News" 1970). Poorly educated women are the ones most likely to be ignorant about birth control, and to trust to luck rather than to use some sort of contraceptive protection.

*

REFERENCES

Beigel, H. G. Illegitimacy. In *The encyclopedia of sexual behavior*, Vol. I, ed. A. Ellis and A. Abarbanel. New York: Hawthorn, 1961.

Christensen, H. T., and Meissner, H. H. Studies in child spacing: III—Premarital pregnancy as a factor in divorce. *Am. Sociol. Rev.* 18 (1953): 641–644.

DeBurger, J. E. Marital problems, help-seeking, and emotional orientation as revealed in help-request letters. *J. Marriage Family* 29 (1967): 712–721.

Kenkel, W. F. *The family in perspective.* 2nd ed. New York: Appleton, 1966.

Kirkendall, L. A. *Premarital intercourse and interpersonal relations.* New York: Julian Press, 1961.

Rodman, H. *Marriage, family, and society.* New York: Random House, 1965.

Udry, J. R. *The social context of marriage.* Philadelphia: Lippincott, 1966.

[37]

Unwed Mothers

READING FOR UNDERSTANDING

Summary

_____ 1. In summary, this passage presents
   a. the *history* of illegitimate motherhood.
   b. the *types* of unmarried mothers there are.
   c. the *reasons* that unmarried mothers have problems.
   d. *methods* for avoiding illegitimate births.

_____ 2. The summary is best stated in the
   a. first paragraph.
   b. second paragraph.
   c. third paragraph.
   d. fourth paragraph.

Vocabulary

_____ 3. If chances of success are **notoriously*** poor, they are
   a. completely unsuccessful.
   b. known widely to be very poor.
   c. not really poor at all.
   d. not certain to be poor.

_____ 4. To **curtail*** education is to
   a. cut it short.
   b. stretch it out.
   c. improve on it.
   d. disapprove of it.

Summary	Number right _____	× 10 =	_____
Vocabulary	Number right _____	× 10 =	_____
Comprehension	Number right _____	× 10 =	_____
		Total score	_____

_____ 5. If a marriage was **precipitated*** by a pregnancy, a pregnancy
    a. destroyed the marriage.
    b. made the marriage happy.
    c. caused the marriage.
    d. dampened the marriage.

Comprehension

_____ 6. If an unmarried pregnant woman marries to make her child legitimate, often such marriages
    a. are filled with hostility.
    b. prevent attendance in college.
    c. have a very low success rate.
    d. create financial difficulties.

_____ 7. The reason that unmarried mothers are more severely criticized than unmarried fathers is probably because
    a. most people do not blame men for what they do.
    b. the Church so disapproves of "illicit sex."
    c. people want such pregnancies to be aborted.
    d. the mothers are more visible than the fathers.

_____ 8. Which of the following is *not* a reason for there being more unwed mothers in the lower class than in the middle class? "In the lower class
    a. sexual relationships are more casual."
    b. the mothers assume that they will have an abortion."
    c. men are less involved with their women."
    d. men are less likely to protect from pregnancy."

_____ 9. Unwed mothers are found in
    a. the lower class.
    b. the middle class.
    c. the upper class.
    d. all classes.

_____ 10. The majority of unwed mothers apparently
    a. end education with grammar school.
    b. have at least some high school education.
    c. have at least some college education.
    d. finish their education in college.

[37]

Unwed Mothers

READING FOR STUDYING

This essay question tests whether students understand the conflict that confronts some unmarried pregnant women:

Criticize this statement: "If an unmarried woman becomes pregnant, she should give birth to her baby even if she knows she will not be married before the baby is born."

Criticize means "give the arguments for and against, and state your conclusion." Give the arguments for and against the statement in the question and state your conclusion about it. **Underline** the parts of the passage needed to answer the question. Then either **summarize** this information under a heading or **write** an answer to the question. End by stating why you agree or disagree with the statement.

_____

_____

_____

_____

_____

_____

_____

_____

_____

_____

_____

_____

_____

_____

_____

_____

Images of Man

There are many different interpretations of the nature of man, but they can be grouped into five fairly distinct viewpoints: (1) The classical or rational view of Western philosophers, held up to and through the period of the Enlightenment. This view has been inherited largely from the world of Greece and Rome. (2) The Western religious view expressed in the Hebraic traditions. Judaism, Christianity, and Islam hold variations on a basic theme; this stance has permeated the history of Western civilizations. (3) In the Oriental world, we have singled out the Hindu and Buddhist heritages as representatives of the Eastern religious view. (4) The opposing images of man in relation to society offered by the philosophers Hobbes and Rousseau. (5) The scientific view, which can be divided into two parts: the biological understanding of man, which is largely the product of the natural sciences, and the behavioristic view, which is largely attributable to certain thinkers in the social sciences. There are various subdivisions, modifications, and transformations, but it is thought that these are the general images produced by civilizations throughout history.

THE RATIONAL VIEW OF MAN

According to the classical rationalistic view of man, inherited mainly from Greece and Rome and revived in a slightly different form during the Renaissance, what most distinguishes man is the fact that he is a rational being. For Plato, reason is the highest part of the soul, and the function of reason is to guide conduct. It is independent and immortal in its essential nature. Only reason is able to penetrate to the very nature of things. For Aristotle, also, reason is the highest faculty of the soul. It is man's prize possession, which sets him apart from subhuman nature. The Stoics believed in a cosmic reason, or *logos,* which pervades all things. The ideal person is the wise man, who suppresses his emotions and governs his world by controlling himself. Reason must

From *Living Issues in Philosophy,* 7th ed., by Harold H. Titus, Marilyn S. Smith, and Richard T. Nolan © 1979 by Litton Educational Publishing, Inc. Reprinted by permission of D. Van Nostrand Company.

check the testimony of the senses, since the "assent of reason" is central in human knowledge.

According to this classical interpretation, man is to be understood primarily from the viewpoint of the nature and the uniqueness of his rational powers. Mind is the unifying principle and, as such, is distinguished from the body. Reason is the pride and glory of man. For Socrates, Plato, and their followers, the intelligent man is the virtuous man. To know the right is to do it. Vice is the result of ignorance. The goal of human effort and the meaning of progress are the harmonious development of all of man's functions and capabilities through the supremacy and the perfection of reason in man and society.

While the classical view of man is optimistic, especially in its confidence in human reason and its view that the intelligent man is virtuous, there is an undertone of melancholy in Graeco-Roman civilization. Many Greek thinkers were impressed by the brevity and mortality of man. They did not believe that large numbers of people could be among the wise. History had little meaning, since it was viewed as a series of cycles or endless recurrences. A few men, such as Democritus, Epicurus, and Lucretius, saw man as wholly a part of nature, but they did not deny the importance of reason; they merely interpreted it in more naturalistic and mechanical terms.

The Renaissance view of man retains a firm, optimistic confidence in man's reason. It differs from the classical view in that man's uniqueness is understood both in terms of his rational independence and his relationship to God. His religious faith, however, was not based upon authoritative pronouncements, but free inquiry and his own choices. With the purpose of understanding and justifying his capacity for initiative in the world, Renaissance man sought harmony between philosophy and theology. Though a Christian orientation set the perspective, he shared with his classical predecessors the focus on practical applications of truths to man's life in society.

THE WESTERN RELIGIOUS VIEW OF MAN: JUDAISM, CHRISTIANITY, AND ISLAM

Engrained in the sacred literature of these traditions is the major motif that man is in a special relationship to the Creator. Human uniqueness is not chiefly in man's reason or in his relation to nature. Instead, each person is a worthwhile, unique individual of divine origin.

In Judaism and Christianity man has the capacity to act under his own initiative; he has the freedom to move within the limits of time and space, to alter the paths of history, but not God's ultimate sovereignty or the final outcome of the historical process. In the sense that man has the capacity to choose and to enter relationships of love, he is made "in the image of God"; that is, the Creator has endowed man with unique attributes of a free agent capable of active love, characteristics analogous to God's own self-expression. However, because man has freedom to make choices, he can resist the call to fellowship with God and neighbor. The choice of false gods, misplaced allegiance with its consequences, is "sin."

In Islam man is also the primary, intentional creation of God. It is more difficult to derive a doctrine of human freedom from the Qur'an[1] than it is from the Bible. With an uncompromising emphasis on the omnipotence of God, Muslims have included a strong sense of predestination in their image of man; God directs all events. In contrast, other themes in the Qur'an point to individual responsibility for actions, the very act of submission to Allah's will presupposing a measure of freedom. It is perhaps most fair to say that there is a problem of reconciling man's free will with God's omnipotence in Islam.

For these three Western religions the criterion for the exercise of human freedom is one's loving submission to the will of God. Each understands the nature of that love and breaches of the relationship (sin) in a variety of ways in their holy writings and traditions. Participation in the community of faith, as each defines that community, is an essential nurturing of persons individually and corporately in their basic goodness as "children of God." It is this participation which empowers them with love. An implication of the Western religious image of man is, therefore, that personal fulfillment requires an individual *and* communal loyalty or affection for God, neighbor, and self.

THE ORIENTAL RELIGIOUS VIEW OF MAN: HINDUISM AND BUDDHISM

The Eastern religions have many varying views of man and his essence. The Hindu religion, or Hinduism, is distinctive for its complexity and it is difficult to delineate one particular view of man in Hindu thought. Nevertheless, the great theme of nearly all schools of Hindu thinking is that man must lay hold of eternal life, which is indestructible and imperishable. He must pierce through all the misleading confusions and appearances of this life to see his true, real self in the context of the eternal life. Man must begin with true knowledge about himself. He must cut through the jungle of delusion, which is revealed by his senses, so that he can know the eternal and permanent life that does not pass in and out of existence.[2]

No aspect of Buddhist thought is more puzzling to the Western mind than the Buddhist view of human nature. Buddhist teaching begins with a diagnosis of the human situation and finds a remedy for that situation in "The Four Noble Truths." Both the diagnosis and the remedy are set in a world view very different from that of the West. Buddhism sees present human existence in terms of migration from one life to another. Turn where we will, nothing in present existence is permanent. In Buddhist thought, existence involves *dukkha*, or "suffering." The term signifies the mental and physical ills which accompany our existence as we know it here and now in contrast to the bliss of *nirvana*. The main problem for the Western mind is that Buddhism also insists that we have no "self" to experience either the suffering or the bliss. Human beings are no exception to the rule that "all is change." There can be no fixed human nature. The Buddhist doctrine asserts that rather than a self or soul, there is instead a coming together of "streams," of bodily sensations, feelings, perceptions, conceptions, and consciousness. Thus, for man to be proud (that is, to have self-regard), he must be vain and deluded, for not only are the attachments the self makes impermanent but anything which can be called the self is also impermanent, subject to change and decay.

Unlike the Western traditions, Hinduism and Buddhism view man's freedom in such a way that he may conform to the flow of migration from one life to another and thereby find eventual release from a self-aware existence; or, he may choose to be out of step with this flow and consequently retard his freedom from selfhood. However, *all* existence will find ultimate destiny in the same *nirvana;* thus, there is no need for a concept of freedom which has any ultimate significance. . . . [A]t this point we should understand that human freedom in Western religious thought is crucial to an individual's and a people's destiny. In Hinduism and Buddhism, on the other hand, the same destiny, *nirvana,* is the identical future for the entire universe.

In the philosophic schools of Hinduism and Buddhism sin is the ignorant clinging to the world which inhibits the process of migration and liberation from the universe. Again one finds a sense of "sin" different from the understandings in the Hebraic traditions. In the East human nature finds its fulfillment in flowing toward *nirvana;* in the West a communal fellowship with a loving Creator is the goal which one may choose or reject.

HUMAN NATURE AND SOCIETY:
HOBBES AND ROUSSEAU

With the advent of the Renaissance, philosophers became aware that an important philosophical consideration had remained untapped in the earlier classical and religious images of man. What they began to ask was not merely how man differed from the animals, but what possibilities he possessed for becoming more human. How could people live together in peace and harmony? Would it be possible for man to create a new form of life, one that would be more worth living? Or is there something so corrupt in the nature of man that he is doomed to repeat the errors of the past and present?

These questions led naturally to a concern for the relation between human nature and society. Is there an unchanging human nature that determines social forms—that makes suffering and war inevitable? Or would it be possible to alter the social form in a fashion that would lead to change and progress?

Two very different pictures of the relation between human nature and society developed. First, in the seventeenth century, Thomas Hobbes (1588–1679) published *Leviathan* (1651), essentially an analysis of political authority. The title for his work came from the Old Testament, where the Leviathan was a magnificent crocodile who ruled the animal kingdom and could never be overthrown. Hobbes, who had witnessed rebellion and civil war in England, was convinced that peace and order required a Levianthanlike state which would be able to resist attack and which had absolute authority over its subjects.

Hobbes based his political position on an analysis of human nature. He argued that human beings were naturally competitive, aggressive, greedy, antisocial, and "brutish." If left to themselves they would be continuously at war with one another. Hobbes attacked the idealistic political philosophies of Plato and Aristotle for being unrealistic and for assuming wrongly that people were naturally capable of virtue and wisdom. He dismissed reason and appealed to human passions, particularly the passion for self-preservation. Man's agreement with the state (the social contract) is, therefore, mainly an agreement of equally selfish and self-seeking persons not to commit mass murder and thereby destroy the human race.

The second picture of the social contract was that developed by the French philosopher Jean Jacques Rousseau (1712–1778). Rousseau, contrary to Hobbes, had an extremely optimistic view of human nature. He believed that people were "naturally good" and it was only the corruptions of society that made them selfish and destructive. Rousseau does not, therefore, take the social contract to be simply a doctrine of protection between mutually brutish individuals. Rather, the function of the state is to allow people to regain the "natural goodness" that they once had in the absence of any state at all. Rousseau's aim is to develop a conception of the state which will allow us to live as morally as possible.

Our basic concern here is not so much with the theory of the state that Hobbes and Rousseau proposed, but with the clear opposition of their views in respect to the moral nature of man. For Hobbes man in the "state of nature" desires only to outdo his fellow man; he mainly seeks gain and glory, always at the expense of another. For Rousseau, on the other hand, "natural man" is "naturally good" and contemporary society has corrupted him. Rousseau further believed it was competition and our lust for private property which was responsible for this corruption; as a result we must reexamine our social institutions. In his famous book, *The Social Contract* (1762), he asserts that man must regain his freedom within society; to be a citizen is to want and to do what is good for the society as well as oneself. Rousseau has properly been regarded as the father of the most liberal and revolutionary theories of our time; they see that he insisted that the rights of the individual be free from government intervention. Man should live according to his own "natural goodness" and that outweighs any claim the state or society may have.

THE SCIENTIFIC VIEWS OF MAN

One strict scientific interpretation of man asserts that man and all his activities are determined by the laws of physics and chemistry. In this view, man is merely a more complex or "higher" form of life, who may be explained by the same laws that govern all other matter. Man is a part of the physical order of nature; like other objects, he has size, weight, shape, and color. Man occupies space and time; the laws of physics, such as the law of gravitation, apply to him as well as to other physical objects.

This scientific view of man does not consider the realm of science to extend beyond the objective "facts" as disclosed by the various natural sciences. Since the nineteenth century, however, the scientific method has been applied in many of the humane studies, which has resulted in the disciplines we know as the social sciences: sociology, political science, anthropology, and psychology. In contemporary behavioral science, human psychology has become the study of man's behavior. According to this scientific view, man can be manipulated, formed, and developed in much the same manner as any other animal.

> The cry of the behaviorist is: "Give me the baby and my world to bring it up in and I'll make it crawl and walk; I'll make it climb and use its hands in constructing buildings of stone or wood; I'll make it a thief, a gunman, or a dope fiend. The possibility of shaping in any direction is almost endless."[3]

A direct forerunner of behaviorism during the nineteenth century was the field of animal psychology, a field which developed from the Darwinian revolution in biology. Animal psychologists undertook vast research on rats, cats, chickens, and chimpanzees as substitutes for the human subject, always claiming a close identity in their methods with those of the natural sciences. As a result of these studies, the behaviorist was led to conclude that the task of a psychologist is to investigate human *behavior* rather than the human mind and its consciousness.

John B. Watson, who founded the behaviorist school of psychology, held that the scientific investigation of man must be limited to the objectively observable. "Now what can we observe? We can observe behavior—what the organism says and does."[4] The far-reaching implication of this limitation is that the scope of observation does not include what the human organism *means* or *intends* by his speech and action; all subjective terms such as *sensation, perception, drive,* and *purpose* are dropped. For Watson, man was simply "an assembled organic machine ready to run."[5] Many contemporary behaviorists, including B. F. Skinner, are fascinated by the possibility that a world of people could be controlled from birth on.

The position of the behavioral scientist is that all individuals are "by nature" identical—empty organisms furnished with the same neural and mechanical equipment, waiting to be formed, accidentally or purposefully, by the forces around them. Heavy criticism has been leveled at this approach; Hannah Arendt, for example, is contemptuous of what she calls the ". . . all-comprehensive pretension of the social sciences which as 'behavioral sciences' aim to reduce man as a whole, in all his activities, to the level of a conditioned and behaving animal."[6]

Behaviorists and atheistic existentialists deny that man has an essential human nature. A strict behaviorist sees man as a robot or a machine; all individuals come equipped with the same potential for manipulation by the world around them. Existentialists such as Sartre hold a directly opposite view: man has no human nature because he exists before he can be defined by any conception of himself. "Man is nothing else but that which he makes of himself. . . . Man is indeed a project which possesses a subjective life, instead of being a kind of moss, or a fungus, or a cauliflower."[7] For Sartre and others, man is condemned to be free, left alone without excuse, for he may use neither God nor society as explanation for his actions. Man is nothing else but the sum of his actions. And indeed, if existence precedes essence, man cannot excuse his actions by reference to a given and specific human nature; "in other words, . . . man *is* freedom."[8]

REFERENCES

1. Often written as "Koran." Contemporary Islamic scholars prefer Qur'an.
2. H. D. Lewis and Robert Lawson Slater, *World Religions* (London: C. A. Watts, 1966), p. 34.
3. John B. Watson, *The Ways of Behaviorism* (New York: Harper, 1928), pp. 35–36.
4. John B. Watson, *Behaviorism* (Chicago: University of Chicago Press, 1958), p. 6.
5. *Ibid.,* p. 269.
6. Hannah Arendt, *The Human Condition* (Chicago: University of Chicago Press, 1958), p. 45.
7. Jean-Paul Sartre, "Existentialism Is a Humanism," p. 291.
8. *Ibid.*

[38]

Images of Man

READING FOR UNDERSTANDING

Summary

_____ 1. In summary, this passage presents
    a. the *types* of natures found in humankind.
    b. the *reasons* men have different natures.
    c. *points of view* about the nature of man.
    d. a *method* for identifying the nature of man.

_____ 2. The summary is best stated in the headings and in the
    a. first paragraph.
    b. second paragraph.
    c. third paragraph.
    d. fourth paragraph.

Vocabulary

_____ 3. A **faculty*** of the soul is
    a. that which instructs the soul.
    b. that which the soul teaches.
    c. a power or ability of the soul.
    d. a part (or parts) of the soul.

_____ 4. A **virtuous*** person
    a. does the right thing.
    b. does the wrong thing.
    c. has low intelligence.
    d. has high intelligence.

Summary	Number right _____	× 10 =	_____
Vocabulary	Number right _____	× 10 =	_____
Comprehension	Number right _____	× 10 =	_____
		Total score	_____

_____ 5. A **motif*** is a
   a. certain and proven truth.
   b. repeated theme or idea.
   c. driving motive or purpose.
   d. major point of disagreement.

Comprehension

_____ 6. Sadness is associated with the classical rationalistic view of man because that view holds that
   a. only a few people can attain wisdom.
   b. great wisdom leads to great pride.
   c. we cannot decide what is "right."
   d. virtuous nations cannot win wars.

_____ 7. One respect in which the Judaic and Christian views of man differ from the classical view of man is that the Judaic and Christian views believe that human imperfection results from
   a. sin, not ignorance.
   b. ignorance, not sin.
   c. intolerance, not lack of virtue.
   d. lack of virtue, not intolerance.

_____ 8. A primary difference between the Western religious view of man and the Oriental religious view of man is that the Western religious view places more emphasis on
   a. passing from one life to the next.
   b. the impermanence of life on earth.
   c. denial of the existence of a self.
   d. human freedom and the individual.

_____ 9. John B. Watson's behavioristic view of man is in agreement with
   a. both Hobbes's view and Rousseau's view.
   b. neither Hobbes's view nor Rousseau's view.
   c. Hobbes's view, but not Rousseau's view.
   d. Rousseau's view, but not Hobbes's view.

_____ 10. Which of the following four viewpoints of the nature of man is *most different* from the other three viewpoints?
   a. rational views
   b. Western religious views
   c. Oriental religious views
   d. scientific views

[38]

Images of Man

READING FOR STUDYING

This essay question tests the student's understanding of important relationships between two viewpoints of the nature of man:

> State how "reason" and "vice" in the classical rationalistic view of man are *related* to parallel concepts in the Judaic-Christian view of man.

To state how things are *related* is to "state what connections exist among them." Identify concepts in the Judaic-Christian view of man that are parallel to "reason" and "vice" in the classical rationalistic view of man; show what connection exists between these two views. **Underline** the parts of the passage needed to answer the question. Then either **summarize** this information under appropriate headings or **write** an answer to the question.

[E L E V E N]

Reading with a Critical Eye

This part of the book contains questions that will help you develop your critical (or evaluative) comprehension of textbooks. *Critical comprehension* is the ability to form judgments about the motives of writers, the methods they use, and the general value of what they write. Following are some examples of critical reading:

> You read in a business textbook about the unionization of workers and, although the author does not so state, you decide that the author is more concerned with the rights of employers than with the rights of workers. You have judged the writer's motives.
>
> In your psychology textbook you observe that the author has included many interesting examples to hold your interest and to make the subject "live" for you. You have judged the writer's methods.
>
> Your algebra textbook makes algebra understandable to you for the first time, so you decide that the writer has done a good job of explaining algebra to you. You have judged the value of what the author wrote.

When you form such judgments, you are reading with a critical eye.

Critical comprehension does not require especially advanced thought processes; we are all capable of making judgments such as those shown in the above examples. Critical comprehension is not based so much on an extraordinarily high level of thinking as it is on the possession of specialized knowledge and the willingness to engage in "conversations" with writers.

For example, if you have seen a television program that I have not seen, and we both read a review of the program in the newspaper, you would be a better judge of the accuracy of the review because you have special knowledge that I do not have. On the other hand, if you and I both read the script for a new play, I might be a better judge of the merits of the script than you are, because I have read the scripts for hundreds of plays, and you may not have.

To read with a critical eye, you must view yourself as worthy of engaging in "conversations" with writers, and you must be willing to make the effort to do this. In addition, to become skillful at reading critically, you must understand both the kinds of questions to ask yourself as you read and also the standards that are most useful for arriving at reasonable judgments.

When you read a novel for pleasure and tell a friend, "I enjoyed it; you will too," this may be all the critical evaluation that is important. But critical evaluation of your college reading requires more than a decision about whether you like or dislike what you read.

The questions in this part of the book will help you understand better the types of questions you can ask to engage in meaningful interactions with the writers of college textbooks. When you discuss possible answers to the questions, you will learn the standards that may be used to arrive at acceptable judgments.

The following questions may be different from those you have thought about before. If they are, you will discover that they may interest you in your reading in an entirely new way. Skillful readers relate what they read to all that they have learned in the past and to the standards that they have acquired as a result of their previous experiences; they look for meanings that may be hidden to other readers.

If you learn to ask yourself the types of questions that follow, reading will become more interesting and enjoyable to you, and you will find yourself better prepared to answer any questions you may be asked about your college textbooks.

1. *Studying.* Questions for this passage appear on page 9.

2. *Job Success.* The author presents four kinds of behavior that people expect of fellow workers. Are these some of the things you expect of fellow workers, relatives, or neighbors? Does your approval or disapproval of the writer's views about getting along with peers affect your acceptance of the six expectations the writer says employers have of workers?

3. *Word Structure.* The writer states, "If you understand English word structure, you will often be able to discover the meanings of unfamiliar words without consulting a dictionary." Is this true? Examine a few pages of a college textbook that you find difficult to read and list some of the derivatives you find there. Do your findings make the writer's statement more or less believable?

4. *Smokers.* The writer describes the types of people who have been smokers in this country since the beginning of the century, but provides no references that we may consult to determine if the information is correct. Should you accept these undocumented statements as correct? Would the information be more believable if it were supported by references?

5. *Human Needs.* The passage states that the majority of people in our society have satisfied physiological, safety, social, and esteem needs to at least some degree. Is this true? Provide evidence that this statement is probably true or probably false.

6. *Fitness.* The writer gives equal attention to three components of physical fitness, because all these elements are equally important to total fitness. But are all three elements of fitness equally important to average people in our society? Is there one component of fitness that is more important to average people than the other? Explain your reasoning.

7. *Purposes of Advertising.* Examine newspapers and magazines to find examples of primary demand advertising and selective advertising that make you want to purchase what is advertised, and find an example of institutional advertising that you feel improves the advertiser's image. Explain why the examples you selected are particularly convincing or appealing to you.

8. *Mate Selection.* Is it believable that people marry those who are similar to them in age, social class, religion, education, and the other categories listed in the passage? Select a married couple you know well and determine the extent to which the couple is similar or dissimilar in the ways discussed in the passage. Does your analysis tend to increase or decrease your acceptance of the statements made in the selection?

9. *Marijuana.* Could Becker's explanation of how people become marijuana users also be applied to explain how other addictions are developed? Describe the steps that lead to marijuana use to somebody you know who started smoking or drinking when very young. Ask if those steps give a reasonable description of how their own smoking or drinking habit was acquired. Does the answer you receive support the conclusion that Becker has identified principles that underlie addictions other than that to marijuana?

10. *Values.* The writer does not state whether he believes that (1) our positive values outweigh our negative values, or (2) our negative values outweigh our positive values. What, if any, evidence is there in the passage that the writer holds one and not the other of these opinions?

11. *Birth Control.* The writer does not state whether he approves or disapproves of the use of birth control measures. What, if any, evidence is there in the passage that the writer favors or does not favor the practice of using birth control methods?

12. *The Wheel Theory of Love.* The writer claims that the "wheel theory" of love can be applied to love relationships and other primary relationships, such as relationships with parents and with close friends. Is this true? Use the "wheel theory" to describe two close relationships you have (make one a love relationship, if you can). In your judgment, is the theory useful for understanding close relationships?

13. *Exercise.* Twenty-year-old Robert wants to achieve fitness in the medium zone. He plans to do this by spending fifteen minutes on Monday, Wednesday, and Saturday jogging for two miles with a heart rate of 155 beats per minute. Evaluate Robert's plan, and give him suggestions on how he might better achieve his objective.

14. *Immigration.* At the beginning of the passage the author states that immigrants came to this country to find better economic opportunity and social equality; however, at the end of the passage he makes it clear

that immigrants also came largely because there was good, cheap transportation and because they were persuaded through the efforts of American entrepreneurs. Is this a contradiction? Explain your reasoning.

15. *Packaging.* The writer does not state whether he believes that (1) the advantages of packaging are so great that the disadvantages should be overlooked, or (2) the disadvantages of packaging are so great that restrictions should be placed on packaging. What, if any, indication is there in the passage that he holds one and not the other of these opinions?

16. *Propaganda.* The writer states that knowing propaganda methods helps us evaluate persuasive arguments logically. Is this true? Find a newspaper or magazine editorial (or letter to the editor) that uses a propaganda technique to convince readers to believe as the writer does; also find one that does not resort to propaganda to persuade. Is it true that knowing propaganda methods helped you to evaluate persuasive arguments more logically?

17. *Demography.* The author of this passage wants readers to understand how to compute the annual growth rate of populations, but many students cannot compute this figure after they have studied the passage. What might the writer have done to make it easier for students to understand how to make this kind of computation?

18. *Relatives.* Are the categories presented in this passage adequate for describing relationships among relatives? Divide a sheet of paper into seven columns and write these headings over each column: "Relatives," "Primary," "Secondary," "Tertiary," "Consanguineous," "Affinal," and "Closeness I Feel." Write the names of your relatives in the first column, check off the appropriate information in the next five columns, and, in the last column, write how close you feel to each relative. Do you notice any patterns in your responses? To what extent are the categories given in the passage adequate or inadequate for describing relationships among relatives?

19. *Self.* Usually we expect that information in textbooks is documented by fairly recent research; however, in 1934, Mead described how the self emerges in three stages. Does the fact that Mead's analysis was reported nearly fifty years ago have any effect on the meaningfulness of this information for us today?

20. *The Ecosystem.* This passage was written for first-year college students who are taking an introductory biology course but are not specializing in biology. In your judgment, did the author of the passage succeed in making information about the ecosystem easily accessible to such students? Give detailed evidence to support your answer.

21. *Business Games.* Do Parkinson's Law, the Peter Principle, and the Radovic Rule actually apply to large organizations? Describe each of

these formulations to someone who works for a large organization; ask if the formulations are descriptive of what goes on there. (Use your own experiences if you have worked for a large organization.) Does your survey tend to increase or decrease your acceptance that these practices exist in large organizations?

22. *Job Hunting.* The book from which this passage was taken is usually read by first-year college students. Does the writer take this fact into account as well as he might? In formulating your decision, examine the examples of a résumé and cover letter to determine if there is anything about the samples that should be different for the intended audience.

23. *Mass Hysteria.* The writer defines *mass hysteria* as behavior that involves (1) "widespread and contagious anxiety" (2) "caused by some unfounded belief." Do the two examples of mass hysteria help readers understand both aspects of this definition? How do you rate the writer's success in providing readers with examples that help them understand mass hysteria?

24. *Social Class.* Does the passage present reasonable descriptions of the social classes in this country? Select the social class most familiar to you and decide if, in your experience, the information given about that class is accurate. Does your opinion about the accuracy of this description have any effect on your willingness to accept the information given about the other social classes?

25. *Intelligence.* You have passed through all the stages of intellectual development described in the passage. As you read about them, did you find any statement about your intellectual development that is true or false? What, if any, effect did this have on your willingness to accept other statements in the passage as being true?

26. *Effects of Advertising.* The author does not state whether he believes that advertising raises costs, is wasteful, or is truthful. What, if any, evidence is there in the passage that the author believes or disbelieves these things about advertising?

27. *Marry?* The author gives six reasons that people should not marry. Is there any truth in the arguments? Think about a marriage you know well and try to determine if the partners enjoy romantic love, provide each other with good companionship, have economic security, are sexually gratified, and enjoy parenthood. Does your analysis suggest that the writer was well advised or ill advised to have unmarried people consider these problems?

28. *Education.* This passage appears in a book usually studied by first-year college students. What purpose did the writer hope to achieve by describing alternative forms of education to readers who are most likely pursuing a college degree? Was it appropriate for him to do this?

29. *Norms.* Did the writer do a good job of making norms understandable to the college students for whom his explanations are intended? In formulating your decision, examine the paragraph about *folkways* to determine if there is anything the writer might have included to make folkways more understandable to his audience.

30. *Spellings.* This passage about the standardization of English spellings is incomplete in a very important way. What is missing?

31. *Long Life.* Could the information in this passage be rearranged to provide a more logical organization? To answer this question, bracket and letter the paragraphs as follows: (a) paragraph 1, (b) paragraphs 2-4, (c) paragraph 5, (d) paragraphs 6-8, and (e) paragraphs 9-10. Explain whether these paragraphs and groups of paragraphs (*a, b, c, d,* and *e*) could be rearranged to give the passage a better organization.

32. *Defenses.* The writer uses examples that suggest that "average" and "normal" people may use defense mechanisms from time to time. If this is true, you should know somebody who has used a defense mechanism. Give an instance in which you, a friend, or a relative has used one of the four defense mechanisms explained in the passage. Does relating this information to your experience increase your understanding and acceptance of it?

33. *Buying.* Is it true that purchases are made for rational or for emotional reasons? Use the criteria in the passage to estimate the extent to which these factors determined the last major purchase you made. Consider the extent to which each of these entered into your decision: cost, dependability, usefulness, fear, pride, sociability, and emulation. Does this analysis add to your understanding or appreciation of the statements in the passage?

34. *Marriage.* The passage states that "research indicates that childless marriages, when they survive, appear to be healthier than marriages with children." The passage then goes on to explain difficulties parents report with child rearing, but it does not give important information you could use to estimate your chances for having a healthy marriage with children. What is the missing information?

35. *Grades.* The passage states three basic opinions about how students should be graded: (1) they should be compared to other students; (2) their achievement should be compared to their potential; or (3) they should not be graded at all. However, your experience has probably revealed to you that only one of these methods is widely used. Which grading method do most schools use? Why aren't the other two methods used widely?

36. *Decisions.* The writer uses the word "d-e-c-i-d-e" to help students remember the steps in the decision-making process. Does using this

device help or hinder the author in achieving his objective? In preparing your answer, consider whether the decision-making process could be summarized in fewer steps and, if so, whether it would be easier to remember fewer steps.

37. *Unwed Mothers.* This passage from a textbook revised in 1978 cites references that are mostly from the 1950s and 1960s. Would more recent citations increase your willingness to accept this information as being valid for today? Why do you think the author did not include more recent citations to support his statements?

38. *Images of Man.* This passage presents five views of the nature of man. In your judgment, is one view more valid than the others? Or do you believe that the nature of man is best understood by taking two or three of the views into account? Explain your reasoning.

{TWELVE}

Records of Progress

On the following pages there are record forms you may use to chart your progress as you answer the questions and do the exercises in *Reading Skills for College Study*. Forms for the Reading for Understanding multiple-choice questions are followed by forms for the Reading for Studying exercises and the Reading with a Critical Eye questions.

The Reading for Understanding forms have been devised so that you can see at a glance where your strengths and weaknesses are in answering Summary, Vocabulary, and Comprehension questions. After you have computed the four scores at the bottom of a Reading for Understanding answer sheet, keep a record of your scores by **circling** the correct numbers on the following record forms.

The Reading for Understanding questions have been written in such a way that few students will consistently achieve a total score of 90 or 100. If your total score averages about 80, you are reading with good understanding. Do not become discouraged if your total scores are not consistently 90 or 100. When you answer questions incorrectly, you will be given an opportunity to understand the reasons for your incorrect answers, and thus you will learn how to answer questions correctly in the future.

However, if you do not achieve an average total score of about 70 by the time you have answered the first twenty sets of Reading for Understanding questions, *Reading Skills for College Study* is probably too difficult for you. If this should happen, it would be wise to seek skills improvement in easier materials and to return to *Reading Skills for College Study* when you are ready for it.

© 1980 by Houghton Mifflin Company.

SCORES FOR READING FOR UNDERSTANDING

	Summary	Vocabulary	Comprehension	Total Score
1 Studying	10 20	10 20 30	10 20 30 40 50	10 20 30 40 50 60 70 80 90 100
2 Job Success	10 (20)	10 20 30	10 20 30 40 50	10 20 30 40 50 60 70 80 90 100
3 Word Structure	10 20	10 20 30	10 20 30 40 50	10 20 30 40 50 60 70 80 90 100
4 Smokers	10 20	10 20 30	10 20 30 40 50	10 20 30 40 50 60 70 80 90 100
5 Human Needs	10 20	10 20 30	10 20 30 40 50	10 20 30 40 50 60 70 80 90 100
6 Fitness	10 20	10 20 30	10 20 30 40 50	10 20 30 40 50 60 70 80 90 100
7 Purposes of Advertising	10 20	10 20 30	10 20 30 40 50	10 20 30 40 50 60 70 80 90 100
8 Mate Selection	10 20	10 20 30	10 20 30 40 50	10 20 30 40 50 60 70 80 90 100
9 Marijuana	10 20	10 20 30	10 20 30 40 50	10 20 30 40 50 60 70 80 90 100
10 Values	10 20	10 20 30	10 20 30 40 50	10 20 30 40 50 60 70 80 90 100
11 Birth Control	10 20	10 20 30	10 20 30 40 50	10 20 30 40 50 60 70 80 90 100
12 The Wheel Theory of Love	10 20	10 20 30	10 20 30 40 50	10 20 30 40 50 60 70 80 90 100
13 Exercise	10 20	10 20 30	10 20 30 40 50	10 20 30 40 50 60 70 80 90 100
14 Immigration	10 20	10 20 30	10 20 30 40 50	10 20 30 40 50 60 70 80 90 100
15 Packaging	10 20	10 20 30	10 20 30 40 50	10 20 30 40 50 60 70 80 90 100
16 Propaganda	10 20	10 20 30	10 20 30 40 50	10 20 30 40 50 60 70 80 90 100
17 Demography	10 20	10 20 30	10 20 30 40 50	10 20 30 40 50 60 70 80 90 100
18 Relatives	10 20	10 20 30	10 20 30 40 50	10 20 30 40 50 60 70 80 90 100
19 Self	10 20	10 20 30	10 20 30 40 50	10 20 30 40 50 60 70 80 90 100
20 The Ecosystem	10 20	10 20 30	10 20 30 40 50	10 20 30 40 50 60 70 80 90 100

SCORES FOR READING FOR UNDERSTANDING

	Summary		Vocabulary			Comprehension					Total Score									
21 Business Games	10	20	10	20	30	10	20	30	40	50	10	20	30	40	50	60	70	80	90	100
22 Job Hunting	10	20	10	20	30	10	20	30	40	50	10	20	30	40	50	60	70	80	90	100
23 Mass Hysteria	10	20	10	20	30	10	20	30	40	50	10	20	30	40	50	60	70	80	90	100
24 Social Class	10	20	10	20	30	10	20	30	40	50	10	20	30	40	50	60	70	80	90	100
25 Intelligence	10	20	10	20	30	10	20	30	40	50	10	20	30	40	50	60	70	80	90	100
26 Effects of Advertising	10	20	10	20	30	10	20	30	40	50	10	20	30	40	50	60	70	80	90	100
27 Marry?	10	20	10	20	30	10	20	30	40	50	10	20	30	40	50	60	70	80	90	100
28 Education	10	20	10	20	30	10	20	30	40	50	10	20	30	40	50	60	70	80	90	100
29 Norms	10	20	10	20	30	10	20	30	40	50	10	20	30	40	50	60	70	80	90	100
30 Spellings	10	20	10	20	30	10	20	30	40	50	10	20	30	40	50	60	70	80	90	100
31 Long Life	10	20	10	20	30	10	20	30	40	50	10	20	30	40	50	60	70	80	90	100
32 Defenses	10	20	10	20	30	10	20	30	40	50	10	20	30	40	50	60	70	80	90	100
33 Buying	10	20	10	20	30	10	20	30	40	50	10	20	30	40	50	60	70	80	90	100
34 Marriage	10	20	10	20	30	10	20	30	40	50	10	20	30	40	50	60	70	80	90	100
35 Grades	10	20	10	20	30	10	20	30	40	50	10	20	30	40	50	60	70	80	90	100
36 Decisions	10	20	10	20	30	10	20	30	40	50	10	20	30	40	50	60	70	80	90	100
37 Unwed Mothers	10	20	10	20	30	10	20	30	40	50	10	20	30	40	50	60	70	80	90	100
38 Images of Man	10	20	10	20	30	10	20	30	40	50	10	20	30	40	50	60	70	80	90	100

SCORES: READING FOR STUDYING AND READING WITH A CRITICAL EYE

	Reading for Studying	*Reading with a Critical Eye*
1 Studying		
2 Job Success		
3 Word Structure		
4 Smokers		
5 Human Needs		
6 Fitness		
7 Purposes of Advertising		
8 Mate Selection		
9 Marijuana		
10 Values		
11 Birth Control		
12 The Wheel Theory of Love		
13 Exercise		
14 Immigration		
15 Packaging		
16 Propaganda		
17 Demography		
18 Relatives		
19 Self		

SCORES: READING FOR STUDYING
AND READING WITH A CRITICAL EYE

	Reading for Studying	Reading with a Critical Eye
20 The Ecosystem		
21 Business Games		
22 Job Hunting		
23 Mass Hysteria		
24 Social Class		
25 Intelligence		
26 Effects of Advertising		
27 Marry?		
28 Education		
29 Norms		
30 Spellings		
31 Long Life		
32 Defenses		
33 Buying		
34 Marriage		
35 Grades		
36 Decisions		
37 Unwed Mothers		
38 Images of Man		

[TO THE STUDENT]

One of the skills that this book teaches is "reading with a critical eye." Please use your critical reading ability to evaluate READING SKILLS FOR COLLEGE STUDY. Answer the following questions and mail your answers to James F. Shepherd, c/o Marketing Services, Houghton Mifflin Company, College Division, One Beacon Street, Boston, MA 02107. I will study your responses and use them to improve future editions of this book.

Thank you,
James Shepherd

Which type of school do you attend? Two-year?_____ Four-year?_____ University?_____

What is the title of the course for which this text is assigned?_____

_____

How many credits are given for this course?_____

1. What do you like most about this book?_____

_____

2. What do you like least about this book?_____

_____

3. Evaluate the instruction that this book gives for developing the following skills, using this key: 1—excellent, 2—satisfactory, 3—fair.

   a. Reading comprehension_____   d. Taking notes on books_____

   b. Finding word meanings   e. Answering multiple-choice

      in context_____   questions_____

   c. Underlining textbooks_____   f. Answering essay questions_____

Use the numbers or titles of the textbook selections to answer questions 4 through 11.

4. Which of the multiple choice questions, if any, are too difficult?_____

5. Which of the written exercises, if any, are too difficult?_____

6. Which of the Reading with a Critical Eye questions, if any, are too difficult?_____

7. Which selections are most interesting?_____

8. Which selections are least interesting?_____

9. Which selections are too difficult?_____

10. What other types of textbook selections should be included in this book?_____

_____

11. What did you learn from this book that was most helpful in your other courses?_____

_____

Please make any additional comments that you wish._____

_____

_____